Fundamental Classroom Music
Skills THEORY AND PERFORMING TECHNIQUES

Holt, Rinehart and Winston Consulting Editor in Music:
Allan W. Schindler, Eastman School of Music

Fundamental Classroom Music Skills
THEORY AND PERFORMING TECHNIQUES

Gustav Wachhaus
University of Maryland, College Park

Terry Lee Kuhn
Kent State University

HARCOURT BRACE JOVANOVICH COLLEGE PUBLISHERS

Fort Worth • Philadelphia • San Diego
New York • Orlando • Austin • San Antonio
Toronto • Montreal • London • Sydney • Tokyo

Library of Congress Cataloging in Publication Data

Wachhaus, Gustav.
    Fundamental classroom music skills.

    Includes indexes.
    1. Music — Theory.   I. Kuhn, Terry Lee, joint author.
II. Title.
MT6.W12F8   781   78-13476
ISBN:0-03-041775-9

Printed in the United States of America

1234   082   1413121110

Cover: Silk-screen print by Ben Shahn, *Silent Music*, 1951. Copyright © Estate of Ben Shahn, 1978.

Preface

To the Student

Countless numbers of people have learned to read music, and an even greater number have learned to play instruments. You too can learn to play instruments and to read music. It is not difficult. The symbols used in this text to represent music are the same symbols that have been in traditional use for centuries, and you have probably seen many of them in school music books, church hymnals, or other music books. Your objective in learning to read music should be to help you to make music. Because the sound of music is not on the printed page, the printed symbols must be brought to life through performance.

Music is often compared to science because in both we represent quantitative aspects on paper. Like musical symbols, the symbols of science have been standardized through use over many years. They are not quantities in themselves, but only represent quantities. So too with the symbols of music. Music notation represents some aspects of sounds occurring in time, but it is not always completely representative of the aural phenomena called music. Unlike symbols of science, the translation of the written symbols of music into sound is open to subjective interpretation.

This subjective aspect of music performance, called "style," cannot be described fully in words. It is one of the experiences of music performance that is learned best through listening and imitation. You will have to learn many aspects of music performance through listening critically to your instructor, your classmates, and yourself. This method of learning music is even older than the symbolic representation of music.

Your task, then, is to learn simultaneously the symbolic representation of music and the appropriate performance practices associated with this music. The symbols of music will be represented in this text in the format referred to as lead sheet notation (pronounced "leed").

A *lead sheet* attempts to communicate the four most important aspects of written music: rhythm, pitch, harmony, and lyrics. The dimensions of tempo and dynamics are sometimes included. Chapter 1 will help you read music rhythm, and Chapter 2 will help you read musical pitch. The remaining chapters in this book explore performance on the many instruments that you can use in classroom or informal music-making situations and also theoretical concepts that will facilitate your musical performance.

To the Instructor

Fundamental Classroom Music Skills is written for college students enrolled in music fundamentals courses, often those students preparing for careers in elementary, early childhood, and special education, as well as recreation. In addition, this text has been used successfully with music majors preparing to become general music teachers at the elementary and junior high school levels.

Some of the unique aspects of this text include: (1) tempo indications for each song, (2) melody picking on autoharp, (3) open tuning and finger-picking patterns for guitar, (4) extensive treatment of the voice and song leading, (5) use of the treble clef for all materials, and (6) multiple verses for songs, with their rhythmic accents. Extra verses provide enjoyable materials for practicing newly learned skills. Lastly, (7) the ranges of many songs have been lowered from traditional pitch levels to encourage students with undeveloped voices to sing. The confidence gained through this type of singing experience can be important in extending the comfortable singing range of these students'voices.

It is the authors' belief that this course should be activity oriented rather than presented in a lecture format. Classroom teachers, music specialists, and camp counselors will all find bountiful opportunities for the practical application of the skills learned from this text, whether in performing with and/or for others or in teaching others to make music.

The emphasis of this text is on the learning of musical skills appropriate for informal and classroom music-making situations. Theoretical concepts are presented in separate chapters for clarity; however, overlapping the study of theoretical concepts with performance on instruments will provide the best learning experiences for students. Because most folk and traditional music is published in lead sheet notation (melody notated in treble clef with chord symbols placed above the staff), the theoretical concepts presented in this text prepare student's to follow a lead sheet, performing melodies and accompanying chords.

The treatment of individual instruments, song leading, and singing is intended to be so complete that a thorough study of an individual chapter will make a student independent in that skill. An instructor, therefore, may choose to eliminate certain chapters, or take the chapters out of order, depending on the institution and the class for which the text is used. The availability of instruments may also be a factor in choosing chapters. We suggest that all classes begin with Chapters 1 and 2 to initiate students in the understanding of rhythm and pitch notation. Then the class could focus on a melody instrument such as the recorder (Chapter 3), bells (Chapter 7), or a keyboard instrument (Chapter 8). Another approach would be to follow Chapters 1 and 2 with a study of lead sheet notation (Chapter 9), and then take up a harmony instrument such as the autoharp (Chapter 10), the left hand of a keyboard instrument (Chapter 12), or guitar (Chapter 13). It would be a rare course in which all of the chapters were studied in their entirety.

A test covering minimal theoretical understanding of concepts presented in this book is provided in Appendix B. This test can be used as a final examination or as a summary review of the theoretical concepts presented throughout the text. The questions are general, and students should be able to answer them in relation to any song.

This text can be used with two different teaching approaches. The first approach requires a sufficient number of instruments to serve an entire class simultaneously, at least one instrument for every two students. Following a brief introduction and demonstration by the teacher, students work through the materials in a given chapter, learning performance techniques and applying theoretical concepts. After a brief period of individual practice, the class performs songs together. After proceeding through the chapter in this manner, students are tested individually by the instructor.

This text can also be used in a learning centers approach, each performance chapter being a different center. This second approach is particularly useful to instructors who do not have adequate supplies to give an entire class the same type of instrument at one time. In the learning centers approach, students all read through the same theoretical chapter. A brief amount of time is spent discussing the reading material. Then students pursue different performance chapters, using whatever instruments are available. The supply of instruments is controlled through a master checkout system consisting of a large poster board with a library-book card and pocket for each available instrument. Students sign up for whatever instrument is desired and available for a given class period. Once a card is removed, other students are made aware that they must choose some other instrument. When a student finishes with an instrument, the card is replaced, thereby letting others know that the instrument is again available. The instructor then has a record of how many times each student in the class has worked with each instrument. In the learning centers approach, the teacher continually moves among the students, assisting wherever help is required. In this teaching approach, students use different sequences of the performance chapters of the text.

Many instructors of music fundamentals classes like to begin the first class meetings with rote singing, call-and-response songs, or singing games. Such activities are approached easily and involve all students, regardless of previous musical experience or ability. The extensive song materials contained in this text include songs appropriate for such opening activities. (See Chapter 5, "Singing Songs."

After students have acquired some skill in singing and playing several instruments, they can realize the greater joy of making music with others. There is a delight in singing a song alone, or in strumming chords together in class on like instruments: No one will deny the intrinsic worth of those experiences. However, a more sophisticated musical response can be elicited by combining voice with various other instruments. The perceptive instructor will find songs throughout this text that accommodate performance on a variety of basic melody and chording instruments.

In addition to being understood, as we imply in the proverb on the title page of Chapter 1, music has aesthetic powers that should also be enjoyed. To enjoy a course in fundamentals, both instructors and students should approach it with optimism and a positive attitude. Reflecting on the joy and satisfaction that both great artists and amateurs can derive from music, we hope that students will learn to make one or more of these performance mediums a part of their lives.

Acknowledgments

We would like to acknowledge the many unnamed students whose learning experiences have contributed to the content, instructional procedures, and revisions of this text. We extend our thanks to Dr. Eugene Troth, Chairman of the Department of Music at the College Park campus of the University of Maryland, for arranging teaching schedules to permit the trial use of the manuscript over two semesters. Dr. Stravroula Fanos is to be credited with the approach we take in Chapter 12, "Playing Accompaniments on Keyboard Instruments." Professor Mary Hoffman and Dr. Marcene Huebner are to be credited for ideas incorporated in Chapter 16.

A special acknowledgment must be given to Harvey Reid. A folk musician and instructor at the College Park campus of the University of Maryland, he has been an inspiration for many students and faculty members. His approach to playing folk music and to life is reflected in many positive suggestions that we have incorporated. In particular, his ideas on folk style, autoharp, guitar, and the theoretical concepts necessary for playing folk music appear throughout these pages.

For their help in reviewing the manuscript, we wish to thank Dawn S. Baker, West Virginia University; Irma H. Collins, Murray State University; John R. Heard, California State University at Fresno; Dorothy T. Kozak, University of Nebraska; John H. Martin, California State University at Fresno; Eunice B. Meske, University of Wisconsin; Earl Norwood, Plymouth State College; Allan W. Schindler, Eastman School of Music; Keith P. Thompson, The Pennsylvania State University; T. Temple Tuttle, Cleveland State University.

We wish to express appreciation to the students — Kathie M. Lawrie, in particular — whose patience, poise, and music competence greatly enhanced the photographs contained in this text.

Gloria Wachhaus served as resource consultant for the selection of song material, as proofreader, and as a multifaceted contributor in the preparation of this manuscript. Finally, Terry would like to thank Liz for her understanding, patience, and support throughout the tasks of writing and rewriting.

College Park, Maryland   **G.W.**
Kent, Ohio   **T.L.K.**
November 1978

Contents

Fundamental Classroom Music Skills THEORY AND PERFORMING TECHNIQUES

CHAPTER ONE
Reading Rhythm

I HEAR, and I FORGET

I SEE, and I REMEMBER

I DO, and I UNDERSTAND

CHAPTER ONE
Reading Rhythm

Rhythm refers to the pulse and duration of musical sounds. One of the most basic methods of responding rhythmically to music is to synchronize some bodily movement with the pulse, or beat, of the music. This movement often takes the form of foot tapping, finger snapping, or swaying in time with the music. Identifying the pulse of music is crucial both to listening and to notating musical sounds. Each pulse that you feel as you listen to music is called a *beat*. The beat rhythm in music is the regular recurrence of points of emphasis separated by equal durations.

In slower-moving music points of emphasis are separated by longer durations.

Beat in music is defined as points of emphasis separated by equal durations. Select a familiar piece of music and clap with the beat as it is performed. A recording can be used for this purpose, or half of the class can sing a familiar song while the other half claps on the beat. Here is a suggestion for this exercise. Clap once for each note.

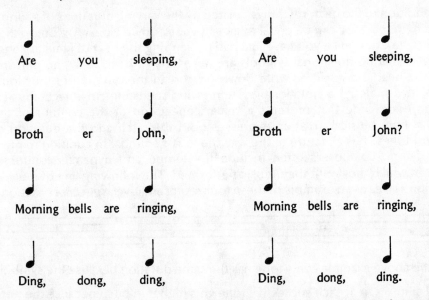

Sometimes a piece of music should be played or sung at a particular *tempo*, or speed. Tempo is usually indicated in beats per minute. Modern notation of tempo includes the type of note value that receives one beat and the speed at which beats progress. Therefore, the indication of ♩ = 80 given below for "Skip to My Lou" means that the tempo is 80 beats per minute and that each quarter note receives one beat.

The *metronome*, a device first marketed by Maelzel in 1816, can reproduce tempos exactly for you. If you have a metronome, set it at 80; it will click 80 times per minute, once for each beat. Now turn it off and clap the beat rhythm as you hear "Skip to My Lou."

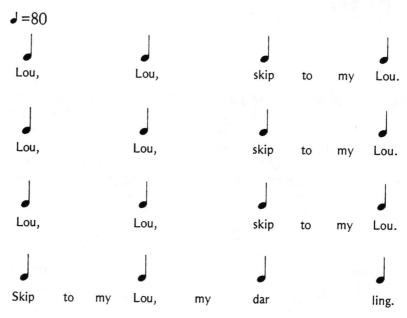

You could perform "Skip to My Lou" at other tempos. Playing a whole piece of music slower or faster does not change the rhythm of the piece.

NOTATING RHYTHMS

In addition to the beat, rhythm is created by the varying durations of sounds. The length of a tone can be equal to a beat, shorter than a beat, or longer than a beat. The experience you have just had in clapping the beat of familiar songs indicates that no notational symbols are necessary to hear, feel, and perform with the beat; however, to write down or to read the duration of individual tones in a melody, a notational system is indispensible. In effect, musical notation is a code that presents a visual conception of the contour of the musical line. Musical notation expresses both the pitch and the duration of musical tones: It is a picture of the way the music sounds. In addition to pitch and rhythm, composers often include the tempo and dynamic (loudness) levels at which they want their music performed. The following line of musical notation serves as an example of these four representative aspects of notation.

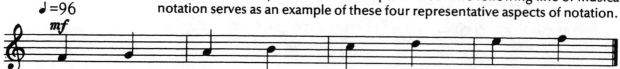

In the above example every tone has the same duration because the symbols are all similar (♩), each successive tone gets higher in pitch because the note heads (the circular part, as opposed to the stem) go from low to high on the staff, the tempo is 96 beats per minute with each quarter note receiving one beat, and the notes are to be played moderately loud (mf).

Beats can be grouped by accenting every second, third, or fourth beat. The groupings of two, three, and four beats are the most common groupings in Western music. The beats in each group are numbered, beginning with the accented beat as number "one." We shall underline the "ones" to indicate that these beats should be clapped slightly louder in order to produce an accent.

Clap the following lines, observing the accents on the ones. Notice that the accents group the beats together.

Number of
Beats per
Group

Two	<u>1</u>	2	<u>1</u>	2	<u>1</u>	2	<u>1</u>	2	<u>1</u>	2	<u>1</u>	2
Three	<u>1</u>	2	3	<u>1</u>	2	3	<u>1</u>	2	3	<u>1</u>	2	3
Four	<u>1</u>	2	3	4	<u>1</u>	2	3	4	<u>1</u>	2	3	4

The grouping of beats, referred to as *meter*, is indicated by a symbol called the *meter signature*. The meter signature of a song consists of two numbers. The upper number indicates how many beats there are in each grouping. In the exercise above, you performed groupings of two, three, and four. The lower number in the meter signature identifies the note value that receives one beat. For example, in the meter signature $\frac{2}{4}$ there are two beats per group, and each beat is equivalent to a quarter note. The meter signature $\frac{4}{4}$ indicates that each measure contains four beats, each equivalent to a quarter note. The $\frac{4}{4}$ meter signature is often written as "C." Meter signatures sometimes prove to be cumbersome and even inaccurate, but their usage is so widespread that we will retain them in this text.

Note Value

In printed music, the structure of a note shows its duration. Notes minimally contain a round part called the head (o ●); they may also contain a stem (|) and perhaps one or more flags (♩) or beams (▬).

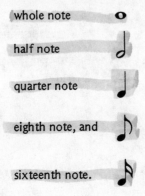

Parts of a note

The most commonly used note values are named the

whole note

half note

quarter note

eighth note, and

sixteenth note.

Each of these notes may be followed by a dot, in which case they are named the

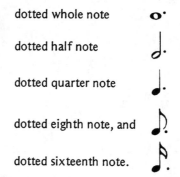

dotted whole note

dotted half note

dotted quarter note

dotted eighth note, and

dotted sixteenth note.

Notes have proportional time values. A whole note is always equal to two half notes,

$$\mathbf{o} \; = \; \rlap{/}d \; \rlap{/}d$$

a half note is always equal to two quarter notes,

$$\rlap{/}d \; = \; \rlap{/}J \; \rlap{/}J$$

a quarter note is always equal to two eighth notes, and

$$\rlap{/}J \; = \; \text{♫} \; = \; \text{♪ ♪}$$

an eighth note is always equal to two sixteenth notes.

$$\text{♪} \; = \; \text{🎵} \; = \; \text{♪ ♪}$$

Notice that flags and beams function identically when affixed to the stem of a note.

Rests

A set of symbols called "rests" is used to represent a duration of silence. Every note value has a corresponding rest value. The following symbols are used:

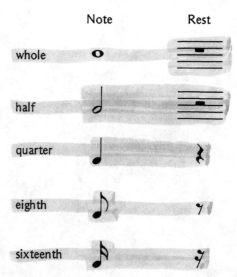

	Note	Rest
whole		
half		
quarter		
eighth		
sixteenth		

Measures

Measures are groupings of beats represented on a staff by vertical lines called *bar lines*. The first beat in each measure usually is performed with an accent. In the following example four beats are grouped together in each measure. Each beat is equal to a quarter note. Keeping these facts in mind, clap the beats, accenting the first of each group.

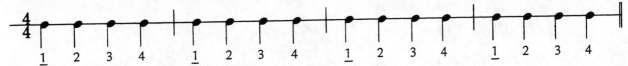

RHYTHMIC COUNTING

When you count to facilitate the performance of rhythms, remember that numbers always occur precisely on a beat. In the following example the second beat of the third measure is divided into two equal eighth notes and is counted "two and." When you clap half notes, clap the third beat, keep your hands clasped, and make a silent downward motion to indicate the fourth beat. A dash between numbers represents a note value whose duration includes more than one beat. Now, divide the class in half and clap the following rhythms on the upper line against the steady beat of the lower line. Count aloud as you clap.

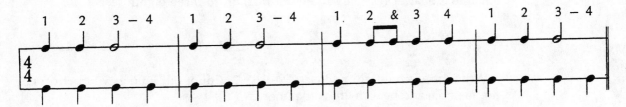

Finish writing out the counting of the beats for each of the following exercises to be sure that you understand the rhythm. Then practice clapping the rhythm of each exercise. The upper line of the two-line staff contains the melodic rhythm and the lower line contains the beat rhythm. *Melodic rhythm is the duration of the tones of a melody.* The melodic and beat rhythms can be played on different rhythm instruments. Always have one or more persons perform the beat rhythm as you clap or play the melodic rhythm. Both parts can be started together by counting one complete measure of preparatory beats to establish the tempo. When learning new songs or new skills, you should use slower tempos, increasing the speed as you gain facility. Tempo indications are suggested rather than absolute.

1

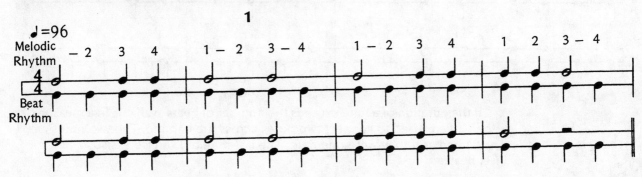

Dotted notes

A dot added to a note extends its duration by one-half. Adding a dot to the following notes has the same effect as using a tie (‿): It combines two written notes into a single duration equal to the sum of both notes. A dotted half note is therefore equal to a half note plus a quarter note, or, to three quarter notes.

In $\frac{4}{4}$ and in $\frac{3}{4}$ meters, the dotted half note receives three beats. Dots can also be added to quarter and eighth notes, with similar effect.

Dotted Rests

A dot added to a rest extends its duration by one-half. A dotted quarter rest is equal to a quarter rest plus an eighth rest, or, to three eighth rests.

Write in the counting; and clap Exercise 2. Count out loud as you perform the melodic and beat rhythms together.

2

If the duration of a tone exceeds the number of beats available in a measure, then a tie is used to connect two notes across the bar line. The two notes are sustained as if they were one note. The last tone of Exercise 3 is sustained for six beats.

3

Eighth notes have one-half the duration of quarter notes; therefore, each beat containing two eighth notes is divided into two equal sounds. Eighth notes are counted "1 and 2 and." The two dots and the double bar at the end of Exercise 4 constitute a *repeat sign*. When you see this sign you should return either to the beginning of the song, or to where a similar set of two bar lines and two dots faces the opposite direction, and repeat the enclosed portion of the song.

4

While some members of the class sing "Paw Paw Patch" (page 286), have the other members perform the following *rhythm score*.

Rhythm scores are designed to be repeated throughout the singing of a song; therefore, students playing the "sticks" line should repeat it until the end of the song. Those playing the other instruments should do likewise.

Exercise 5 contains the dotted-quarter-note rhythm. A good way to figure out this rhythm is to (1) feel the beat, (2) divide all beats into the shortest note value in the melodic rhythm, (3) tie beat divisions together to produce the original melodic rhythm, and then (4) clap the melodic rhythm while speaking the counting syllables for the divisions. In the dotted-quarter-note rhythm, the dot extends the duration of a note by one-half of the note's duration. Since the undotted quarter note is one full beat, the dot extends the duration of the tone through one-half of the next beat. Study the step-by-step explanation below.

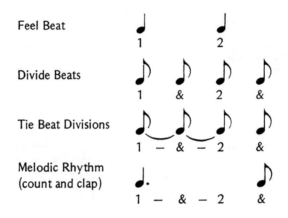

Be sure that you "feel" the beat that is represented by the dot before performing the eighth notes that follow dotted quarter notes in Exercises 5 through 7.

5

6

7

When you count a rhythm, remember to divide the beats into the fastest-moving note value in the melodic rhythm and then add ties to produce the rhythm desired. Figuring rhythms out in this manner will help you understand them. The first measure of Exercise 8 is counted as follows:

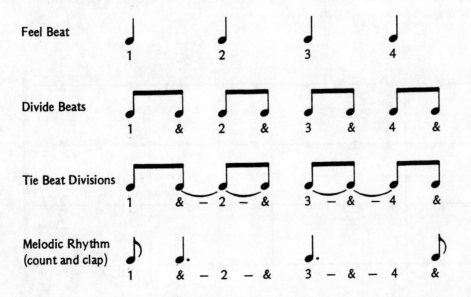

Perform Exercises 8 and 9, paying particular attention to the dotted-note rhythms.

While some members of the class sing the round "Music Alone Shall Live" (page 103), perform the following rhythm score for percussion instruments, dividing the lines among the class.

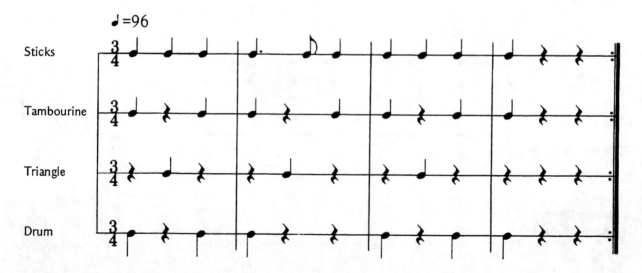

Sixteenth notes are played four per beat in $\frac{2}{4}$ meter. The basic sixteenth-note subdivision is counted "1 e & a   2 e & a." It is pronounced "one ee and uh, two ee and uh."

The following illustration explains several common sixteenth-note rhythms.

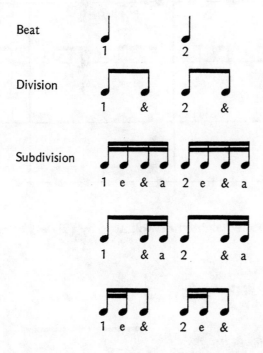

Practice counting the rhythms in Exercises 10 and 11, then clap each exercise.

10

11

Perform the following rhythm score to the singing of "This Old Man" (page 101).

The duration of a dotted eighth note followed by a sixteenth note is counted as follows:

Exercises 12 and 13 use dotted eighth notes followed by a sixteenth note. Clap these exercises carefully, observing this new rhythm.

12

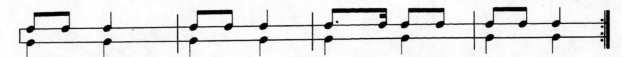

13

The first three notes in the following exercise make what is known as a syncopated rhythm. *Syncopation* is the rhythmic technique of displacing the normal accent implied by beat groupings. This displacement can be facilitated by (1) sustaining a long tone from a weak beat, or the unaccented part of a beat, through a strong beat; (2) placing a rest on a strong beat; or (3) accenting a weak beat. In the following exercises the syncopated tone begins on the unaccented part of a beat and is sustained through the accented portion of the following beat. The quarter note displaces the accent of the melodic rhythm by beginning on the unaccented (the "&") part of the first beat and then sustaining through the accented part (the "2") of the second beat.

Here is how to figure out the counting of the syncopated rhythm in the following exercises.

Practice Exercises 14, 15, and 16 until you can perform them by yourself accurately.

14

15

16

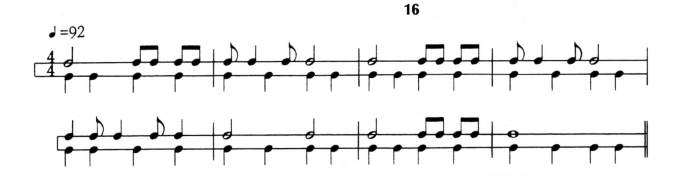

The following rhythm score can be used to accompany the signing of "Tom Dooley" (page 239).

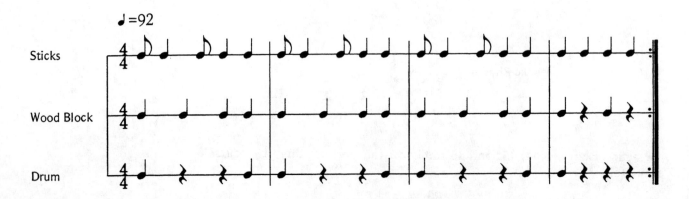

The rhythm ♪♩♩ is contained within the duration of one quarter note. It is counted as follows when it occupies the second beat of a measure in $\frac{2}{4}$ meter:

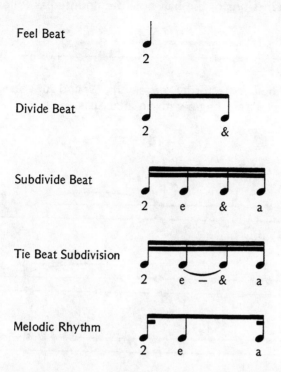

Exercise 17 begins with an *anacrusis,* sometimes referred to as an *upbeat* or *pick-up note(s)*. An anacrusis is a note or notes constituting less than a full measure of beats that precede the first full measure. To maintain the symmetry of the total song, the last measure supplies the beats needed to make a complete measure when added to the beats in the anacrusis. Start the class together by counting "one and two and, one and two and" and begin clapping on the "and" of the second "two."

17

The remaining exercises in this chapter use note values other than the quarter note as the beat-note. The meter signature $\frac{2}{2}$, sometimes indicated as ¢, means that there are two beats per measure, and that each half note receives one beat. The subdivisions of the half note are counted as follows:

Write in the counting and perform Exercises 18, 19, and 20. You will notice that all three of these exercises begin with an anacrusis.

18

19

20

Songs notated in $\frac{6}{8}$ meter can be interpreted in two ways. In the first way, you feel six beats per measure with each eighth note receiving one beat ($\frac{6}{\flat}$). In the second way, you feel two beats per measure with each dotted quarter note receiving one beat ($\frac{2}{\flat}$). The melody, harmony, and text of the song will aid you in deciding how to interpret the meter of songs notated in $\frac{6}{8}$ meter. Exercise 21 requires the first meter interpretation, and Exercises 22 and 23 require the second meter interpretation. Here are some common $\frac{6}{8}$ rhythmic patterns of the first type, and the counting syllables for each.

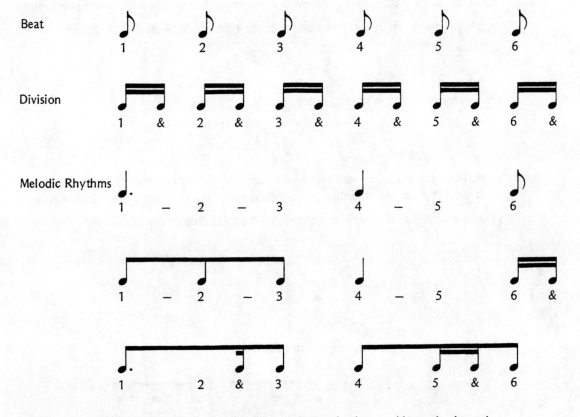

Alternate halves of the class may clap the melodic rhythm and beat rhythm of Exercise 21. Keep your hands clasped together to indicate the sustained notes. Ties are used to connect notes within measures in this exercise.

Some songs notated in $\frac{6}{8}$ meter are intended to be felt with two beats per measure, rather than six. In such cases, the basic six beats per measure

1   2   3   4   5   6

are performed with a strong pulse on beats 1 and 4

<u>1</u>   2   3   <u>4</u>   5   6

so that in each measure you feel two beats, each of which has three divisions. Each beat is then represented by a dotted quarter note. Because each beat is given a number in rhythmic counting, the beats in this interpretation of $\frac{6}{8}$ meter are

and the rhythm syllables for the divisions are

(pronounced "one nah nee, two nah nee"). Observe that each dotted quarter note divides into three eighth notes. Common rhythms in $\frac{6}{8}$ when it is intended to be performed in $\frac{2}{?}$ are shown below.

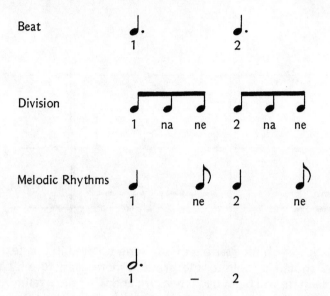

Complete the rhythmic counting for all the notes in the melodic rhythm lines, and then perform Exercises 22 and 23, observing the $\frac{2}{?}$ interpretation of $\frac{6}{8}$ meter.

22

The sign "D. C. al Fine" at the end of Exercise 23 is an abbreviation for *da capo al fine,* which means "go back to the beginning and play to the end." The end is the double bar marked with the word "Fine" (pronounced "fee-nay"). The repeat sign is not observed during the D. C. repetition.

23

Perform the following rhythm score throughout the singing of the round, "Three Blind Mice ." Select different instruments for each line of the score. Play through the rhythm score once as an introduction before beginning to sing.

You can practice rhythmic reading of any song notated in this text or in any songbook. You should be able to interpret the meter signature by explaining how many beats there will be in each measure and what note value will receive one beat. After you have determined the beat groupings and the note value that equals one beat, write out the counting of the beats for the melodic rhythm. Then you should be able to perform the rhythm of the melody by clapping or playing a percussion instrument.

WORKSHEET

(1) Write in the counting above each of the following exercises:

(2) Write in an appropriate meter signature for each line of notes.

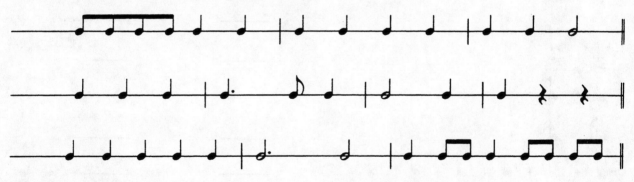

(3) Complete the rhythmic duration of each measure by filling in *one* note.

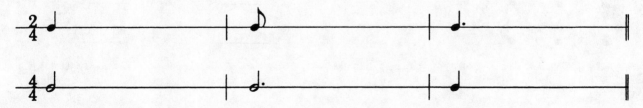

(4) Complete the rhythmic duration of each measure by filling in *one* rest.

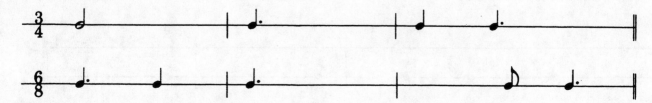

(5) Write the answer to each of the following sums in a single note value and a single rest value. Some notes and rests should be dotted.

	Note Value	Rest Value
𝅗𝅥 + 𝅗𝅥 =	𝅝	▬
♩ + ♩ =	____	____
♪ + ♪ =	____	____
𝅗𝅥 + ♩ =	____	____
♩ + ♪ =	____	____
♪ + ♪ + ♪ =	____	____
♪ + ♪ + ♪ + ♪ =	____	____
𝅗𝅥. + 𝅗𝅥. =	____	____
♪ + ♪ + ♪ =	____	____
♩ + ♩ + ♩ =	____	____
𝅗𝅥 + ♩ + ♩ =	____	____
♩ + ♪ + ♪ + ♩ =	____	____
♪. + ♪ =	____	____
♩ + ♪ + ♩ + ♪ + ♩ =	____	____
♪ + ♪ + ♪ + ♪ =	____	____
𝅗𝅥. + ♩ + ♪ =	____	____

(6) Listen carefully as your instructor claps a rhythm. Notate it on the staff provided below. Each rhythm will be performed six times.

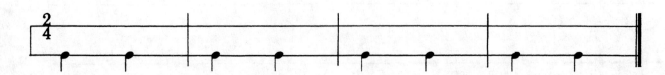

CHAPTER TWO
Reading Pitch

CHAPTER TWO
Reading Pitch

Pitch is the relative highness or lowness of the sounds that you hear. Pitch results when vibrating bodies, such as vocal cords, guitar strings, or columns of air, are set into motion. In addition to pitch, each tone of a melody also contains the properties of duration, tone color, and dynamics.

Pitches are represented visually by placing a note on a *staff*. The staff is made up of five horizontal lines of equal length and distance from each other. The spaces between, above, and below these lines also are used for the placement of notes. The lines and spaces of the staff always are numbered from low to high.

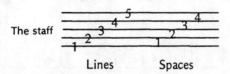

Pitches take their names from the first seven letters of the English alphabet: A, B, C, D, E, F, and G. Each of these seven pitch names is assigned to particular lines and spaces of the staff by the use of a device called a *clef sign*. Although four clefs are used in music notation today, the treble, or G, clef (𝄞) is most commonly used to denote the pitches played by the instruments that you will study. When this sign is placed at the beginning (left-hand side) of the staff, the pitch G will always occur on the second line. All other pitches on the staff are named consecutively from low to high with reference to that line.

Test how well you know the pitch names on the staff by figuring out what words the following notes spell. Bar lines separate words.

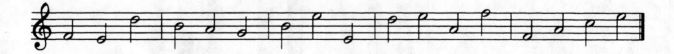

PITCHES ON THE KEYBOARD

Now that you can recognize the names of pitches on the staff, you must apply those names to specific positions on a keyboard. At this point, you should refer to a keyboard to help you to identify and visualize the names of pitches as they occur in music. All keyboard instruments are constructed alike, and each white key has a letter name which corresponds to a line or space of the staff. In order to locate a particular white key, it is necessary to use the groupings of black keys for reference. Notice in the illustration below that the black keys (ebonies) are grouped in alternate sets of two and three. These groupings enable you to identify the white keys (ivories) that surround them.

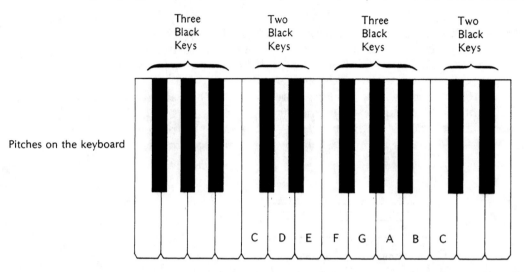

Pitches on the keyboard

Look first at a group of two black keys. The pitch C, a white key, is located immediately to the left of this group of black keys; D is between the two black keys; and E is the white key to the right of two black keys.

Now look at a group of three black keys. The pitch F can be found on the left of these three black keys, and B is found to the right of the three black keys, while G and A are between those outer tones — G to the right of F and A to the left of B.

Each white key of the keyboard has a letter name which is represented on one line or space of the staff. Now look at the diagram below, which relates the keyboard to the pitches of the notes of the staff. The pitch name of the note found on the second line corresponds to the note G on the keyboard. Notice that the pitches on the staff relate directly to the white keys on the keyboard.

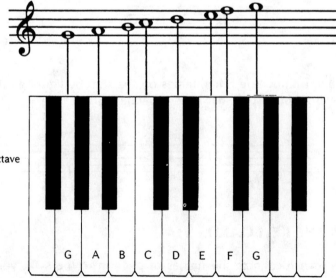

The keyboard and the upper staff octave

Because many of the tones used in singing extend below the lower limit of the staff, lines must be added to accommodate the range of some melodies. *Ledger lines* are short lines that extend the staff either downward or upward. These lines, plus the spaces above and below them, are named consecutively from the last given letter name above or below the staff. Notice in the next diagram that ledger lines are a little longer than the notes that are placed on, below, or above them, and that they are spaced like the lines of the staff itself. The name of the first pitch given in the space below the second ledger line below the staff is G. This G is *one octave* lower in pitch than the next G, which is found on the second line of the staff. The series of letter names of the notes continues alphabetically.

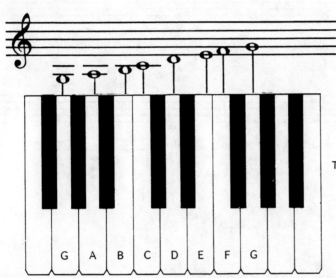

The keyboard and the lower staff octave

In summary, notes placed on the lines and spaces of the staff (without accidentals) correspond to the white keys of the keyboard. The names of the lines of the staff are E, G, B, D, and F, and the names of the spaces of the staff are F, A, C, and E. The space above the staff is G, and the space below the staff is D. Ledger lines extend the staff to accommodate tones lower or higher than the staff can represent.

Reading the pitches contained in melodies is like reading the letters that make up words, in that the symbols are interpreted from left to right. Reading music is different from reading words in that you must also learn to read up and down while reading from left to right.

Name the pitch of each note in the following song. Writing the letter name in pencil under the note is a good way to keep track of where you are. When you have practiced naming the pitches often enough to feel that you have them memorized, test yourself by erasing the penciled letters and reading them again. (*Note:* The capital letters printed above the staff are *not* the names of pitches. You will learn about them in Chapters 9 and 11.)

On Top of Old Smoky

United States

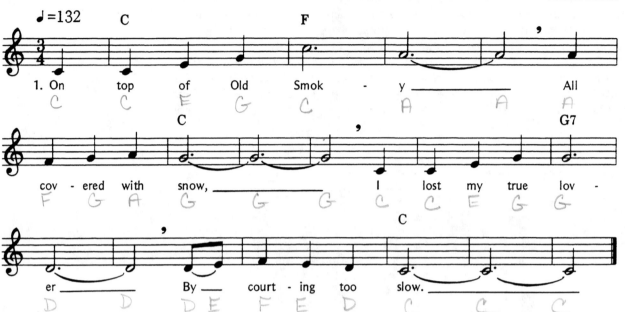

♩=132

1. On top of Old Smok - y _____ All
C C E G C A A A

cov - ered with snow, _____ I lost my true lov -
F G A G G G C C E G G

er _____ By _ court - ing too slow. _____
D D D E F E D C C C

2. Oh, courting is pleasure and parting is grief,
   But a false-hearted lover is worse than a thief.

3. A thief will just rob you of all that you save,
   But a false-hearted lover will send you to the grave.

4. The grave will decay you and turn you to dust.
   Not a boy in a million a poor girl can trust.

5. They'll hug you and squeeze you and tell you more lies
   Than the rain drops in heaven, or stars in the skies.

6. They'll swear that they love you, your heart for to please,
   But as soon as your back's turned, they'll love whom they please.

7. It's raining, it's hailing, this dark, stormy night.
   Your horses can't travel for the moon gives no light.

8. Go put up your horses, and give them some hay,
   And sit down beside me for long as you stay.

9. My horses ain't hungry, they won't eat your hay,
   I'm leaving for Georgia, I'll be on my way.

10. I'll go by Old Smoky, the mountains so high,
    Where the wild birds and turtle doves can hear my sad cry.

ACCIDENTALS

Black keys are named in relation to white keys through the use of sharps (♯) and flats (♭), called *accidentals*. Look again at your keyboard and locate the F key. A sharp sign in front of the note F on the staff directs you to play the key with the next highest pitch after F. This key is not G, but the black key to the right of F. In this case we call that key F-sharp.

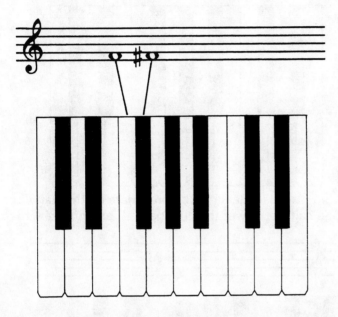

The distance between any key on the keyboard and the next highest or lowest key is called a *half step*. In going from F to F-sharp you move up one half step. If you go up by half steps on the keyboard from F up to the next highest F, you will cover twelve different keys. These keys constitute a *chromatic scale*. (You will learn more about scales in Chapter 4.)

Through the use of accidentals, all twelve tones of the chromatic scale can be presented on a staff that uses only seven different letter names. Find the key represented by each of the sharped notes:

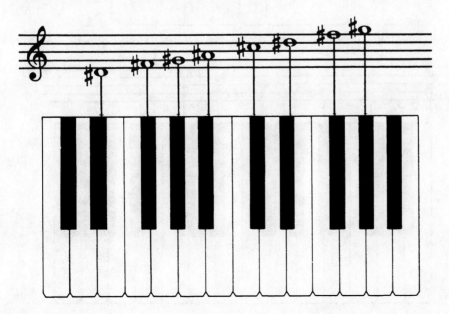

A sharp always fulfills its function of raising the pitch of a notated tone one half step, even when it does not result in playing a black key. For instance, E-sharp on the staff directs you to play F, and B-sharp directs you to play C.

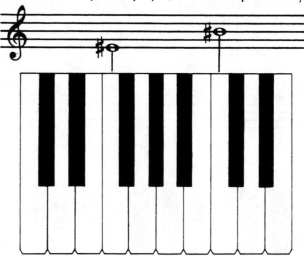

A flat sign (♭) placed immediately before a note on the staff directs you to play the key one half step lower than the natural, or white-key, tone.

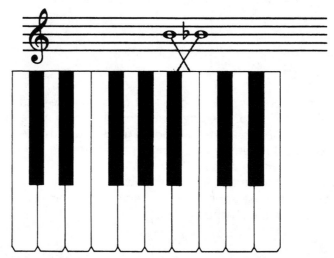

Study which key is played for each of the following flatted notes on the staff:

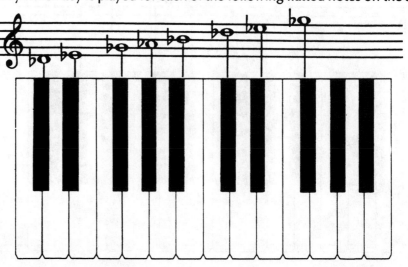

Should you see this symbol, ♮ , placed to the left of a note, it indicates that a previously used sharp or flat has been canceled. This sign, called a *natural,* is used to indicate that a particular pitch is neither flat nor sharp. The effect of a natural is to lower the pitch of a sharped note, or to raise the pitch of a flatted note. In both cases the raising or lowering is always the distance of one half step. The effect of the natural sign, like the other accidentals, is canceled by a bar line.

Review of Pitch Names

Try to name each of the black keys of the keyboard with two different pitch names. Also name the four white keys that can be notated with two different pitch names. Two different notes which indicate the same pitch are called *enharmonic tones.* Your answers to the first two sentences in this paragraph specify the enharmonic notes most common in music: C♯-D♭, D♯-E♭, F♯-G♭, G♯-A♭, A♯-B♭, E♯-F, E-F♭, B♯-C, and B-C♭. Each of these pairs represents two ways of notating a single pitch.

KEY SIGNATURES

In music notation, the raising or lowering of notes may be accomplished in either of two ways: (1) by using accidentals within a measure, or (2) by using a key signature. A *key signature* consists of sharps or flats placed next to the clef sign at the beginning of a staff.

As an accidental, the sharp, flat, or natural sign is placed on the line or in the space immediately to the left of the note to be altered. The effect of the accidental lasts only until the next bar line. A bar line cancels the effect of an accidental. The names of the notes in the following example are

Observe that the sharp is written before the note but is named after saying the pitch of the note, that is, "F♯" ("F-sharp").

When notes are altered through the use of a key signature, sharps or flats are placed next to the clef sign at the beginning of each staff. All notes of the same name — regardless of the octave in which they occur — are changed. In the following example, all Fs, Cs, and Gs are raised one half step. Unless superseded by accidentals; such accidentals affect only the specific pitch to which they are affixed for the duration of that one measure.

Write the letter name of each note in the following song. Be careful to observe both the key signature and the accidentals written next to the notes.

Greensleeves

England

d. = 44

Dm ... C

1. A - las my love _____ you do me wrong, _____ To

Bb ... A ... Dm

cast me off _____ dis - court - eous - ly And I have loved _____ you

C ... Bb ... A ... Dm

for so long, _____ De - light - ing in _____ your com - pa - ny.

CHORUS

F ... C ... Dm ... A

Green - sleeves ___ was all my joy, _____ Green - sleeves ___ was my de - light,

F ... C ... Dm ... A ... Dm

Green - sleeves was my heart of gold, ___ And who but my la - dy Green - sleeves.

2. I long have waited at your hand
   To do your bidding as your slave,
   And waged, have I, both life and land
   Your love and affection for to have.
   Chorus

3. If you intend thus to disdain
   It does the more enrapture me,
   And even so, I will remain
   Your lover in captivity.
   Chorus

4. Alas, my love, that yours should be
   A heart of faithless vanity,
   So here I meditate alone
   Upon your insincerity.
   Chorus

5. Ah, Greensleeves, now farewell, adieu,
   To God I pray to prosper thee,
   For I remain thy lover true,
   Come once again and be with me.
   Chorus

WORKSHEET

(1) Write the letter name of each note given below;

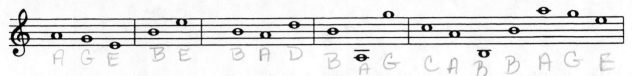

A G E   B E   B A D   B A G   C A B B A G E

(2) Write a quarter note on the staff for each letter name given;

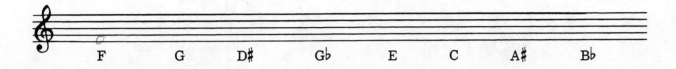

F   G   D♯   G♭   E   C   A♯   B♭

(3) Label all of the E, G♯, B♭, and C keys on the keyboard below;

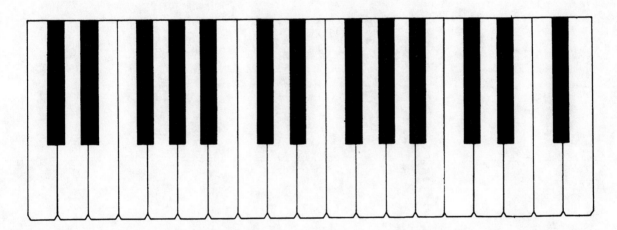

(4) Write and name the enharmonic note for each of the following:

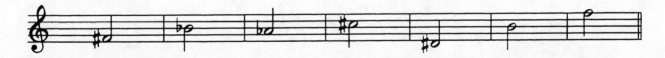

(5) Name the notes in the following line of music:

CHAPTER THREE
Playing the
Soprano Recorder

CHAPTER THREE
Playing the Soprano Recorder

The recorder is a small wind instrument that has been popular for periods of time spanning the last six centuries, especially in Elizabethan England. There are five popular sizes of recorders: sopranino, soprano, alto, tenor, and bass; the soprano is the most popular size. However, the alto has the ideal solo tone quality, combining the dynamic brilliance of the soprano with the mellowness of the tenor. Bach, Handel, and Telemann all wrote extensively for the alto recorder. The recorder is commonly used both in school music programs and elsewhere. Groups such as the American Recorder Society publish music for recorder ensembles and sponsor group activities for recorder players. Since the recorder is relatively easy to play, it provides a means for musical expression while you are still learning about music.

The sections of the recorder are named the head joint, middle joint, and foot joint. The recorder is much like a whistle, in that it is played by blowing into the end of the head joint (through the windway). The recorder has seven holes along the upper side of the middle and foot joints, and one hole on the underside at the top of the middle joint. The last two holes on the upper side each comprise two smaller holes. When we count the number of holes on the recorder, each pair of small holes is considered as one. Figure 3.1 shows the parts of a recorder.

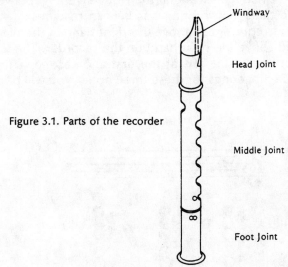

Figure 3.1. Parts of the recorder

Windway

Head Joint

Middle Joint

Foot Joint

When you hold the recorder, your left thumb covers the hole on the back of the recorder and the first three fingers of your left hand cover the first three holes on the upper side of the instrument. The right-hand fingers cover the four remaining holes at the foot joint end of the instrument. The weight of the instrument is supported by your lips and right thumb, leaving your fingers and left thumb free to cover and uncover the holes. Your left little finger is not used in playing the recorder. Study the picture on the chapter title page.

The recorder should be held at approximately a forty-five degree angle to the body. Your arms should fall toward the sides of your body and your shoulders should be relaxed. Maintain a good posture: (1) standing straight with your feet slightly apart or, (2) sitting forward without leaning back.

Cover the holes with the pads of your fingers, not the fingertips. When your fingers are not being used to cover the holes, you should hold them in readiness directly above and close to the hole each respective finger normally plays.

The recorder should be placed between your lips, but it should not touch your teeth. Only the very tip of the windway should be between your lips. In preparing to blow, build up an adequate supply of air by inhaling through your mouth (not through your nose). Then start the flow of air by releasing the tongue from the roof of the mouth, as in saying "doo." Release it very gently, being careful not to explode the air, or the beginning of the tone will sound harsh and perhaps "chirpy." Do start the tone by releasing the air pressure with the tongue, not just by exhaling. An attack started by exhaling alone will produce an indistinct *glissando* or scooping quality at the beginning of the tone.

To end a tone, stop the flow of air by placing your tongue on the roof of the mouth just behind the teeth, as in preparing to articulate the letter "d." The attack, duration, and termination of each tone may be diagramed as follows:

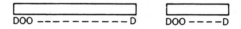

Intonation (being in tune) is greatly affected by overblowing or underblowing. Blowing too hard makes the tone harsh and the pitch sharp. Blowing too softly makes the tone weak and the pitch flat. Low notes require less breath pressure than high notes; therefore, you must blow more softly on low tones and increase breath pressure slightly on higher tones.

Fingerings for the notes B, A, and G on the recorder are given in the following diagram. A solid circle indicates that the respective finger covers its hole. An empty circle indicates that the finger is held in readiness just above the hole. The left hand is represented above the right hand in the diagram, since the left hand is held above the right hand on the recorder. The left thumb is diagramed between and to the left of the first and second left-hand finger holes. By learning the fingerings for these three notes, you will be able to play "BAG" and "GAB."

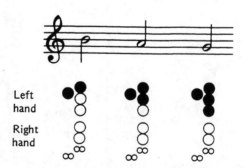

Practice the following two songs, "BAG" and "GAB," until you have mastered them, playing with perfect rhythm and good tone quality. (The letters above the staff of these songs represent chords and may be played on autoharp, piano, or guitar: you do not use these letters in playing the recorder.)

BAG

GAB

In the melody of "ED" two new notes are introduced: low E and low D.
These notes are fingered as follows:

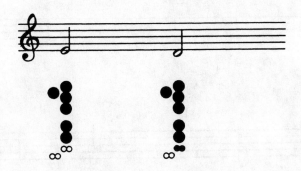

ED

You can practice the notes you have learned so far on the songs, "Jolly Old Saint Nicholas" and "Worried Man Blues."

Jolly Old Saint Nicholas

United States

Worried Man Blues

United States

$\quad\downarrow=112$

"Dance," "Hush Little Baby," and "Indian Dance" all require the use of the note C, which is fingered this way:

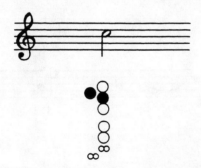

Dance

$\quad\downarrow=132$

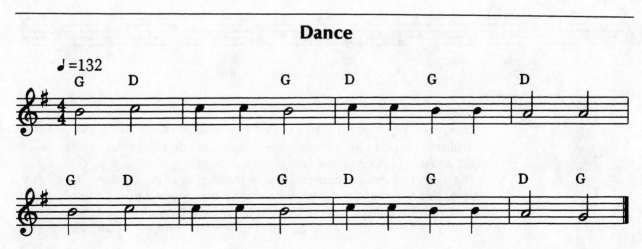

Hush Little Baby

United States

Indian Dance

The symbol ( ) in "Indian Dance" is a breath mark. It is used in wind instrument music to indicate the best places for the performer to breathe to avoid awkward phrasing and lack of air support.

The note F-sharp is required to play the theme from Brahms's First Symphony. You may need to favor this pitch by using only a portion or all of the pad of your little finger on the bottom hole. Each recorder is different. Listen carefully to determine how to play this note in tune on your particular instrument.

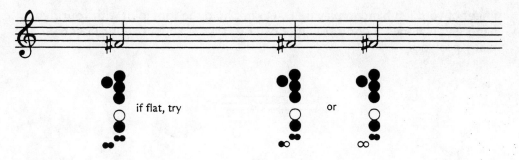

if flat, try   or

Theme
First Symphony

Johannes Brahms

Michael Row

United States

Learn to finger high D so that you can play the following songs. Remember to support your recorder with your lips, right thumb, and second finger of your left hand in playing D. Do not hold the foot joint with your right hand. Do maintain a good playing position, always keeping your fingers in a ready position.

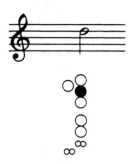

Largo

Anton Dvořák

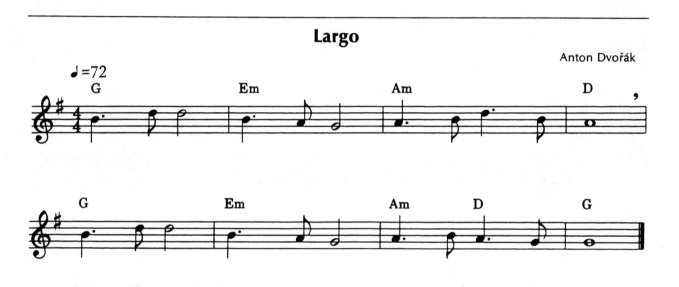

Go Tell Aunt Rhody

United States

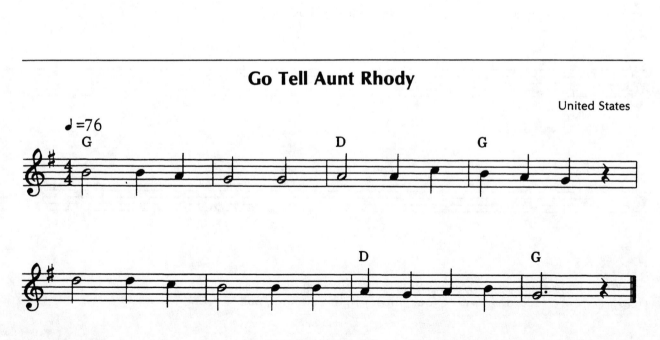

Skye Boat Song

Scotland

Amazing Grace

United States

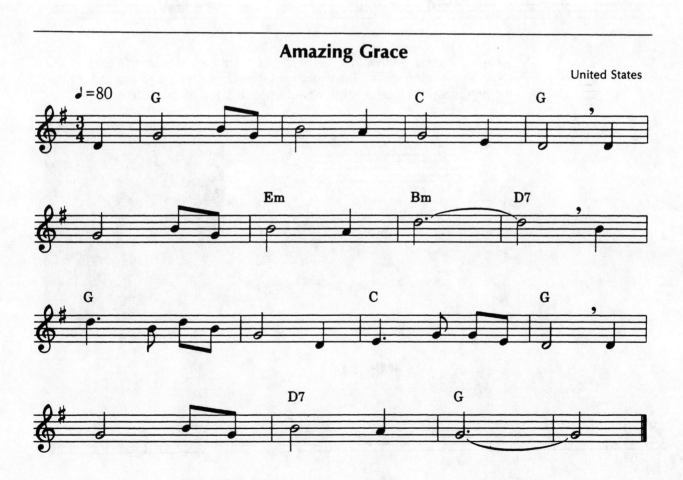

Ode to Joy
Ninth Symphony

Ludwig van Beethoven

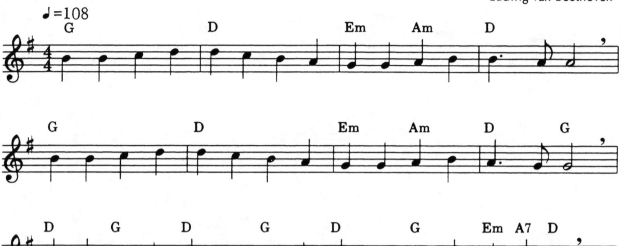

High E is fingered like low E except that the thumbhole on the back of the recorder is slightly open. The thumbnail should be pivoted so the nail divides the hole, leaving one-fourth to one-third of the top of the hole open.

Thumb in half-hole position

High E

Riddle Song

United States

The term D. S. al Fine occurs in "Long Long Ago." "D. S." stands for "dal segno," which indicates a repetition from a point in the piece marked by the sign %. The entire expression D. S. al Fine tells the performer to return to the sign and continue to the end, which is marked with the word "Fine."

Long, Long Ago

Thomas H. Bayly

D. S. al Fine

Now that you have control over nine notes on your recorder, try them out on the following songs. You can play the rounds with your classmates. Try to accompany your friends on autoharp, piano, guitar; and/or with rhythm instruments as they play the melodies.

Hey, Ho! Nobody Home
Round

England, arranged by Terry Lee Kuhn

A Minor Brother
Round

Gustav Mahler, arranged by Terry Lee Kuhn

The Tailor and the Mouse

England

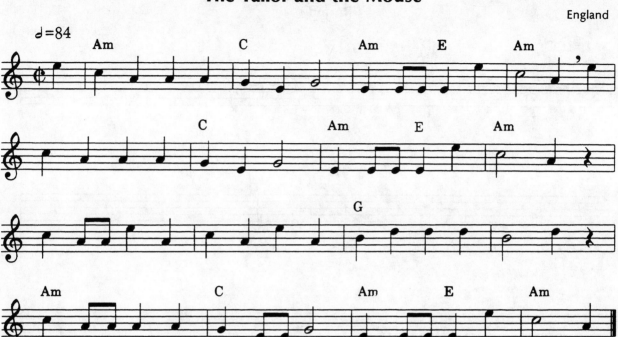

Se Vuol Ballare

Wolfgang Amadeus Mozart

Let Us Sing Together
Round

Czechoslovakia

Jig

Ireland

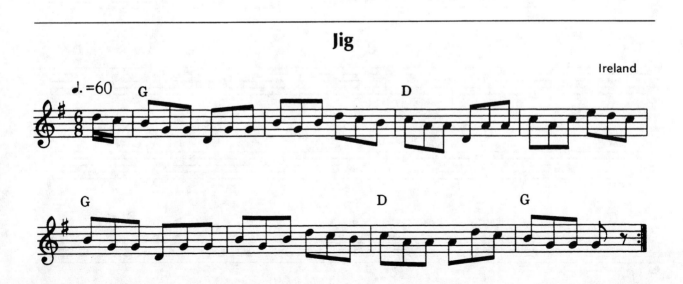

Bile Them Cabbage Down

United States

Theme
Polovetsian Dances

Alexander Borodin

"Tune of the Tay" introduces the *slur*, a curved line connecting two notes of different pitch. The slur directs a performer to connect the two tones as *legato* (smoothly) as possible. Accomplish this effect on the recorder by not tonguing; that is, maintain steady breath support while moving your fingers precisely together.

Tune of the Tay

England

"In the Shining Moonlight" introduces two commonly used pitches in the lower register of the recorder, F and C. C is fingered like this:

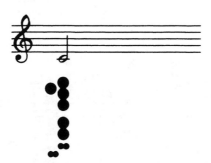

The fingering for F depends upon the particular hole pattern of your instrument. Recorders are constructed with either Baroque or German fingering systems. Look at the line of holes on the upper side of the middle joint, and count down from the head joint; if the fifth hole is larger than the fourth hole, then your recorder has a Baroque fingering system.

Baroque

However, if the fourth hole is larger than the fifth hole, then you have a German fingering system.

German

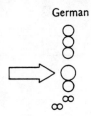

Professional performers use Baroque-fingered instruments; however, some beginners start on the German fingering system because their teachers consider it easier in the early stages of learning. Be sure to choose the correct fingering for F.

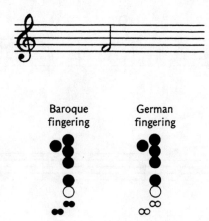

Baroque fingering   German fingering

Blow very softly on the low C in the following songs, and be sure to finger F correctly.

In the Shining Moonlight

France

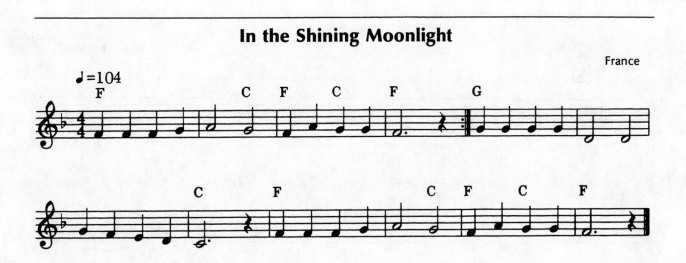

The Ash Grove

Wales

Psalm 23

Scotland

Kum Ba Ya

United States/Africa

Voice or
Bells and Drum

Shady Grove

United States

The "Coventry Carol" utilizes the note B-flat in addition to the B-natural at the end. B-flat is fingered this way:

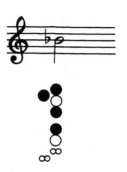

Coventry Carol

England

Jingle Bells

James Pierpont

Pavane

Thoinet Arbeau

Playing the ostinato rhythm on a hand drum will help evoke the original stately dance feeling of "Pavane."

Hand Drum
Ostinato Rhythm

Hineh Mah Tov
Round

Israel

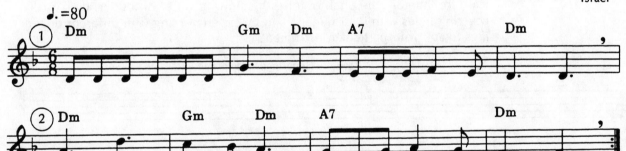

A note indicated with a *fermata,* or hold ( ), is held longer than the note's value, at the discretion of the performer. In "Old Hundredth" you would hold the notes with fermatas about twice as long.

Old Hundredth

Genevan Psalter

God Rest Ye Merry, Gentlemen

England

There are many notes on the recorder that have not been introduced in this chapter. Some of the more common notes and their fingerings are given in the following chart. As you gain experience in proficiency on the recorder, all of these tones, and many more, will become part of your technique. You will also learn to "humor" the pitch of tones by blowing softer or louder, by partially covering holes with your fingers, and by experimenting with different fingerings to suit your particular instrument.

Baroque Fingerings for Soprano Recorder

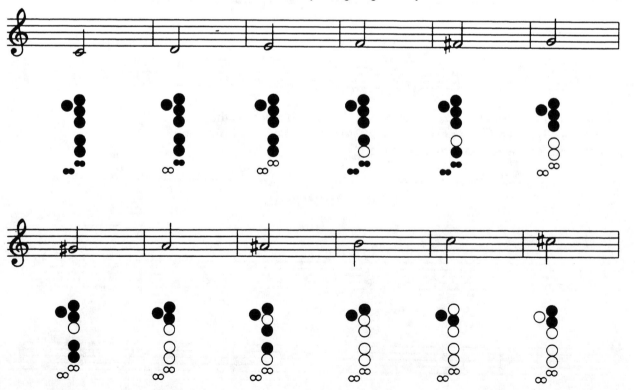

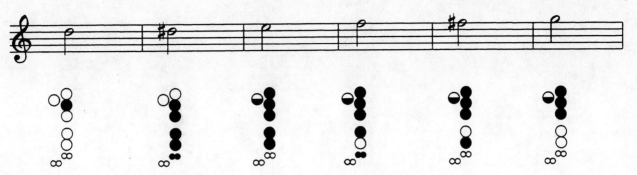

German Fingerings

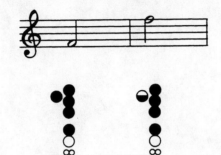

CHAPTER FOUR
Understanding Scales and Key Signatures

CHAPTER FOUR
Understanding Scales and Key Signatures

In music of the Western nations, the octave is divided into twelve equally spaced tones, which, when played consecutively, are called the *chromatic scale.*

Most songs use fewer than all twelve tones in the melody; the most common type of song uses seven tones. Played consecutively, these tones form a *diatonic scale.*

In order to construct any scale, you must be familiar with the intervals of half step and whole step. A *half step* is the distance between any white key and the black key immediately to its right or left. Some examples are D to D♯, A♭ to G, and F♯ to G. Find other examples of half steps between white and black keys. A half step is also the distance between two white keys where there is no intervening black key. The examples are E to F and C to B.

A *whole step* is two adjacent half steps. Some examples of whole steps are C to D (white key to white key with one black key in between), G♯ to A♯ (black key to black key with one white key in between), B to C♯ (white key to black key with one white key in between), and E♭ to F (black key to white key with one white key in between). The pairs of keys marked "X" on the following keyboard are all separated by whole steps.

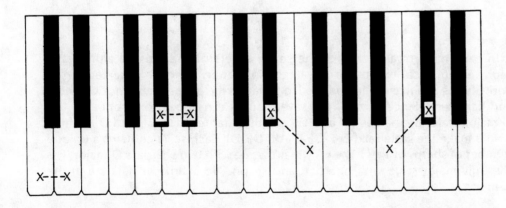

MAJOR SCALE PATTERNS

The sound of a *major scale* is the familiar do-re-mi-fa-sol-la-ti-do, which starts and ends on tones an octave apart; that is, the scale begins and ends on the same letter name, and including that name twice, spans eight tones. A major scale can be built on each of the twelve tones that make up the chromatic scale, and each major scale carries the name of the tone on which it begins. For instance, the C-major scale contains the tones

The C-major scale, D-major scale, Bb-major scale, F#-major scale, and all the others have the same structure; they merely differ in their starting pitches. The tones of each major scale follow this pattern of whole steps (W) and half steps (H):

There is a whole step between consecutive degrees of the major scale, except between the third and fourth degrees (here, E and F) and between the seventh and eighth degrees (here, B and C), each of which contains a half step interval.

You can use the chromatic scale and this pattern to figure out any major scale. If, for instance, you wanted to know the notes in the D-major scale, you would make the first tone D and use the pattern as follows:

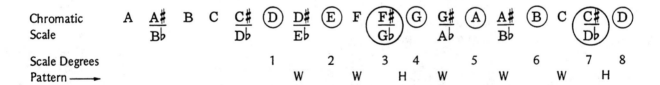

In each major scale, each of the seven letters of the musical alphabet is represented once, except for the beginning letter, which is repeated at the end. Sharps and flats are introduced to produce the proper sequence of whole and half steps. Since each of the seven letters can appear only once, in the D-major scale, the names F♯ and C♯ are used rather than G♭ and D♭ (which would make the scale read D-E-G♭-G-A-B-D♭-D). Each scale contains a unique number of sharps or flats: The only major scale with two sharps is D-major, F is the only major scale with one flat, and so on. No sharps or flats are in the C-major scale.

MAJOR KEY SIGNATURES

It is a convention to place sharps or flats at the beginning of each line of music to automatically raise or lower the notes to the pitches that are used consistently in that key. You will recall from Chapter 2 that notes placed on the lines and spaces of the staff refer only to white keys unless a sharp or flat is placed before the note head. Placing the sharps or flats at the beginning of the staff is a great convenience; if a song lies in the G-major scale, then the note F usually will be sharped and rarely natural. Placing the F♯ at the beginning of each line is simpler than placing one next to each F. This method also helps to identify the major scale being used; in fact, this group of sharps or flats at the beginning of each line is called the *key signature*.

Since each major scale has a unique number of sharps or flats, there is no confusion among key signatures. For example, this signature

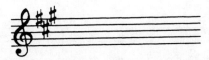

designates the A-major scale, since that is the only scale with the notes F, C, and G sharped. In the following chart the key signatures for the most common major scales are given.

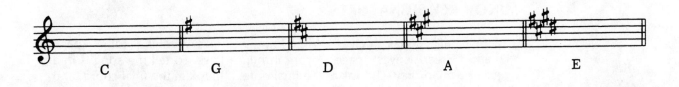

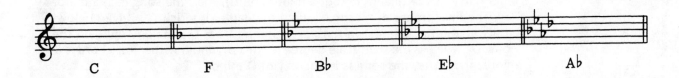

Look up the following songs in this text and identify the major key in which each is written from the key signature.

Title	Page	Key
"Gonna Sing"	162	F major
"Lightly Row"	155	＿＿ major
"You're a Grand Old Flag"	137	＿＿ major
"Kookaburra"	129	＿＿ major
"America the Beautiful"	87	＿＿ major

MINOR SCALE PATTERNS

Minor scales exist in three forms: natural minor, harmonic minor, and melodic minor. Each form of the minor scale has a specific pattern. The melodic-minor scale pattern is the only one that is different in its ascending and descending forms.

D Natural Minor

Scale Degrees	1	2	3	4	5	6	7	8	7	6	5	4	3	2	1
Ascending Pattern ⟶		W	H	W	W	H	W	W							
Descending Pattern ⟶									W	W	H	W	W	H	W

D Harmonic Minor

Scale Degrees	1	2	3	4	5	6·	7	8	7	6	5	4	3	2	1
Ascending Pattern ⟶		W	H	W	W	H	W+H	H							
Descending Pattern ⟶									H	W+H	H	W	W	H	W

D Melodic Minor

Scale Degrees	1	2	3	4	5	6	7	8	7	6	5	4	3	2	1
Ascending Pattern ⟶		W	H	W	W	W	W	H							
Descending Pattern ⟶									W	W	H	W	W	H	W

MINOR KEY SIGNATURES

Many familiar songs, such as "When Johnny Comes Marching Home" (page 113) and "Greensleeves" (page 36), are in minor keys. To tell if a song is in a major or a minor key, (1) look at the final note, (2) look at the final chord, and (3) look at the key signature. If the final note is the sixth scale degree of the major scale indicated by the key signature, and if the final chord is the same letter name as the final note (but a minor chord), then the song is in a minor key. The final phrase of "Joshua Fought the Battle of Jericho" is given below. Notice that it has one flat in the key signature, that the melody ends on the note D which is the sixth scale degree in F major, and that the final chord is D minor; therefore, the song is in the key of D minor.

Now the following names of minor keys can be added to the key signature chart on page 69. Notice that the tonic of each minor key is the sixth degree of the major key that shares its key signature. The two keys, one major and one minor, that share the same key signature are referred to as *relative keys*.

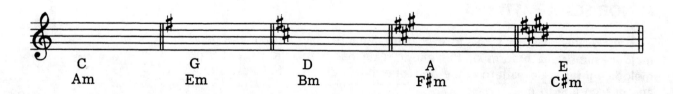

C	G	D	A	E
Am	Em	Bm	F♯m	C♯m

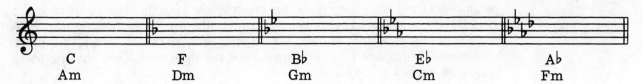

TONIC

The first (and last) note of a scale has a special significance, evidenced by the fact that the scale carries its name. The note upon which the scale is based is called the *tonic*. The seven tones that form a major or minor scale are chosen because one can hear a certain relationship among them. The basis of this relationship is their distance from the tonic.

Melodies tend to "gravitate" toward the tonic; its presence at the end of a melody usually indicates that melodic activity has come to rest. For this reason, the final note in a song is usually the tonic in both major and minor keys. Most songs end with the tonic; in fact, the ear can hardly accept any ending of a song other than the tonic. For this reason, one of the best ways to determine the tonic is to look at the final note of a song's melody.

Listen for the tendency of a song to gravitate toward the tonic as either a temporary or a final resting place in these two lines of "Home on the Range." This song is in the key of F-major, and the first line ends on the note G, not the tonic.

As you can hear, there is no finality at the end of this first phrase, so the song must continue. The second line is nearly identical to the first, except that the line does end on the tonic, F, and the song sounds finished.

Just as the melody of a song tends toward the tonic as a resting place, so the chords in the accompaniment to the melody fluctuate and then usually come to rest on the most stable chord. *Chords* are groups of notes played simultaneously (see Chapter 11). Depending on what notes make them up, they sound harmonious or dissonant and stable or unstable. A seventh chord, for example is relatively unstable and wants to "resolve" or gravitate toward a more stable chord, usually the chord built on the tonic. The tonic chord is the most harmonious, stable, and tension-free. This fact gives you a third clue to the key of a song: The final chord tends to be the chord that is built on the tonic note. Some songs, for the sake of variety or interest or surprise, may not end on the tonic note or on the corresponding chord, but you easily can hear these surprise endings and determine what note and chord is "expected" for the end of the song.

In summary, the key of a song can be determined by looking for agreement among (1) the final note, (2) the final chord, and (3) the key signature. For example, a song that ended (1) on the melody note E, (2) on the E-major chord, and (3) with four sharps in the key signature undoubtedly would be in the key of E-major. A song that ended (1) on the melody note C#, and (2) on the C#-minor chord, with (3) four sharps in the key signature would just as obviously be the key of C#-minor.

Look up each of the following songs and identify its key.

Title	Page	Key
"The Bear Song"	248	D major
"River Theme"	231	E minor
"Scarborough Fair"	252	_____
"Roll On, Columbia, Roll On"	253	_____
"Frère Jacques"	211	_____
"Little Tom Tinker"	212	_____
"Zum Gali, Gali"	215	_____
"Wayfaring Stranger"	119	_____

WORKSHEET

(1) Write the names of the chromatic scale tones ascending from C:

___ ___ ___ ___ ___ ___ ___ ___ ___ ___ ___ ___

(2) Write the whole and half step interval pattern that separates scale degrees in an ascending major scale:

___ ___ ___ ___ ___ ___ ___

(3) Write the pitch names for the ascending major scale which begins on each of the following tones:

E ___ ___ ___ ___ ___ ___ ___ ___

F ___ ___ ___ ___ ___ ___ ___ ___

A ___ ___ ___ ___ ___ ___ ___ ___

B♭ ___ ___ ___ ___ ___ ___ ___ ___

(4) Write the ascending D, G, and E♭-major scales on the staffs below:

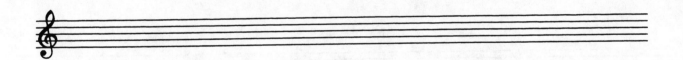

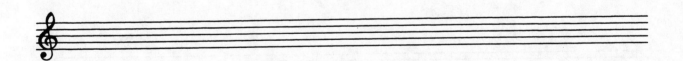

(5) Write out the key signatures for each of the following major scales:

D   C   E♭   F   G   A   B♭

(6) Write the whole and half step interval pattern that separates scale degrees in an ascending natural minor scale:

___ ___ ___ ___ ___ ___ ___

73

(7) Write the ascending natural minor scale for the following key signatures:

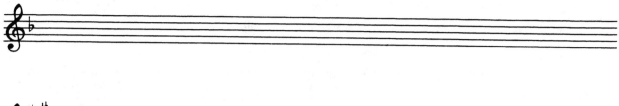

(8) The final measures of twelve songs are given below. Identify the key of each of these songs.

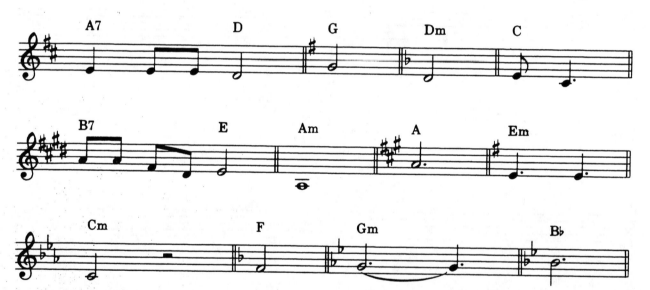

CHAPTER FIVE
Singing Songs

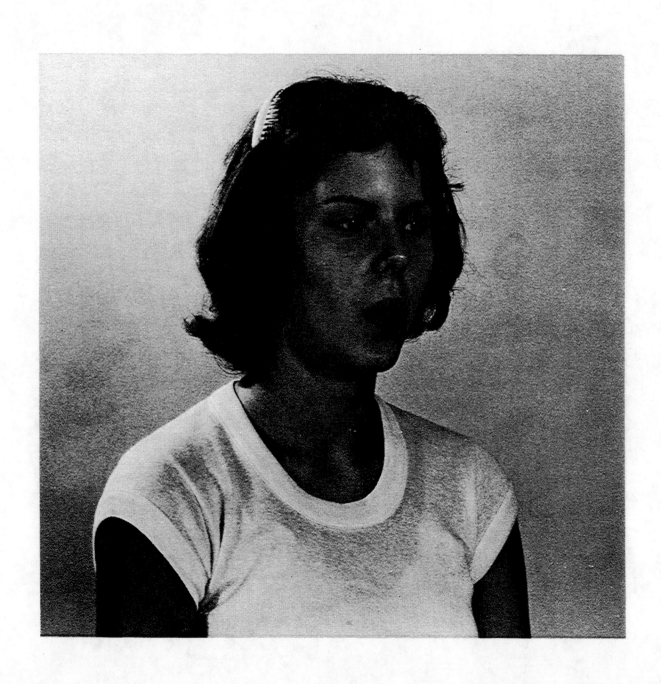

CHAPTER FIVE
Singing Songs

It is often said that the human voice is the most expressive of all musical instruments. People everywhere laugh, sob, wail, and yell as means of communicating feelings, evidence that the voice can convey the "language of the soul." Singing, then, is the process of organizing and controlling the pitch and rhythm of sounds produced within your body in order to communicate emotion. The addition of words sung to specific pitches and rhythms in order to communicate verbal ideas also gives rise to the definition of singing as "tuned speech."

VOICE PRODUCTION

The vocal mechanism, although hidden from view, can be understood from a mechanical standpoint (See Figure 5.1). There are three parts: the "bellows," which provide air; the "vibrators," which produce pitches; and the "resonating cavities," which amplify and color the tone. All of these bodily functions can be brought under conscious control. The processes of vocalizing and singing should not be thought of as mysterious or only for the musically gifted. Anyone who is capable of speaking also is able to adjust that speech in different pitch ranges in order to become a singer.

The "bellows" are the lungs. The loudness and steadiness of your singing depend upon control of your diaphragm and lower rib cage, which allow your lungs to contract and expand. To feel how your body behaves when you

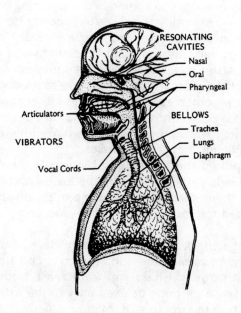

Figure 5.1. The vocal mechanism

Correct singing posture

breathe deeply, place both your hands above your hips in the area of your waist between your ribs and hip bones and press in. Take a deep breath through your mouth. You should be aware of the expanding lungs pressing against your ribs and diaphragm, which, in turn, will force your hands apart. Exhale through your mouth while pressing your hands inward. Do the exhalations several different ways: Hissing, panting, and coughing will allow you to gain conscious control of the air supply for your singing.

Maintaining correct posture will allow the rest of your rib cage to support your lungs. Place your fingertips on your shoulders (right hand on right shoulder and left hand on left shoulder). Pull your elbows in toward your sides until you feel your shoulders pulling down, not back. Slowly drop your hands and arms without changing the set of your shoulders. This is the posture that permits the maximum expansion of your lungs.

The "vibrators" are the two folds of mucous membrane, called *vocal cords*, found at the top of the larynx (Figure 5.2). The lungs force air up through the trachea and past the vocal cords, which in turn begin to vibrate at a given rate according to the tension placed upon them.

Figure 5.2. Vocal cords

Low pitch   High pitch

You can become aware of your vocal cords and their location by placing your fingertips on your neck below your chin just above the bump known as the "Adam's apple." This area is most pronounced in men. Women may locate it best by humming and locating the source of greatest vibration with their fingers.

While singing a comfortable pitch on the open vowel sound "ah," press against this area with your fingers. You should hear a lowering of the pitch that you are singing, since you are causing the cords to separate from each other.

The vocal cords differ in physical size and shape in every individual. The variables include age, sex, and physical maturity. Some vocal cords are thin and short and vibrate at faster rates, producing high pitches. Other persons' vocal cords are thick and long, vibrating at slower rates to produce low pitches. Generally, sexually mature women are categorized as either sopranos or altos, and men as tenors or basses, according to the physical construction and resulting pitch ranges of their vocal cords. Sopranos have a higher vocal range than altos, and tenors a higher range than basses.

If you have never explored the full range of your voice before, the next exercise (Figure 5.3) will help you to determine the lowest and highest pitches (and the *range* between them) that you are capable of producing at this time. The numbers are provided for your convenience in locating a specific pitch.

The results of this range check should not be considered fixed for all time. Factors such as maturity, physical condition, exercise, and training through feedback from your instructor will help you to increase both ends of your range. Most adults can sing about one octave between the extremes of the G below middle C to high D in the treble staff. Mature males automatically make the vocal shift necessary to sing one octave below females and children whose voices have not matured.

NAME _____   SEX: male _____ female _____

Listen to the pitch being played on the piano. It is E, also numbered as zero. Hum by closing your lips over an open jaw (teeth not touching). If you can match the E comfortably at the exact pitch, then check "at pitch." If your voice is an octave lower, then check "octave lower."

> I am humming (check one) _____ at pitch _____ octave lower

Those singing at pitch and those singing an octave lower will be tested separately.

The instructor will play each of the following descending notes at a very slow tempo and call out the name and number of each note. Cross out with an "X" each note that you can match comfortably by humming. When you reach the point at which you can no longer comfortably match the pitches, sit quietly until everyone has found the low note of his/her vocal range.

The instructor will now play the following ascending notes at a slow tempo and call out the name and number of each note. Hum by closing your lips over an open jaw and cross out with an "X" each note you can match comfortably. When you reach your highest comfortable note, sit quietly until the class has completed the exercise.

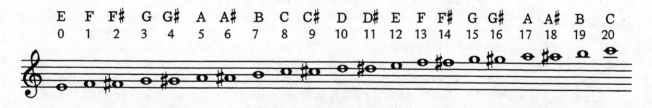

Figure 5.3. Vocal range check

Be aware that your vocal range places limitations on the keys you choose for song performance. The key of a song may have to be lowered until the highest pitch can be sung comfortably. This act of lowering, or *transposition* (Chapter 14), also affects the lowest pitch of the song. Make sure when you transpose a song down that you can also sing the lowest note in the new key.

One way to increase your low range is to take the following scale pattern and sing it slowly, using a comfortable volume and vowel sound such as "ah" or "oo." The curved line under each group of five notes is called a *slur*. Slurs indicate that notes of different pitch are to be played or sung smoothly without taking a breath.

Exercise for Lower Range

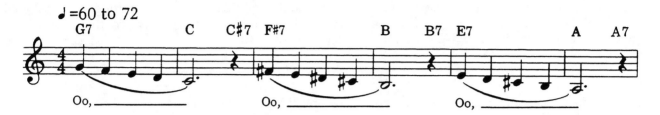

Continue transposing this pattern down by half steps until the lowest pitch of your range is reached. Repeated use of this exercise will gradually relax the vocal cords, allowing them to vibrate freely and at a slower rate, thus producing lower pitches.

The muscles that control the vocal cords also relax during the process of yawning. Place your forefinger and middle finger next to each other and insert the tips of both fingers between your teeth. The fingers should be placed vertically rather than horizontally, so that the jaws are opened at least one inch.

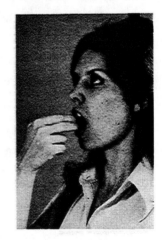

Open jaw position

While your fingers are in this position take several slow, deep yawning breaths. Slowly expel the air. Now remove your fingers and yawn again with your jaws in the same open position. Try to keep the jaw in the same open position when you sing. This position, much different from the position that you usually use for speech, is essential for maximum extension of your range.

Another exercise may be used to gradually extend your upper vocal register. Begin on a comfortable pitch in the middle of your range singing the vowel sound "ee." Sing the scale pattern C, D, E, F, G using this vowel sound to sing smoothly (*legato*) from one note up to another.

Exercise for Upper Range

Transpose this exercise up a half step at a time until you reach your highest comfortable pitch. The resulting sound should not be forced or harsh.

Women may find this exercise easier to perform than men because of the physiological phenomenon known as *falsetto* that occurs in mature males. In falsetto singing only the thin edges of the vocal cords vibrate. The resulting sound is thinner and lighter than that of the lower register. The volume of this sound can be increased by using more air and by using the resonant cavities of the head to amplify the sound.

The resonators used for amplification and tone color adjustment are the cavities of the nasal, oral, and pharyngeal areas of the head. Depending on where the air stream from the lungs is directed or focused, the resulting tone quality, called *timbre,* will be thin (nasal), normal (oral), or heavy (pharyngeal). These cavities also may be manipulated consciously to produce further refinements of the three basic tone colors. The proper tone color for a song varies according to the demands of the text, its tempo and dynamic markings, and the traditional performance practice associated with it. A lullaby should not sound the same as a work song, nor should a patriotic song sound like a spiritual.

To become aware of the resonators you have available to color tone, try the following exercises.

(1) While humming a comfortable pitch with jaws closed, place your fingertips on either side of your nose on the bones that lie beneath your eyes. Move your fingertips around these bones and over the bridge of your nose to locate the sources of greatest vibration. These areas are your nasal cavities or sinuses. Think the syllables "mm" and "n" alternately to feel how the tongue can be used to change the focus of the air stream and produce a change in tone color. If you have difficulty hearing these changes in timbre, try placing one hand over one of your ears.

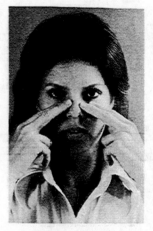

The nasal cavities

(2) While humming a comfortable pitch with your jaws closed, slowly open your jaws without opening your lips. You should feel the source of vibration move from your nose to your lips, cheeks, and teeth (the oral cavity). Try this exercise with both "mm" and "n" sounds.

(3) Start by humming "mm" with your jaws closed. Drop your jaw open about one inch but keep your lips closed. Slowly open your lips while changing to the vowel sound "ah." You should feel a gradual shift in the resonance of the pitch which you are humming. Next, try the same exercise but at the end open your lips and sing the vowel sound "uh" instead of "ah." Notice how the resonance feels as if it were emanating from the back of your tongue and upper throat (the pharyngeal area).

A good singer will hear differences in coloration between the sounds he or she produces while singing, and will feel the physical changes that affect these sounds. You must remember these physical sensations in order to continue improving your singing skills.

READING SONGS

When reading a song for the first time, look it over and analyze the contour of the melody. Do the note heads proceed up or down? Are the intervals small or large? What is the relation of the last note in a line to the first note of the next line? Are any of the phrases repeated? Such questions will help you to sight-read vocal music.

After you have learned the rhythm and pitches of a song, give careful attention to the lyrics. Try reading the words as if they were poetry without pitch. Read each word aloud with clear resonant tone, giving particular attention to the correct formation of the vowels *a, e, i, o,* and *u.* Try saying the words of the text with your eyes closed and a hand placed over one ear. Really listen to yourself. Also, try reading the words of the text to a friend who is located twenty feet away from you. Ask your friend to tell you whether you are communicating all the words.

The following songs are arranged in order by their range. The first song has just four different pitches, all within the span of a major third. (For an explanation of such intervals, see Chapter 11.) After you have sung it in the given key try transposing it up as well as down to find the keys in which you can sing it comfortably.

Teacher Don't 'Low

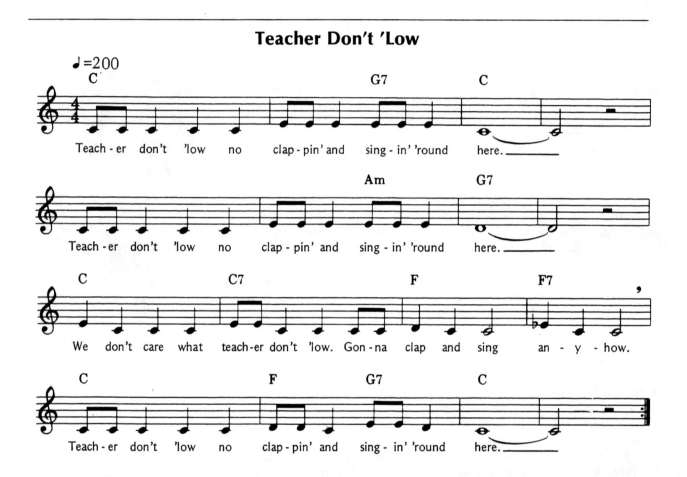

For additional verses, substitute for "clappin' & singin' " such phrases as

"pickin' & grinnin' "
"finger poppin' "
"eyeball rollin' "
"toe touchin' "
"tummy rubbin' "

Make up other phrases that will fit the three-beat rhythm of "clappin' & singin'."

The following song contains just four different pitches in its melody and spans the interval of a perfect fifth. Try creating additional verses that resolve Billy's fate.

Mary Had a Billy Goat

♩=88

1. Ma - ry had a bil - ly goat, bil - ly goat, bil - ly goat.

Ma - ry had a bil - ly goat and he was lined with steel.

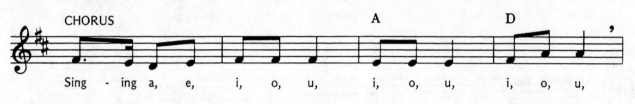

CHORUS

Sing - ing a, e, i, o, u, i, o, u, i, o, u,

Sing - ing a, e, i, o, u, a, e, i, o, u.

2. He fed on nails and circulars, circulars, circulars.
   He fed on nails and circulars and relished miniskirts.
   Chorus

3. One day he ate an oyster can, oyster can, oyster can.
   One day he ate an oyster can and a clothesline full of shirts.
   Chorus

4. The shirts can do no harm you know, harm you know, harm you know.
   The shirts can do no harm you know, but oh! that oyster can!
   Chorus

5. The can was filled with dynamite, dynamite, dynamite,
   The can was filled with dynamite which he mistook for cheese.
   Chorus

The next song's melody contains six different pitches within the range of a minor sixth. Try dividing the class in half and having one group sing the question (the first four measures) and the other group sing the replies (the last six measure plus one beat).

Where Are You Going, My Pretty Maid?

England

1. Where are you go - ing, my pret - ty maid? Where are you go - ing,

my pret - ty maid? "I'm go - ing a' - milk - ing, sir," she said,

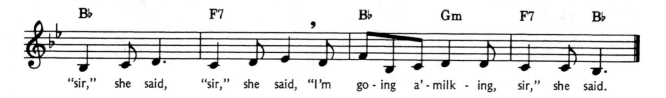

"sir," she said, "sir," she said, "I'm go - ing a' - milk - ing, sir," she said.

2. <u>Shall</u> I go with you, <u>my</u> pretty maid? *(Repeat)*
   "Oh, <u>yes</u>, if you please, kind <u>sir</u>," she said. *(Repeat)*

3. <u>What</u> is your fortune, <u>my</u> pretty maid? *(Repeat)*
   "My <u>face</u> is my fortune, <u>sir</u>," she said. *(Repeat)*

4. <u>Then</u> I can't marry you, <u>my</u> pretty maid! *(Repeat)*
   "<u>No</u>body asked you, <u>sir</u>," she said. *(Repeat)*

"Aura Lea," a popular song of the Civil War period, contains seven different pitches within the range of a minor seventh. Usually, the pitch indicated with a *fermata*, or hold (⌢), is held approximately twice as long as the note's value (see Appendix).

Aura Lea

W. W. Fosdick

George R. Poulton

1. As the black-bird in the spring, 'Neath the wil-low tree, ____
Sat and piped, I heard him sing, Sing-ing Au-ra Lea.

CHORUS
Au-ra Lea, Au-ra Lea, Maid of gold-en hair,
Sun-shine came a-long with thee, And swal-lows in the air.

2. In her blush the rose was born,
Music when she spoke,
In her eyes the glow of morn
Into splendor broke.
Chorus

The following words can be sung to the tune of "Aura Lea." They were written by George R. Poulton for the use of cadets at West Point.

Army Blue

1. We've not much longer here to stay
For in a month or two
We'll bid farewell to Cadet Gray,
And don the Army Blue!

CHORUS:
Army Blue! Army Blue!
Hurrah for the Army Blue!
We'll bid farewell to Cadet Gray
And don the Army Blue.

2. With pipe and song we'll jog along
'Til this short time is through,
And all among our jovial throng
Have donned the Army Blue.
Chorus

The melody of "The Cuckoo" consists of eight different pitches within the range of an octave. The holds at the beginning of the Chorus are to be held at the discretion of the song leader.

The Cuckoo

Austria

2. When I've married my maiden fair what then can I desire?
   Oh, a home for our children and some wood for the fire.
   Chorus

3. After winter come sunny days that will melt all the snow.
   Then I'll marry my maiden fair. We'll be happy, I know.
   Chorus

The following motions may be added to the Chorus:
   Measure 1: Rapidly pat hands alternately on knees.
   Measure 2: Beat 1 — Slap both hands on both thighs once.
             Beat 2 — Clap hands once.
             Beat 3 — Snap fingers on both hands once.
On the second verse add one beat each time the word "cuckoo" is sung by

repeating the word and adding the snapping of fingers once. Do it three times when singing the third verse.

Recorder Descant for Chorus

This patriotic hymn dates from the late nineteenth century. Its melody contains nine different pitches within the range of a major ninth.

America the Beautiful

Katharine Lee Bates

Samuel A. Ward

♩=108

1. O beau - ti - ful for spa - cious skies, For am - ber waves of grain, For pur - ple moun - tain maj - es - ties A - bove the fruit - ed plain! A - mer - i - ca! A - mer - i - ca! God shed his grace on thee, And crown thy good with broth - er - hood From sea to shin - ing sea!

2. O beautiful for Pilgrim feet,
   Whose stern impassioned stress
   A thoroughfare for freedom beat
   Across the wilderness.
   America! America! God mend thine every flaw,
   Confirm thy soul in self-control,
   Thy liberty in law.

3. O beautiful for heroes proved
   In liberating strife,
   Who more than self their country loved,
   And mercy more than life.
   America! America! May God thy gold refine
   Till all success be nobleness
   And every gain divine.

4. O beautiful for patriot dream
   That sees beyond the years,
   Thine alabaster cities gleam
   Undimmed by human tears.
   America! America! God shed His grace on thee,
   And crown thy good with brotherhood
   From sea to shining sea.

The Star-Spangled Banner

Francis Scott Key

John Stafford Smith

1. O_____ say! Can you see, by the dawn's ear - ly
light, What so proud - ly we hail'd At the twi - light's last
gleam - ing? Whose broad stripes and bright stars, thro' the per - il - ous
fight, O'er the ram - parts we watch'd, were so gal - lant - ly
stream - ing! And the rock - ets' red glare, the bombs burst - ing in
air, Gave proof thro' the night that our flag was still there.
O say, does that __ Star - Span - gled Ban - ner __ yet __
wave __ O'er the land __ of the free and the home of the brave?

2. On that shore, dimly seen thro' the mists of the deep,
   Where the foe's haughty host in dread silence reposes,
   What is that which the breeze, o'er the towering steep,
   As it fitfully blows, half conceals, half discloses?
   Now it catches the gleam of the morning's first beam,
   In full glory reflected now shines on the stream;
   'Tis the Star-Spangled Banner, O long may it wave
   O'er the land of the free and the home of the brave!

3. O thus be it ever when free men shall stand
   Between their loved homes and the war's desolation!
   Blest with vict'ry and peace, may the heav'n-rescued land
   Praise the Pow'r that hath made and preserved us a nation.
   Then conquer we must, for our cause it is just,
   And this be our motto: "In God is our trust."
   And the Star-Spangled Banner in triumph shall wave
   O'er the land of the free and the home of the brave.

Alouette

Canada

1. A - lou - et - te, gen - tille a - lou - et - te,
A - lou - et - te, je te plu - me - rai.
Je te plu - me - rai la tete, je te plu - me - rai la tete,
Et la tete, Et la tete, Oh!

In subsequent verses substitute the following phrases for "la tête":
   2. le bec
   3. le nez
   4. le dos
   5. les pattes
   6. le cou

The Orchestra Song
Round

Austria

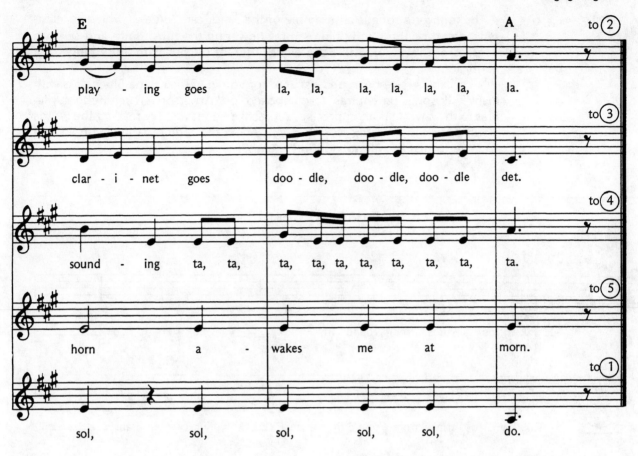

play - ing goes la, la, la, la, la, la, la.

clar - i - net goes doo - dle, doo - dle, doo - dle det.

sound - ing ta, ta, ta, ta, ta, ta, ta, ta, ta.

horn a - wakes me at morn.

sol, sol, sol, sol, sol, do.

Make New Friends
Round

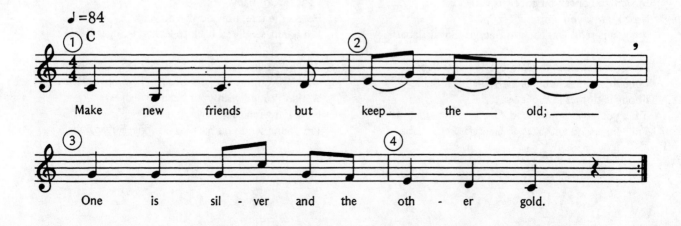

Make new friends but keep____ the ____ old; ____

One is sil - ver and the oth - er gold.

The following song is an example of the American "blues," which contains syncopated rhythms and "blue" notes (lowering the third, fifth, and seventh degrees of the scale). There are eight different pitches within the range of a minor tenth.

No syllables have been underscored for you in "Sugar Babe Blues." As with many folk songs (in contrast to composed, or "Art," songs), setting the syllables to the rhythm is an imprecise, subjective endeavor. Try reading the words aloud before attempting to sing them. Allow the tempo to fluctuate so that your performance will not sound "square."

Sugar Babe Blues

United States

1. Take your arms from 'round my neck ___ Sug - ar Babe, ___
Take your arms from 'round my neck ___ Sug - ar Babe, ___
Take your arms from 'round my neck, ___ You're a no good cheat - in' wreck, ___
'I'm gon - na send you back to Geor - gia, Sug - ar Babe. ___

2. I loved you once you got right Sugar Babe,
I loved you once you got right Sugar Babe,
I loved you once you got right,
Now I know you ain't my type;
I'm gonna send you back to Georgia, Sugar Babe.

3. I bought clothes in the latest style Sugar Babe,
I bought clothes in the latest style Sugar Babe,
I bought clothes in the latest style
Then you go a'runnin' wild,
I'm gonna send you back to Georgia, Sugar Babe.

4. I got sick of baby talk Sugar Babe,
I got sick of baby talk Sugar Babe,
I got sick of baby talk;
Here's the fare, now don't you walk!
I'm gonna send you back to Georgia, Sugar Babe.

5. Walkin' 'round with your head so high Sugar Babe,
Walkin' 'round with your head so high Sugar Babe.
Walkin' 'round with your head so high,
Now I'm gonna say "Bye, bye."
I'm gonna send you back to Georgia, Sugar Babe.

CHAPTER SIX
Song Leading

CHAPTER SIX
Song Leading

The purposes of song leading, or *conducting*, are:
1. Teaching the rhythm, melody, and words of a song.
2. Starting the group together on the same pitch.
3. Starting and stopping the group together on the same beat.
4. Regulating the tempo of the group's singing.
5. Regulating the dynamic level of the group's singing.
6. Giving feedback to the group about the quality of its performance.
7. Communicating enthusiasm and a sense of accomplishment during the learning process.

The tools with which these purposes are achieved are your hands, arms, and face, particularly your eyes. You must know the song that you want to teach well enough so that you can look up to *cue* or direct singers.

Certain patterns of hand and arm movement have become traditional over the past two centuries. These conducting patterns vary depending upon the conductor's experience as well as the demands of the music. Many conductors of instrumental music groups such as bands and orchestras prefer to use a *baton*, a thin, tapered piece of wood or fiberglass. Most informal group singing is conducted without a baton.

CONDUCTING PATTERNS

You should understand one general principle before studying any conducting patterns. The slower the tempo of a song, the larger the physical size of the beat pattern; the faster the tempo of a song, the smaller the physical size of the beat pattern.

Keeping this fact in mind, try conducting the songs in this chapter with either hand or both hands while humming or singing the melody. Left-handed persons may prefer left-hand patterns, while right-handed persons may prefer right-hand patterns when conducting. Let both hands mirror the patterns for emphasis or to conduct large groups.

In our diagrams of conducting patterns, a dot represents the point at which a beat occurs, while an "X" is the approximate point at which a pause occurs before the beginning of the following beat. A beat is always followed by a bounce and a bounce is always followed by a pause. When you conduct songs that move at a slow, smooth tempo, the beats will flow into each other without pauses.

Two Beats per Measure

The first conducting pattern (Figure 6.1) is used for songs that have two beats per measure. Keep your palms down, your fingers together, and your wrists still while you conduct this pattern.

The seven songs that follow begin on the accented first beat of the measure. You should prepare a group of singers to sing by first giving the starting pitch of the melody in a key which is comfortable for both you and the majority of the singers. Next, give at least two preparatory beats in your preselected tempo by saying or singing "Ready, sing," at the same speed as beats 1 and 2 of the

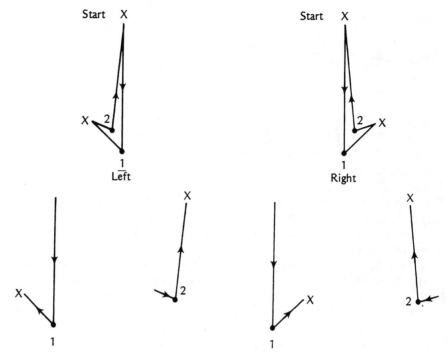

Figure 6.1. Conducting two beats per measure

song. Practice with a small group of friends until you feel confident that you can control the tempo of the song.

Each of the seven songs ends after the last full beat of the last measure. A conductor must indicate a *cutoff* so that the performing group knows when to stop singing. A cutoff is shown by bringing your hand (or hands) to a complete stop in front of your body with a small circular motion. The direction of this circular motion may be either clockwise or counterclockwise.

Now try conducting each of the following songs with two beats per measure. Observe the metronome markings and maintain a steady beat.

Mary Had a Little Lamb

Sara J. Hale

2. Everywhere that Mary went, Mary went, Mary went,
   Everywhere that Mary went the lamb was sure to go.

3. It followed her to school one day, school one day, school one day,
   It followed her to school one day which was against the rule.

4. It <u>made</u> the children <u>shout</u> and play, <u>shout</u> and play, <u>shout</u> and play,
   It <u>made</u> the children <u>shout</u> and play to <u>see</u> the lamb in <u>school</u>.

5. And <u>so</u> the teacher <u>turned</u> it out, <u>turned</u> it out, <u>turned</u> it out,
   And <u>so</u> the teacher <u>turned</u> it out but <u>home</u> it would not <u>go</u>.

6. It <u>waited</u> there 'til <u>school</u> was out, <u>school</u> was out, <u>school</u> was out,
   It <u>waited</u> there 'til <u>school</u> was out for <u>it</u> loved Mary <u>so</u>.

7. "What <u>makes</u> the lamb love <u>Mary</u> so, <u>Mary</u> so, <u>Mary</u> so?
   What <u>makes</u> the lamb love <u>Mary</u> so?" the <u>eager</u> children <u>cry</u>.

8. "Oh, <u>Mary</u> loves the <u>lamb</u>, you know, <u>lamb</u>, you know, <u>lamb</u>, you know,
   Oh, <u>Mary</u> loves the <u>lamb</u>, you know," the <u>teacher</u> did re<u>ply</u>.

All songs in meters that group two beats per measure are conducted with the same conducting pattern. These meters include $\frac{2}{4}, \frac{2}{2},$ and $\frac{2}{}$ ($\frac{6}{8}$ meter performed at a fast tempo). Try to conduct each of the following songs at the indicated tempo while you hum the melody or sing the words.

"Row, Row, Row Your Boat" may be performed as a round by dividing the class into four groups, each with its own conductor. Group 1 begins alone, group 2 starts when group 1 reaches number 2. Group 3 starts when group 1 reaches number 3. Group 4 starts when group 1 reaches number 4. Each group should sing the entire song twice.

Row, Row, Row Your Boat
Round

United States

Jacob's Ladder

United States

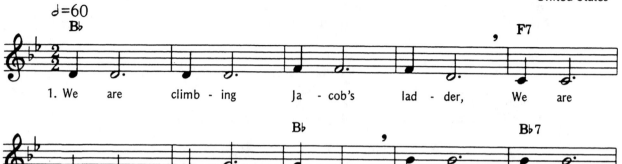

1. We are climb - ing Ja - cob's lad - der, We are
climb - ing Ja - cob's lad - der, We are climb - ing
Ja - cob's lad - der, Sol - diers of the cross. _____

2. Every round goes higher, higher...

3. Brother, do you love my Master?...

4. If you love Him, you must serve Him...

5. We are climbing higher, higher...

Bow, Belinda

United States

1. Bow, bow, bow, Be - lin - da; Bow, bow, bow, Be - lin - da;
Bow, bow, bow, Be - lin - da; Won't you be my dar - ling?

2. Right hand 'round, Belinda; Right hand 'round Belinda;
Right hand 'round, Belinda; Won't you be my darling?

3. Left hand 'round, Belinda; Left hand 'round, Belinda;
Left hand 'round, Belinda; Won't you be my darling?

4. Both hands 'round, Belinda...

5. Shake your foot, Belinda...

6. Join right hands, Belinda...

7. Join left hands, Belinda...

8. Promenade, Belinda...

9. Circle all, Belinda...

Chords indicated in parentheses are alternate ways of harmonizing the melody. Which chords sound best to you?

Drill, Ye Tarriers

Words and music by Thomas Casey

1. Every morning at seven o'clock There's twenty tarriers a'-working at the rock, And the boss comes along and he says, "Keep still, And come down heavy on the cast iron drill."

CHORUS
So drill, ye tarriers drill, And drill ye tarriers drill! Oh, it's work all day for sugar in your "tay," Down beyond the railway, And drill, ye tarriers drill, and blast, and fire!

3. Next time pay day came around
Jim Goff was short one buck, he found,
"What for?" says he, then this reply,
"You're docked for the time you were up in the sky."
Chorus

2. Our new foreman is Dan McCann,
I'll tell you true, he's a real mean man;
Last week a premature blast went off,
And a mile in the air went Big Jim Goff.
Chorus

Thanksgiving Day
Over the River and Through the Wood

Lydia Maria Childs

United States

2. Over the river and through the wood and straight to the barnyard gate,
   We seem to go so very slow, and it's so hard to wait,
   Over the river and through the wood, now grandmother's cap I spy.
   Hurrah for the fun, the pudding's done, hurrah for the pumpkin pie!

3. Over the river and through the wood, now soon we'll be on our way,
   There's feasting and fun for everyone, for this is Thanksgiving day,
   Over the river and through the wood, get on, my dapple grey,
   The woods will ring with songs we sing, for this is Thanksgiving day.

This Old Man

England

1. This old man, he played one, He played knick - knack

on my thumb, With a knick - knack pad - dy whack,

give the dog a bone! This old man came roll - ing home.

2. This old man, he played two, He played knick-knack on my shoe.
   With a knick-knack paddy whack, give the dog a bone!
   This old man came rolling home.

3. This old man, he played three, He played knick-knack on my knee.
   With a knick-knack paddy whack, give the dog a bone!
   This old man came rolling home.

4. This old man, he played four,
   He played knick-knack on my door.

5. This old man, he played five,
   He played knick-knack on my hive.

6. This old man, he played six,
   He played knick-knack on my sticks.

7. This old man, he played seven,
   He played knick-knack up in heaven.

8. This old man, he played eight,
   He played knick-knack on my pate.

9. This old man, he played nine,
   He played knick-knack on my spine.

10. This old man, he played ten,
    He played knick-knack once again.

Three Beats per Measure

Songs written with three beats per measure are conducted with one downbeat, one beat to the outside of the body and one upbeat (Figure 6.2). Give the starting pitch and prepare the singers to begin by saying or singing "one, ready, sing" in the rhythm of beats 1, 2, and 3. Cut the performers off at the end of the last beat of the melody.

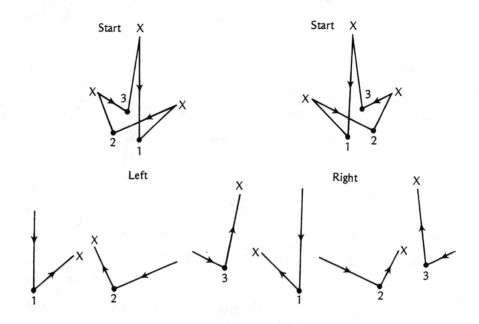

Figure 6.2. Conducting three beats per measure

Try out this pattern by conducting "America" and "Music Alone Shall Live."

2. My native country, thee, land of the noble free,
Thy name I love.
I love thy rocks and rills, thy woods and templed hills,
My heart with rapture thrills
Like that above.

3. Let music swell the breeze, and ring from all the trees
Sweet freedom's song.
Let mortal tongues awake, let all that breathe partake,
Let rocks their silence break,
The sound prolong.

4. Our fathers' God, to Thee, Author of liberty,
To Thee we sing.
Long may our land be bright with freedom's holy light,
Protect us by Thy might,
Great God, our King!

Music Alone Shall Live
Round

Germany

Some songs written with three beats per measure are performed at a fast tempo that makes it physically impractical to indicate where each of the three beats occurs. In these situations all three beats are incorporated into one accented pulse. The resulting conducting pattern looks oval in shape with the accented point (beat 1) at the bottom (Figure 6.3). There are no points of rest in these motions. At least two of these patterns should be given as preparatory beats before singing begins.

The cutoff beat that is given after the last measure is similar to those you have learned previously. Bring your hand (or hands) in toward the center of your body and stop all motion.

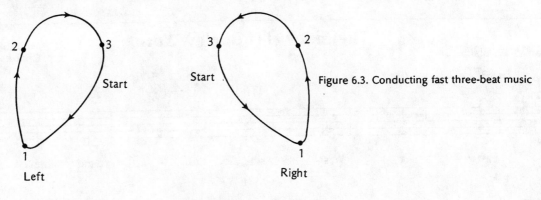

Figure 6.3. Conducting fast three-beat music

Practice conducting "Home" and "Sidewalks of New York," as examples of fast songs with three beats per measure.

Home

Germany

2. Home, home, why did I leave thee?
   Dear, dear friends, do not mourn.
   Home, home, once more receive me,
   Quickly to thee I'll return.
   Home, home, home, home,
   Dearest and happiest home.

The Sidewalks of New York

James W. Blake

Charles B. Lawlor

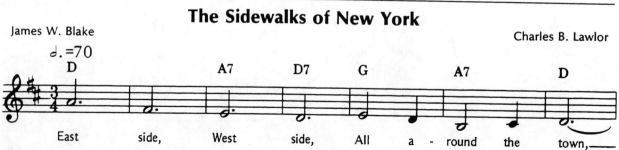

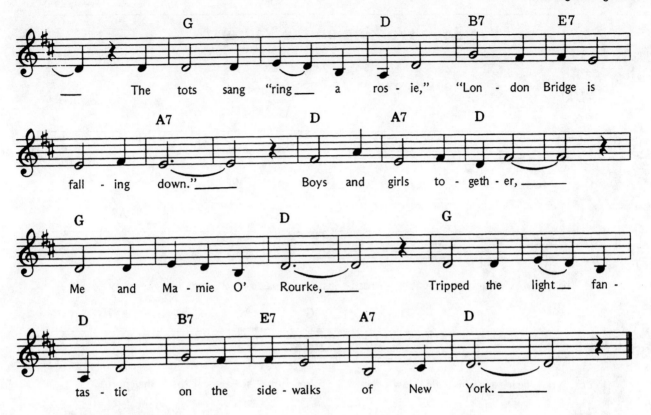

The tots sang "ring __ a ros - ie," "Lon - don Bridge is fall - ing down." __ Boys and girls to - geth - er, __ Me and Ma - mie O' Rourke, __ Tripped the light __ fan - tas - tic on the side - walks of New York. __

Four Beats per Measure

Songs written with four beats per measure are conducted with one downbeat, a second beat across the body, a third beat toward the outside of the body, and an upbeat (Figure 6.4). If you conduct these patterns with both arms, your hands will overlap slightly in front of your body on the second beat. Give the starting pitch and prepare the group to begin by saying or singing "one, two, ready, sing" in the tempo that you have chosen for the performance of the song. Try out this pattern with "I've Been Working on the Railroad."

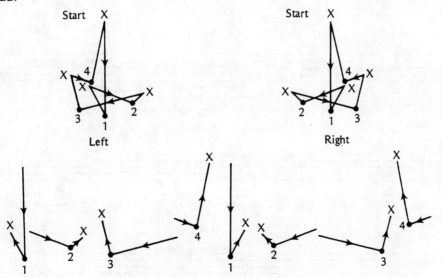

Figure 6.4. Conducting four beats per measure

I've Been Working on the Railroad

United States

Fee, fie, fid-dle-dee - i - o, Fee, fie, fid-dle-dee - i - o, _____

Fee, fie, fid - dle-dee - i - o, Strum - min' on the old ban - jo.

* For autoharp accompaniment.

To quicken the tempo for the section of the song beginning with the words "Someone's in the kitchen with Dinah" (measure 25), change your conducting pattern to two beats per measure (as if the song were written in $\frac{2}{2}$ meter). Two quarter notes will equal one beat.

In measure 30 of the song there is a fermata on the third beat (above the syllable "-nah"). During the preceding measure you should revert to conducting a $\frac{4}{4}$ meter pattern to slow down (*ritard*) the tempo. When you reach the fermata, move your hands slowly and steadily away from your body to "stretch" out the third beat. You should pull your arms away from each other in such a way that there is some degree of tension and anticipation about when this beat will end. Release this fermata by abruptly stopping the sideward motion of your arms and then move your hands into an upbeat motion. This upbeat will allow your singers to breathe and prepare you and the group to perform the next downbeat together.

In measure 33 begin conducting in $\frac{2}{2}$ to speed up the tempo again. Anticipate the fermata in measure 38 by conducting in four during measure 37. Continue conducting in four to the end of the song and cut off the singing after the last beat.

One of the intangibles that can help you to become a successful conductor is the way in which you reflect the musical and verbal content of the songs you conduct. You must look like the music. Facial expressions and movements of the hands, arms, and upper torso must be reflective of the music's style and the meaning of the lyrics.

Two contrasting styles that are employed often in familiar songs are called marcato and legato. A *legato* style of conducting is continuous; beats flow smoothly into each other without interruption. A *marcato* style of conducting is discontinuous; beats are abrupt stops.

One way to become physically aware of these contrasting styles is to pound your right fist into your left palm while you forcefully say aloud, "Mar-ca-to means PUNCHED mu-sic!" Then try conducting "I've Been Working on the Railroad" with this same sensation of "pounding" on each beat.

To become physically aware of the legato feeling, move your hand and arm in a continuous arc from one side of your body, up over your head, stopping when you reach the full extension of your arm on the opposite side of your body. While you do this, say "Leg-a-to means smoo-oo-oo-th mu-sic" without emphasizing any of the words. Now try conducting "Sleep, Baby, Sleep" with the same feeling of smoothness.

Sleep, Baby, Sleep

Germany

1. Sleep, ba - by, sleep, thy fa - ther guards the sheep. Thy

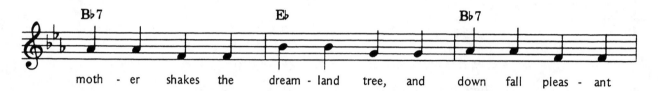

moth - er shakes the dream - land tree, and down fall pleas - ant

dreams for thee. Sleep, ba - by, sleep. Sleep, ba - by, sleep.

2. Sleep, baby, sleep, the white clouds are the sheep,
   The stars like lambs run up and down, the moon, their shepherd, leads them on,
   Sleep, baby, sleep, sleep, baby, sleep.

3. Sleep, baby, sleep, I'll give to you a sheep
   Who wears a tinkling bell so bright, and he'll be with you all the night,
   Sleep, baby, sleep, sleep, baby, sleep.

ANACRUSIS

Many songs do not begin on a downbeat; they begin instead with an *anacrusis,* or pick-up beat. The anacrusis is particularly characteristic of songs whose lyrics begin with an article of speech such as "the." In these instances you must give the beat or beats that precede the anacrusis as preparatory beats. In the following song you would prepare a group to sing by saying or singing "One, ready, sing." This is equivalent to counting "1, 2, 1" and beginning on the following "2."

Notice that at the end of the song you must cut off the singing at the end of the first beat. You do so by bringing the second beat in toward your body, ending with a small circular motion.

Billy Boy

d = 104   England

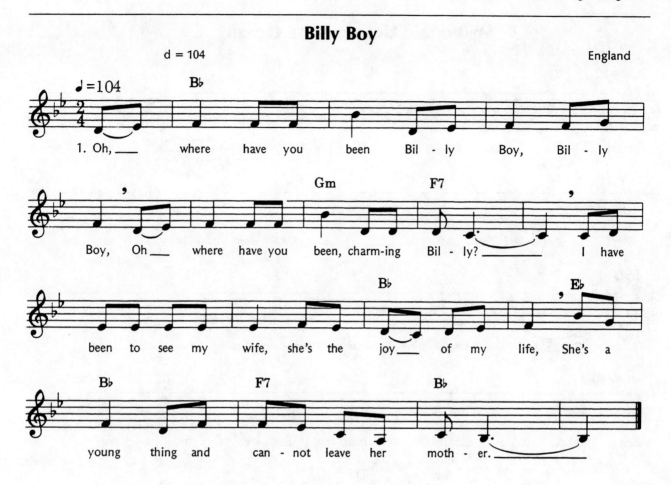

2. Did she <u>bid</u> you to come <u>in</u>, Billy <u>Boy</u>, Billy <u>Boy</u>,
   Did she <u>bid</u> you to come <u>in</u>, charming <u>Bil</u>ly?
   Yes, she <u>bade</u> me to come <u>in</u>, there's a <u>dim</u>ple in her <u>chin</u>,
   She's a <u>young</u> thing and <u>can</u>not leave her <u>moth</u>er.

3. Can she <u>bake</u> a cherry <u>pie</u>, Billy <u>Boy</u>, Billy <u>Boy</u>,
   Can she <u>bake</u> a cherry <u>pie</u>, charming <u>Bil</u>ly?
   She can <u>bake</u> a cherry <u>pie</u>, quick's a <u>cat</u> can wink an <u>eye</u>,
   She's a <u>young</u> thing and <u>can</u>not leave her <u>moth</u>er.

4. How <u>old</u> is <u>she</u>, Billy <u>Boy</u>, Billy <u>Boy</u>,
   How <u>old</u> is <u>she</u>, charming <u>Bil</u>ly?
   She's three times <u>six</u> and four times <u>seven</u>, twenty-<u>eight</u> and e<u>lev</u>en,
   She's a <u>young</u> thing and <u>can</u>not leave her <u>moth</u>er.

Each of the following four songs begins with an anacrusis. Anticipate the
anacrusis by counting, singing, and conducting enough beats to start securely
and confidently. When the anacrusis is more than a half-measure in length,
you prepare the group to perform by conducting one complete measure of
preparatory beats before the measure in which they are to begin singing.

Start this song by conducting beats 1 and 2 while saying "ready, sing," and
bring in the group on beat 3. Maintain eye contact with the group while you do
so.

My Bonnie Lies over the Ocean

H. J. Fuller

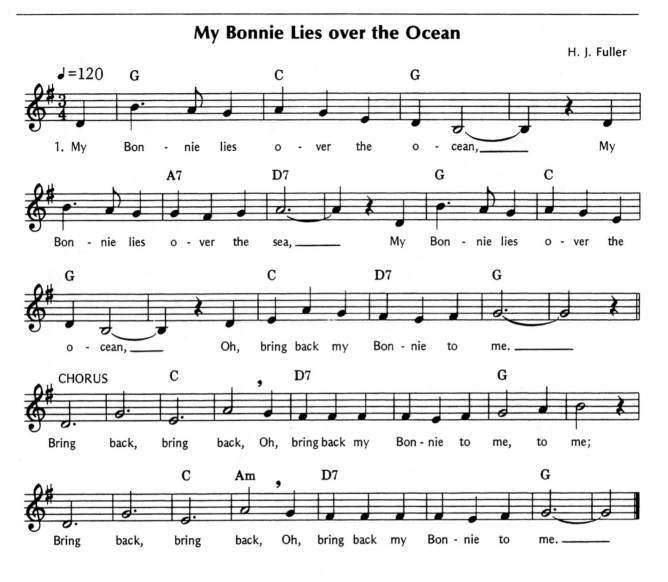

♩=120

1. My Bon - nie lies o - ver the o - cean,_____ My Bon - nie lies o - ver the sea,_____ My Bon - nie lies o - ver the o - cean,_____ Oh, bring back my Bon - nie to me._____

CHORUS

Bring back, bring back, Oh, bring back my Bon - nie to me, to me; Bring back, bring back, Oh, bring back my Bon - nie to me._____

2. Oh, <u>blow</u>, ye winds, <u>o</u>ver the <u>o</u>cean,
   Oh, <u>blow</u>, ye winds, <u>o</u>ver the <u>sea</u>,
   Oh, <u>blow</u>, ye winds, <u>o</u>ver the <u>o</u>cean,
   And <u>bring</u> back my <u>Bonnie</u> to <u>me</u>.
   Chorus

3. Last <u>night</u> as I <u>lay</u> on my <u>pillow</u>,
   Last <u>night</u> as I <u>lay</u> on my <u>bed</u>,
   I <u>stuck</u> my big <u>feet</u> out the <u>window</u>.
   Next <u>morning</u> my <u>neighbors</u> were <u>dead</u>.
   Chorus

Acres of Clams

United States

♩=126

1. I've wan - dered all o - ver this coun - try,_____ Pros -

pect - ing and dig - ging for gold;_____ I've tun - neled, hy

drau - lic'd, and cra - dled,_____ This sto - ry I've fre - quent - ly

told;_____ This sto - ry I've fre - quent - ly

told;_____ This sto - ry I've fre - quent - ly told;_____

_____ I've tun - neled, hy - drau - lic'd, and cra - dled, ____

_____ This sto - ry I've fre - quent - ly told. _____

2. For each one who gets rich by mining
   I saw there were hundreds grew poor;
   I made up my mind to try farming,
   The only pursuit that is sure,
   The only pursuit that is sure,
   The only pursuit that is sure,
   I made up my mind to try farming,
   The only pursuit that is sure.

3. So, rolling my grub in my blanket,
   I left all my tools on the ground,
   And started one morning to shank it
   To country they call Puget Sound,
   To country they call Puget Sound,
   To country they call Puget Sound,
   I started one morning to shank it,
   To country they call Puget Sound.

4. I aimed to get out of the country,
   But poverty forced me to stay,
   And now I've become a settler
   And nothing could drive me away,
   And nothing could drive me away,
   And nothing could drive me away,
   And now I've become a settler
   And nothing could drive me away.

5. No longer a slave of ambition,
   I laugh at the world and its shams,
   And think of my happy condition
   Surrounded by acres of clams,
   Surrounded by acres of clams,
   Surrounded by acres of clams,
   I think of my happy condition
   Surrounded by acres of clams.

The rhythms ♩♩♩ (3) and ♩♪ (3) are called triplets. These rhythmic figures direct one to put three notes (or their equivalent) into the duration usually occupied by two notes.

Nine Hundred Miles

United States

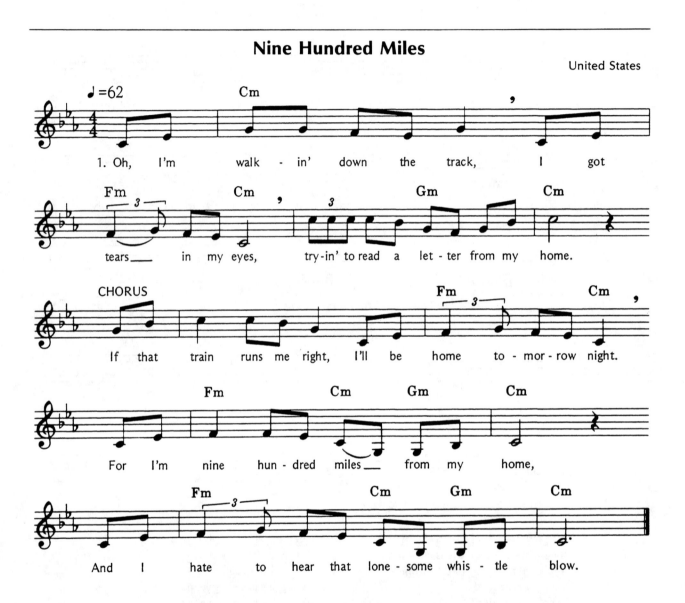

2. Oh, this <u>train</u> that I ride on is a <u>hundred</u> coaches long.
   <u>You</u> can hear the whistle blow for miles and <u>miles</u>.
   Chorus

3. Oh, I'm <u>gonna</u>. pawn my watch, and I'm <u>gonna</u>' pawn my chain.
   <u>I'm</u> gonna' pawn my gold and diamond <u>ring</u>.
   Chorus

4. If my <u>love</u> bids me stay, I will <u>never</u> go away,
   <u>For</u> it's near her I always want to <u>be</u>.
   Chorus

For Health and Strength
Round

For health and strength and dai - ly food we praise Thy name, O Lord.

Some songs, such as the next five, begin on an incomplete beat — usually the second half of the first or last beat of a measure. These songs should be conducted by giving at least the first half of the incomplete beat as preparation to sing. It is usually best to give at least one complete measure as additional preparation before the measure in which you want to begin.

When Johnny Comes Marching Home

Louis Lambert

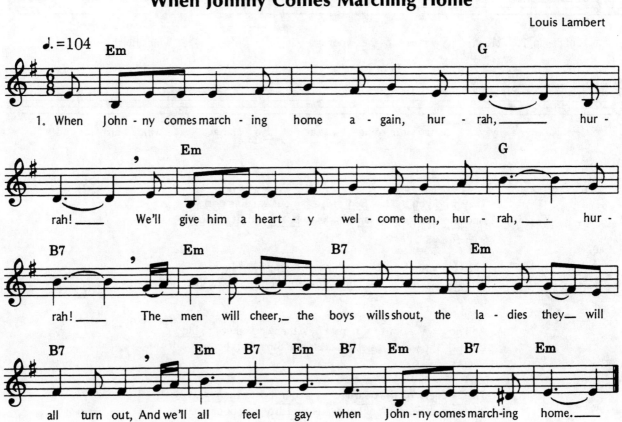

1. When John - ny comes march - ing home a - gain, hur - rah,____ hur -
rah!____ We'll give him a heart - y wel - come then, hur - rah,____ hur -
rah!____ The__ men will cheer,__ the boys wills shout, the la - dies they__ will
all turn out, And we'll all feel gay when John - ny comes march - ing home.____

2. The old church bell will peal with joy, hurrah, hurrah!
To welcome home our darling boy, hurrah, hurrah!
The village lads and lassies say,
With roses they will strew the way,
And we'll all feel gay when Johnny comes marching home.

Blow, Ye Winds

United States

1. 'Tis ad - ver - tised in Bos - ton, New York and Buf - fa - lo, Five hun - dred brave A - mer - i - cans a' - whal - ing for to go.

CHORUS

Sing - ing, blow, ye winds in the morn - ing, blow, ye winds, heigh ho,

Haul a - way your run - ning gear, and blow, ye winds heigh ho!

2. They send you to New Bedford, a famous whaling port,
   And give you to some landsharks to board and fit you out.
   Chorus

3. They tell you of the clipperships a'running in and out,
   And say you'll take five hundred sperm before you're six months out.
   Chorus

4. And now we're out to sea, my boys, the wind comes to blow;
   One-half the watch is sick on deck, the other half below.
   Chorus

5. The Skipper's on the quarterdeck a'squintin' at the sails,
   When up above the lookout sights a mighty school of whales.
   Chorus

6. Then lower down the boats, my boys, and after him we'll travel,
   But if you get too near his fluke he'll kick you to the devil.
   Chorus

7. And now that he is ours, my boys, we'll tow him alongside;
   Then over with our blubberhooks and rob him of his hide.
   Chorus

Every Time I Feel the Spirit

United States

2. Looked all around me, it sure looked fine;
   And I asked my Lord if it were mine.
   Looked all around me, it sure looked fine;
   And I asked my Lord if it were mine.
   Chorus

Golden Slippers

Words and music
by James A. Bland

2. There's the long white robe that I bought last June,
   That I must go and change because it fits too soon,
   And the old grey horse that I always drive,
   I will hitch up to the chariot in the morn.
   Chorus

3. And my banjo still is hanging on the wall,
   For it hasn't had a tune-up since away last fall,
   But the folks all say we'll have a fine old time,
   When we ride up in the chariot in the morn.
   Chorus

4. So it's goodbye, children, I will have to go
   Where the rain can't fall and the wind won't blow,
   And your ulster coats you never there will need
   When we ride up in the chariot in the morn.
   Chorus

5. Now, your golden slippers must be shiny clean,
   And your gloves the very whitest that were ever seen,
   And be sure you're ready when it's time to go,
   When we ride up in the chariot in the morn.
   Chorus

He's Got the Whole World

United States

2. He's got the wind and the rain in His hands. . .

3. He's got the little tiny baby in His hands. . .

4. He's got you and me, brother, in His hands. . .

5. He's got you and me, sister, in His hands. . .

6. He's got the sun and the moon in His hands. . .

7. He's got the whole world in His hands. . .

USING THE HANDS INDEPENDENTLY

Once you have mastered the basic patterns of two, three, and four beats per measure and are able to start and stop group singing efficiently, you should then learn to use one hand to control entrances and *dynamics* (the loudness or softness of the music). Assuming that you are right-handed (left-handed persons may prefer to reverse all subsequent directions), you would use your left hand to indicate the entrance of parts in rounds and part-singing by pointing to, and looking at, the appropriate group.

The left palm held upward with fingers spread indicates that a *forte* (loud) volume of sound is desired and the palm held downward with fingers together indicates that a *piano* (soft) level of sound is desired by the conductor. In addition, moving a raised palm slowly upward indicates a *crescendo* (gradually increasing the volume of sound) while moving the lowered palm slowly downward indicates a *diminuendo* (gradually decreasing the volume of sound). Maintain eye contact with the group, particularly when starting, stopping, changing tempo, or changing dynamics.

Some common notation for dynamics occurs in the next few songs. This symbol, ◁▭ , indicates a crescendo; pointed the opposite way, ▭▷ , it indicates a decrescendo. The letter "p" written over music means it is to be sung piano, while "mf" stands for *mezzo-forte* or medium loud, and "f" stands for forte.

Practice conducting the following songs using the right hand to beat time and the left hand to control the volume level. Strive for independence of motion in the use of your hands. Anticipate when the left hand will move and in which direction. When the left hand is not needed let it hang at your side in a relaxed position. Conduct a beat pattern with either hand while simultaneously raising and lowering the opposite hand. Reverse the motion and function of each hand.

Shenandoah

United States

2. Oh, Shenandoah, I love your daughter,
   Weigh, hey, you rolling river!
   Oh, Shenandoah, I love your daughter,
   Weigh, hey, we're bound away,
   'Cross the wide Missouri.

3. Oh, Shenandoah, I love her truly,
   Weigh, hey, you rolling river!
   Oh, Shenandoah, I love her truly,
   Weigh, hey, we're bound away,
   'Cross the wide Missouri.

4. I long to see your fertile valley,
   Weigh, hey, you rolling river!
   I long to see your fertile valley,
   Weigh, hey, we're bound away,
   'Cross the wide Missouri.

5. Oh, Shenandoah, I'm bound to leave you,
   Weigh, hey, you rolling river!
   Oh, Shenandoah, I'm bound to leave you,
   Weigh, hey, we're bound away,
   'Cross the wide Missouri.

Wayfaring Stranger

United States

In each subsequent verse, substitute the following words for "Father":
2. Mother
3. Sister
4. Brother

Kum Ba Ya

United States/Africa

2. Someone's crying, Lord, kum ba ya. . .

3. Someone's sleeping, Lord, kum ba ya. . .

4. Someone's praying, Lord, kum ba ya. . .

5. Someone's shouting, Lord, kum ba ya. . .

6. Someone's singing, Lord, kum ba ya. . .

7. Someone's weeping, Lord, kum ba ya. . .

8. Someone's kneeling, Lord, kum ba ya. . .

9. Someone's praising, Lord, kum ba ya. . .

Erie Canal

United States

♩=50

Bm   Em   F#7   Bm

1. I've got a mule, her name is Sal, Fif - teen miles on the

2. We'd better get along, old pal, Fifteen miles on the Erie Canal,
   You can bet your life I'd never part from Sal, Fifteen miles on the Erie Canal.
   Get up there, mule, here comes a lock, We'll make Rome by six o'clock,
   One more trip and back we'll go, Back we'll go to Buffalo.
   Chorus

CHAPTER SEVEN
Playing Melodies on Bells

CHAPTER SEVEN
Playing Melodies on Bells

"Bells" is a generic name for many types of pitch-producing instruments. Although a bell usually is thought of as a hollow metal instrument that emits a metallic sound when struck by a clapper, we extend the term to other, similar instruments, in different sizes, shapes, and materials, that communicate definite musical pitches. In most cases, tubes or bars of differing lengths and thicknesses are tuned to the pitches of a diatonic or chromatic scale. The pitches may match or exceed the range of children's singing voices. The bars are mounted over resonant cavities. Tone is produced by bouncing a mallet on the center of a bar or tube, directly over the resonating chamber.

Bells are made from a variety of materials. Alloyed metals such as brass, bronze, copper, gold, lead, silver, steel, tin, zinc, and aluminum commonly are used in the construction of bars or tubes; so is Rio Jacaranda, or Brazilian rosewood. The resonating chambers are made of spruce, limba wood, plastic, or styrene. The mallet has a rounded handle of wood or plastic, five to ten inches in length, with an attached spherical head. Mallet heads are made from wood, cork, felt, fiberglass, brass, plastic, string, yarn, hard rubber, or soft rubber. You must select a mallet of the right material for a given set of bells in order to produce the best tone quality. A hard mallet will produce a bright, loud tone with many overtones, while a soft mallet will produce a soft tone with few overtones. The mallet must have good rebounding quality since the resonance of the pitch is dulled by prolonged contact of the mallet with the bar.

Matched sets of bells are given various names depending on the materials from which they are constructed. Every musical organization, whether it be a symphony orchestra, marching band, jazz band, or church choir, may employ them. They are variously termed xylophone, marimba, vibraphone (or vibraharp), metallophone, chimes, bell lyre, celesta, glockenspiel, carillon, resonator bells, song bells, step bells, hand bells, Swiss Melode bells, tubular bells, tubaphone, cymbala, nolae, campanae, and tintinnabula. We will discuss two basic types of bell sets: diatonic bells and chromatic bells. (The diatonic and chromatic scales are explained in Chapter 4.)

DIATONIC BELLS

Diatonic bells (Figure 7.1) usually conform to an eight-note major scale beginning on middle C. The bells may be mounted on a wooden frame in the shape of a ladder to show the location visually of half steps and whole steps, and the relationship between pitch and elevation. The lowest pitches are on the left side or bottom of the ladder, and the highest pitches are on the right side or top of the ladder. The low-pitched bells are proportionately longer than the high-pitched bells. Usually the individual pitch name is stamped into each bar.

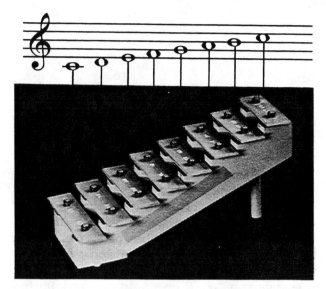

Figure 7.1. Eight-note diatonic step bells

A hard mallet made from maple is used. The mallet must be held in the hand between the thumb and first two fingers so that it can rebound quickly after striking the bars. Snapping the wrist will help.

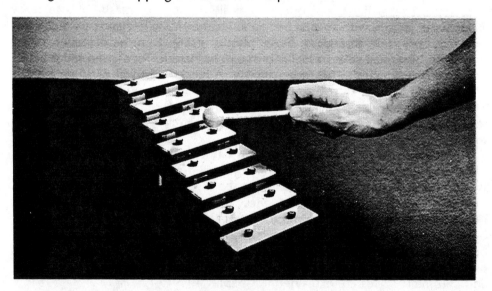

Mallet position

The following songs may be performed on diatonic bells pitched in the key of C major. First, name the pitches used in the melodies. Next, point to the bells that match the names of the notes. Then try playing the bells at a slow tempo while mentally counting the rhythm of the melody. Notice that some of the bells will not be needed. When you can play the entire song at an acceptable tempo without hesitation, try singing along while playing. Make sure that your voice matches the pitches of the individual bells. Men will have to match the pitches one octave lower than the bells.

When the Saints Go Marching In

United States

Oh, when the saints _____ go march - ing in, _____

_____ Oh, when the saints go march - ing in, _____

_____ How I want to be in that num - ber, _____

When the saints go march - ing in. _____

Sally Go 'Round the Sun

United States

Sal - ly go 'round the sun, Sal - ly go 'round the moon,

Sal - ly go 'round the chim - ney pots on a Sun - day af - ter - noon.

CHROMATIC BELLS

Chromatic bells consist of two rows of pitched bars mounted on a frame or placed in individual compartments in a carrying case. The lower row, with more bells in it, contains the pitches of a C-major diatonic scale. Usually these bars are colored with white enamel. The upper row of bells contains the remaining pitches of the chromatic scale (the accidentals — see Chapter 2). They are labeled enharmonically — G♯/A♭, A♯/B♭, C♯/D♭, D♯/E♭, and F♯/G♭ — and are covered with black enamel.

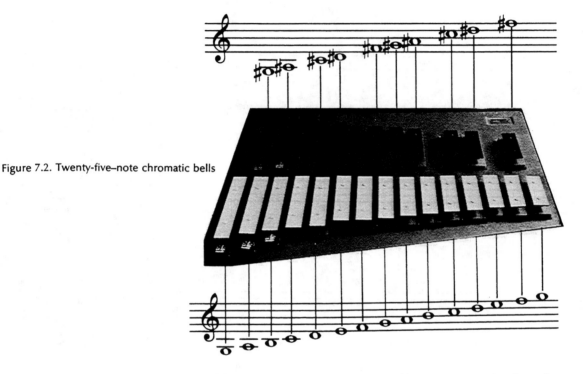

Figure 7.2. Twenty-five–note chromatic bells

The resemblance of a set of chromatic bells to a piano's keyboard is not an accident. Since both instruments can play melodies in all keys, you can transfer your performing skill from one instrument to the other for a change in tone color. Bells have advantages over pianos: they do not have to be tuned regularly, they are less expensive, and they are easily moved.

Although the chromatic bells may be arranged in front of you so that the long bells (those lowest in pitch) are closest to you and the short bells (those highest in pitch) are furthest from you, there is one disadvantage in doing so: you will have to remember their pitches. The letter names stamped into the bars are readable only when the long, low-pitched bars are to your left and the short, high-pitched bars are to your right. The black bells are placed above the white diatonic bars.

Some sets of bells contain the chromatic pitches from middle C to G above the treble staff. These are twenty-bell sets. Some of the following songs may be played on such sets, but many will have to be transposed to higher keys (see Chapter 14) in order that the lowest pitch will not be below middle C. A higher key may preclude singing along while playing the instrument; therefore, we recommend a twenty-five–bell set (Figure 7.2). The five extra bells extend the range down to the G below middle C. Mallets with soft heads should be used to play these bells.

Two versions of "Kookaburra" follow. The first arrangement is written in the key of B♭ major. In order to perform it, you will need a set of bells which has

the Bb below middle C. The second version is written in the key of C major.
Both arrangements may be performed as four-part rounds.

Kookaburra
Round

Australia

2. Kookaburra sits on the <u>old</u> gum tree,
   Eating all the gumdrops <u>he</u> can see.
   <u>Stop</u>, kookaburra! <u>Stop</u>, kookaburra!
   <u>Leave</u> some drops for <u>me</u>.

3. <u>Koo</u>kaburra sits on the <u>old</u> gum tree,
   <u>Coun</u>ting all the monkeys <u>he</u> can see.
   Stop, kookaburra! <u>Stop</u>, kookaburra!
   <u>That's</u> no monk — that's <u>me</u>!

4. Kookaburra sits on the <u>old</u> gum tree,
   He fell off the tree and <u>skinned</u> his knee.
   Poor kookaburra! <u>Poor</u> kookaburra!
   <u>Glad</u> that was not <u>me</u>.

5. <u>Koo</u>kaburra sits on a <u>rail</u>road track.
   '<u>Long</u> came a train and <u>squashed</u> him flat.
   Poor kookaburra! <u>Poor</u> kookaburra!
   <u>That's</u> the end of <u>that</u>!

Kookaburra
Round

Australia

1. Koo - ka - burr - a   sits   on   the   old   gum   tree,_____

Mer - ry,   mer - ry   king   of   the   bush   is   he,_____

Laugh,   koo - ka - burr - a!   Laugh,   koo - ka - burr - a!

Hap - py   your   life   must   be.

2. Kookaburra sits on the old gum tree,
   Eating all the gumdrops he can see.
   Stop, kookaburra! Stop, kookaburra!
   Leave some drops for me.

3. Kookaburra sits on the old gum tree,
   Counting all the monkeys he can see.
   Stop, kookaburra! Stop, kookaburra!
   That's no monk — that's me!

4. Kookaburra sits on the old gum tree,
   He fell off the tree and skinned his knee.
   Poor kookaburra! Poor kookaburra!
   Glad that was not me.

5. Kookaburra sits on a railroad track.
   'Long came a train and squashed him flat.
   Poor kookaburra! Poor kookaburra!
   That's the end of that!

The Little Bells of Westminster
Round

England

The lit-tle bells of West-min-ster go ding, dong, ding, dong, dong.

Song

Birds sing gai-ly from the trees, sweet-ly ring,

as they sing. Bees are fly-ing on their way, bring no

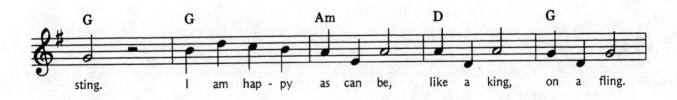

sting. I am hap-py as can be, like a king, on a fling.

Bells ring out my joy each day, ding, dong, ding.

Easy Descant for Bells or Recorders

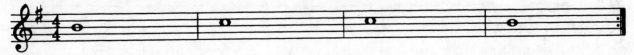

"Jingle Bells," a song written in 1857, is a favorite song of the holiday season. If you are using a twenty-bell set, either play the chorus only or substitute low Ds for the low As and Bs in the melody of the verse.

Jingle Bells

Words and music
by James Pierpont

♩=120

1. Dash - ing through the snow, in a one - horse o - pen sleigh,

O'er the fields we go, Laugh - ing all the way;___

Bells on bob - tail ring, mak - ing spir - its bright,

Oh, what fun it is to sing a sleigh - ing song to - night.

CHORUS

Jin - gle bells, jin - gle bells, jin - gle all the way,

Oh, what fun it is to ride in a one - horse o - pen sleigh!___

Jin - gle bells, jin - gle bells, jin - gle all the way,

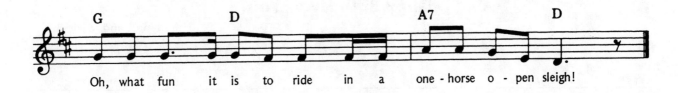

Oh, what fun it is to ride in a one - horse o - pen sleigh!

2. A <u>day</u> or two ago, I <u>thought</u> I'd take a ride,
   And <u>soon</u> Miss Fannie Bright was <u>seated</u> by my side;
   The <u>horse</u> was lean and lank, mis<u>for</u>tune seemed his lot,
   He <u>got</u> into a drifted bank, and <u>we</u>, we got upsot.
   Chorus

3. <u>Now</u> the ground is white, <u>go</u> it while you're young,
   <u>Take</u> the girls tonight, and <u>sing</u> this sleighing song;
   Just <u>get</u> a bobtailed nag, two-<u>forty</u> for his speed,
   Then <u>hitch</u> him to an open sleigh, and <u>crack</u>! you'll take the lead.
   Chorus

Each of the next three songs uses eight different pitches. Select only those bells that correspond to the needed pitches. Remove the needed bells from the case, or remove the unneeded bars from the frame, then regroup the pitches in whatever order makes them most accessible for your performance. The bells need not always be grouped with the lowest pitches on your left and the highest pitches on your right. The flexible arrangement of pitches is one of the advantages of performing songs on bells.

Happy Birthday to You

Words and music by
Mildred J. Hill
and Patty S. Hill

Hap - py birth - day to you. Hap - py birth - day to you. Hap - py birth - day dear _____ _____. Hap - py birth - day to you.

The following arrangement of "Happy Birthday To You" is written in the key of F major. It can be played on chromatic bell sets which do not contain the pitches below middle C.

Happy Birthday to You

Words and music by
Mildred J. Hill
and Patty S. Hill

Hap - py birth - day to you. Hap - py birth - day to you. Hap - py birth - day dear _____ _____ Hap - py birth - day to you.

Don Gato

Margaret Marks
(for English lyrics)

Mexico

1. Oh, Se - ñor Don Ga - to was a cat, _____ _____ On a high red roof Don Ga - to sat. _____ . He went there to read a let - ter (meow, meow, meow), Where the read - ing light was

bet - ter (meow,meow,meow).'Twas a love note for Don Ga-to!_____

2. "I adore you!" wrote the lady cat,
Who was fluffy, white, and nice and fat.
There was not a sweeter kitty (meow, meow, meow),
In the country or the city (meow, meow, meow),
And she said she'd wed Don Gato.

3. Oh, Don Gato jumped so happily
He fell off the roof and broke his knee,
Broke his ribs and all his whiskers (meow, meow, meow),
And his little solar plexus (meow, meow, meow),
"¡Ay, carramba!" cried Don Gato!

4. Then the doctors all came on the run
Just to see if something could be done,
And they held a consultation (meow, meow, meow),
About how to save their patient (meow, meow, meow),
How to save Señor Don Gato!

5. But in spite of everything they tried,
Poor Señor Don Gato up and died.
Oh, it wasn't very merry (meow, meow, meow)
Going to the cemetery (meow, meow, meow)
For the ending of Don Gato.

6. When the funeral passed the market square
Such a smell of fish was in the air;
Though his burial was slated (meow, meow, meow)
He became reanimated (meow, meow, meow)!
He came back to life, Don Gato!

Romance
Eine Kleine Nachtmusick
(A Little Night Music)

Wolfgang Amadeus Mozart

Each of the following songs is playable only on a full set of twenty-five resonator bells unless the song is transposed, or unless the pitches below middle C are transposed one octave higher. Although the latter method may not be faithful to the original line of the melody, the rhythm and harmony will be preserved.

Theme
Symphony No. 94, "Surprise"

Franz Joseph Haydn

When Love Is Kind

England

1. When love is kind,_____ cheer - ful and free_____

Love's sure to find _____ wel - come from me.

But when love brings _____ heart - ache and pang, _____

Tears and such things, _____ love may go hang.

2. If love can sigh for one alone
Well pleas'd am I to be that one,
But should I see love giv'n to rove
To two or three, then goodbye love!

3. Love must in short keep fond and true,
Through good report and evil too.
Else here I swear young love may go
For aught I care to Jericho!

You're a Grand Old Flag

Words and Music by
George M. Cohan

You're a grand old flag, you're a high-fly-ing flag; And for-
ev-er in peace may you wave; _____ You're the em-blem of the
land I love, The home of the free and the brave. _____
Eve-ry heart beats true un-der red, white and blue, Where there's
nev-er a boast or brag; _____ But should auld ac-quaint-ance
be for-got, Keep your eye on the grand old flag. _____

Some songs, particularly those intended to be performed at slow tempos, do not sound as good as they should because of the lack of sustaining power, or continuing resonance, of the individual bells. This defect can be remedied by playing on one bell with two mallets. This effect, called *tremolo,* is created by rapidly alternating the strokes of mallets held in each hand on one bell. This effect should be reserved for notes which last for two beats or more. Try it in the next three songs.

Take Me Out to the Ball Game

Jack Norworth

Albert von Tilzer

On the Beautiful Blue Danube

Johann Strauss II

Sleepers, Wake!

Phillip Nicolai

"The Entertainer," which contains 13 different pitches, may be performed by using mallets held in each hand to play the quick syncopated rhythms. At the end of the sixteenth complete measure of this song there is a first ending and repeat sign, which indicate that you must return to the first complete measure and repeat the entire first section. After replaying this section, skip the first ending and play the second ending. Go then to the next line and play the second section up to the thirty-second complete measure — another first ending. Go back to the beginning of the second section, repeat it, and play the second ending of the second section. At this point observe the *Dal Segno al Fine* (D. S. al Fine). Go back to the sign (𝄋) at the beginning of the first section and play the entire first section. Do not play the first or second endings. Finish by playing the third (Fine) ending.

The Entertainer

Scott Joplin

"Chopsticks" may be performed either as a solo or as a duet between two persons. Both parts require the use of diatonic bell sets pitched above middle C.

Chopsticks

Melody

De Lulli

This arrangement of "That Ringing So Glorious" from Mozart's opera *The Magic Flute* may be performed as a solo; a duet combining the solo with part A, or part A with part B; a trio combining the solo with both A and B, or combining parts A, B, and C; or a quartet combining all four parts. The effect may be enhanced by using a bell set made of steel for the solo part and aluminum alloy or wood sets for the accompanying parts.

That Ringing So Glorious
The Magic Flute

Wolfgang Amadeus Mozart

Accompaniment
Part A

Accompaniment
Part B

Accompaniment
Part C

CHAPTER EIGHT
Playing Melodies on Keyboard Instruments

CHAPTER EIGHT
Playing Melodies on Keyboard Instruments

Although the acoustic piano is the traditional keyboard instrument, there are a number of alternatives. Pianicas, Magnus chord organs, Hohner Organettas, and electric pianos and organs may be used to perform the compositions in this chapter.

In order to perform these compositions you should have access to a keyboard instrument which has at least nine black keys and twelve white keys, corresponding to pitches from G below middle C of the treble staff up to D# on the fourth line in the staff (Figure 8.1). Notice that the keys go up in pitch when you move to the right and go down in pitch when you move to the left on the keyboard.

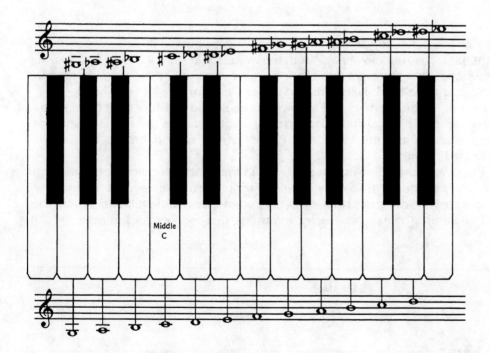

Figure 8.1

If you are using a traditional acoustic or electric piano, seat yourself on the bench so that your right hand is under the brand name of the instrument. If there is no brand name on the instrument, look at the pedals (in the center of the instrument near the floor) and place your right hand over the keys that are centered over the pedals.

BLACK KEY GROUPINGS

Place the thumb and fingers of your right hand on the black keys of the piano as shown in Figure 8.2. Notice that the thumb rests on its left side, the index, middle, and ring fingers are curved, and the little finger is straight. This posi-

Figure 8.2. Black-key grouping beginning on C♯

tion of the hand will be called the *black-key grouping*. In this grouping the right hand does not move away from the five black keys: C♯, D♯, F♯, G♯, and, A♯. Notice that there are two black keys grouped under the left side of your hand and three black keys grouped under the right side of your hand.

Each of the three songs that follow is to be played with the right hand in the black-key grouping position. The numbers written above the staff indicate that the thumb (1) and the successive fingers of the right hand are to play the indicated pitches.

The keys of the following six songs are in the pentatonic mode beginning on F♯. The *pentatonic mode* is a five-note scale having consecutive intervals of whole step, whole step, step-and-a-half, whole step, and step-and-a-half. The key signatures contain six sharps, indicating that the key is F♯ major.

Lucille

G. Wachhaus

There's a Hole in the Bucket, Dear 'Liza

United States

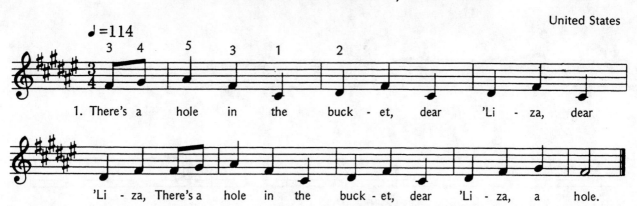

1. There's a hole in the buck - et, dear 'Li - za, dear 'Li - za, There's a hole in the buck - et, dear 'Li - za, a hole.

2. Mend the hole, then, dear Georgie, dear Georgie, dear Georgie,
Mend the hole, then, dear Georgie, dear Georgie, the hole.

3. With what shall I mend it, dear 'Liza, dear 'Liza?
With what shall I mend it, dear 'Liza, with what?

4. With a straw, then, dear Georgie, dear Georgie, dear Georgie.
With a straw, then, dear Georgie, dear Georgie, a straw.

5. If the straw is too long, then, dear 'Liza, dear 'Liza?
If the straw is too long, then, dear 'Liza, what then?

6. Cut the straw, then, dear Georgie, dear Georgie, dear Georgie.
Cut the straw, then, dear Georgie, dear Georgie, the straw.

7. With what shall I cut it, dear 'Liza, dear 'Liza?
With what shall I cut it, dear 'Liza, with what?

8. With a knife, then, dear Georgie, dear Georgie, dear Georgie.
With a knife, then, dear Georgie, dear Georgie, a knife.

9. If the knife be too dull, then, dear 'Liza, dear 'Liza?
If the knife be too dull, then, dear 'Liza, what then?

10. Whet the knife, then, dear Georgie, dear Georgie, dear Georgie.
Whet the knife, then, dear Georgie, dear Georgie, the knife.

11. With what shall I whet it, dear 'Liza, dear 'Liza?
With what shall I whet it, dear 'Liza, with what?

12. With a stone, then, dear Georgie, dear Georgie, dear Georgie.
With a stone, then, dear Georgie, dear Georgie, a stone.

13. If the stone is too rough, then, dear 'Liza, dear 'Liza?
If the stone is too rough, then, dear 'Liza, what then?

14. Smooth the stone, then, dear Georgie, dear Georgie, dear Georgie.
Smooth the stone, then, dear Georgie, dear Georgie, smooth it.

15. With what shall I smooth it, dear 'Liza, dear 'Liza?
With what shall I smooth it, dear 'Liza, with what?

16. With water, dear Georgie, dear Georgie, dear Georgie.
With water, dear Georgie, dear Georgie, water.

17. In what shall I fetch it, dear 'Liza, dear 'Liza?
In what shall I fetch it, dear 'Liza, in what?

18. In a bucket, dear Georgie, dear Georgie, dear Georgie.
In a bucket, dear Georgie, dear Georgie, a bucket.

Peter, Peter, Pumpkin Eater

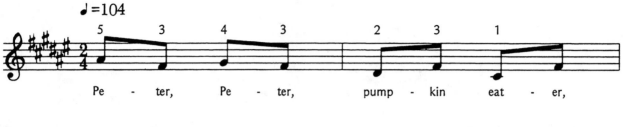

Pe - ter,   Pe - ter,   pump - kin   eat - er,

had   a   wife   and   could - n't   keep   her.   Put   her   in   a

pump - kin   shell,   and   there   he   kept   her   ver - y   well!

Move your right hand up and to the right until your thumb is on F♯, the key formerly used by your middle finger. Place your other fingers on G♯, A♯, C♯, and D♯. This position is also a black-key grouping, but now there are three black keys grouped under the left side of your hand and two black keys grouped under the right side of your hand.

Figure 8.3. Black-key grouping beginning on F♯

Merrily We Roll Along

Goodby, Old Paint

Tongo

Polynesia

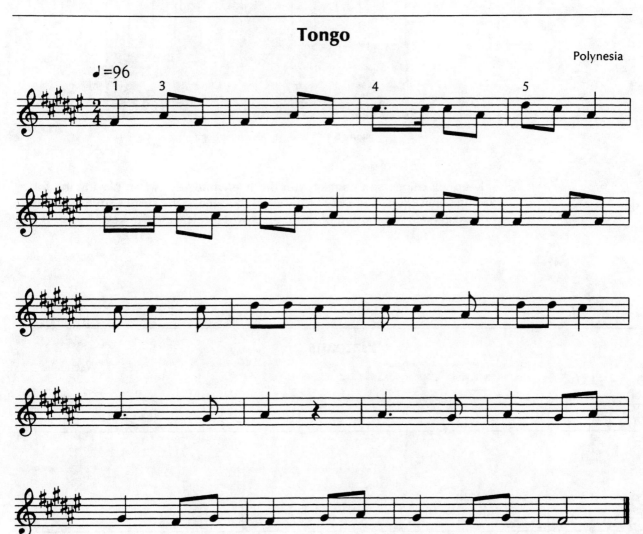

WHITE-KEY GROUPINGS

Now move your right hand down to your left over the white keys until your thumb is over C. Place your other fingers in the curved position shown in Figure 8.4. The index finger is over D, the middle finger is over E, the ring finger is over F, and, the little finger is over G. This position is known as a *white-key grouping* beginning on C.

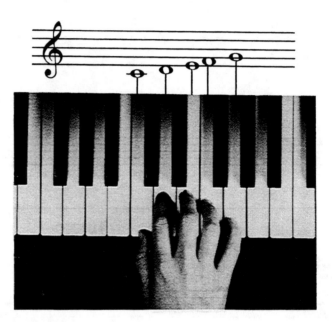

Figure 8.4. White-key grouping beginning on C

Keep your fingers in contact with the five white keys when playing the following songs. Press each key firmly enough to make the strings sound, but do not exaggerate the motion of the fingers when releasing the key.

Plateaus

G. Wachhaus

Roses

A. M. Charles

Lightly Row

1. Light - ly row, light - ly row, o'er the shin - ing waves we go;

Smooth - ly glide, smooth - ly glide, on the si - lent tide.

Let the winds and wa - ters be min - gled with our mel - o - dy,

Sing and float, sing and float, in our lit - tle boat.

2. Far away, far away, echo in the rocks at play,
   Calling not, calling not, to this lonely spot.
   Only with the sea bird's note shall our dying music float,
   Lightly row, lightly row, echo's voice is low.

3. Happy we, full of glee, sailing o'er the wavy sea,
   Happy we, full of glee, sailing o'er the sea.
   Luna sheds her clearest light, stars are sparkling, twinkling bright,
   Happy we, full of glee, sailing o'er the sea.

Move your right hand up to the right over the white keys until your thumb is over G. Place the rest of your fingers on the next four consecutive white keys. Your index finger should be over A, your middle finger over B, your ring finger over C, and your little finger should be over D. This position is the white-key grouping beginning on G (Figure 8.5).

Figure 8.5. White-key grouping beginning on G

Round

♩=116

① 1   3   2   ②   5   4

G G B B A A G   B B D D   C C   B

③   ④

D D G G D D D D   G A B C   D D G

Joy

Johann Sebastian Bach

The Deaf Woman's Courtship

United States

2. Old woman, old woman, will you do my ironing?
   Old woman, old woman, will you do my ironing?
   Speak a little louder, sir; I'm very hard of hearing.
   Speak a little louder, sir; I'm very hard of hearing.

3. Old woman, old woman, will you do my sewing?
   Old woman, old woman, will you do my sewing?
   Speak a little louder, sir; I'm very hard of hearing.
   Speak a little louder, sir; I'm very hard of hearing.

4. Old woman, old woman, may I come a'courting?
   Old woman, old woman, may I come a'courting?
   Speak a little louder, sir; I think I almost heard you.
   Speak a little louder, sir; I think I almost heard you.

5. Old woman, old woman, marry me tomorrow.
   Old woman, old woman, marry me tomorrow.
   Goodness gracious, mercy's sakes! Now I really heard you!
   Goodness gracious, mercy's sakes! Now I really heard you!

The next white-key grouping begins on F and includes a black key in addition to four white keys (Figure 8.6). Move your right hand so that your thumb is over

Figure 8.6. White-key grouping beginning on F

F, your index finger is over G, your middle finger is over A, your ring finger is over B♭ (the black key), and your little finger is over C. Be sure that your ring finger extends out over the black key, B♭, or these next three songs will not sound quite right. If notes are connected with slurs (⌣), the first key should not be released until the second key has been struck.

Ding, Dong, Bell

England

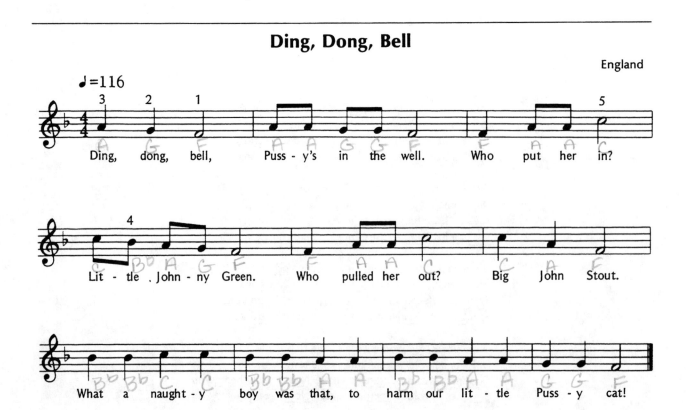

Whistle, Daughter, Whistle

United States

♩=144

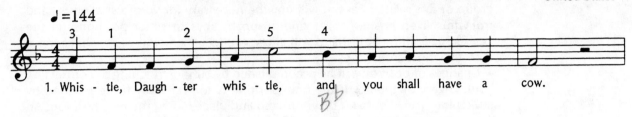

1. Whis - tle, Daugh - ter whis - tle, and you shall have a cow.

Bb

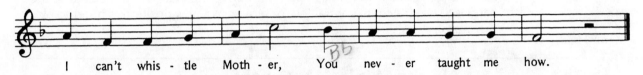

I can't whis - tle Moth - er, You nev - er taught me how.

Bb

2. Whistle, Daughter, whistle, and you shall have a goat.
   I can't whistle, Mother, because it hurts my throat.

3. Whistle, Daughter, whistle, and you shall have a pig.
   I can't whistle, Mother, because I am too big.

4. Whistle, Daughter, whistle, and you shall have a man.
   (whistle _____), Oh, yes! Oh, yes! I can!

Cradle Song

Isaac Watts

Jean Jacques Rousseau

♩=60

Hush, my____ babe, lie still and slum - ber.

Ho - ly____ an - gels guard __ thy __ bed. Heav'n - ly____ bless - ings

with - out num - ber Gen - tly____ fall - ing on __ thy __ head.

CHANGING HAND POSITIONS

Until now, your right hand has been confined to a fixed position over a group of five related keys. It will now be necessary for you to shift your hand from this fixed position over one group of keys to other positions on the keyboard. Shifting your hand will allow you to play melodies that have more than five different pitches.

Changes of position can be accomplished by either stretching or contracting your fingers or thumb. If the new position is too far away to be reached by stretching, you should lift up your hand and place it over the new position. An asterisk placed next to a finger number above the staff will indicate that the hand is to be stretched, contracted, or moved to a new position in order to play that note.

In the Shining Moonlight
Au Clair de la Lune

France

In the shin - ing moon - light, my dear friend Pier - rot,

Came to ask a fa - vor, but I told him "no."

He came far too late, and I had gone to bed.

"Come a - gain to - mor - row. Ask me then in - stead."

1. "Au clair de la lune, mon ami Pierrot,
   Prêtes moi ta plume, pour écrire un mot;
   Ma chandelle est morte, je n'ai plus de feu;
   Ouvres moi ta porte, pour l'amour de Dieu."

2. Au clair de la lune, Pierrot répondit,
   "Je n'ai pas de plume, je suis dans mon lit;
   Va chez la voisine, je crois qu'elle y est,
   Car, dans sa cuisine on bat le briquet."

Twinkle, Twinkle, Little Star

Nicholas Dezede

1. Twin - kle, twin - kle, lit - tle star, how I won - der what you are.

Up a - bove the world so high, Like a dia - mond in the sky,

Twin - kle, twin - kle, lit - tle star, how I won - der what you are.

2. When our daily sun is gone, other lands he shines upon.
   Then you show your little light, twinkle, twinkle, all the night.
   Twinkle, twinkle, little star, how I wonder what you are.

3. While your bright and tiny spark lights the trav'ler in the dark,
   Then you never shut your eye, 'til the sun is in the sky.
   Twinkle, twinkle, little star, how I wonder what you are.

Other lyrics that may be sung to the same melody:

Baa, baa, black sheep, have you any wool? "Yes, sir! Yes, sir! Three bags full.
One for my master, one for my dame, and one for the little boy who lives in the lane."
Baa, baa, black sheep, have you any wool? "Yes, sir! Yes, sir! Three bags full."

A, B, C, D, E, F, G, H, I, J, K, L, M, N, O, P,
Q, R, S, and T, U, V, W, and X, Y, Z.
Now I've learned my "A, B, C." Tell me what you think of me.

Ah! vous dirai je maman, ce qui cause mon tourment?
Papa veut que je raisonne comme une grande personne;
Moi je dis que les bonbons valent mieux que la raison.

Gonna Sing

United States

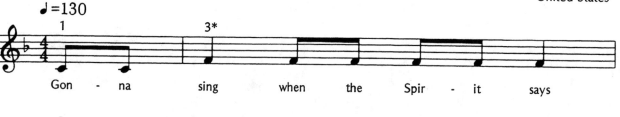

Gon - na sing when the Spir - it says

"sing." Gon - na sing when the Spir - it says

"sing."__ Gon - na sing when the Spir - it says

"sing," And o - bey the Spir - it of the Lord.

If you sing additional verses, substitute any of the following words for "sing":

clap	mourn
cry	praise
groan	pray
jump	roll
kneel	shout
laugh	weep
moan	wail

Another technique will allow you to play melodies that contain scale-like passages. The thumb can be used as a pivot to allow the fingers to pass over it, and fingers can serve as pivots to allow the thumb to pass under them. The thumb, index, and middle fingers are the digits usually involved in passing over or under.

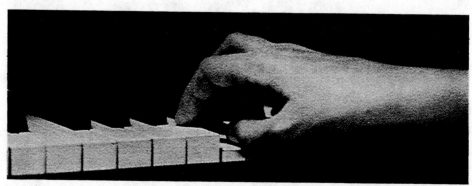

Thumb pivot

In the following songs, we indicate that you should use a finger to pivot by placing its finger number in parentheses. Notice carefully the movement required of the fingers and hand after the pivot.

The Cowboy's Lament

United States

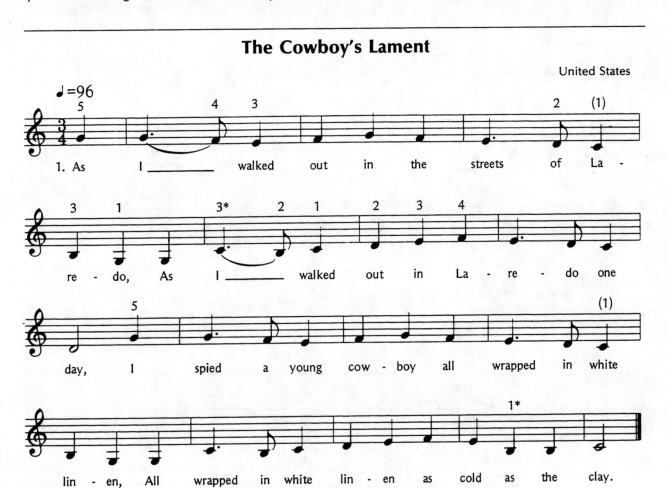

2. "I see by your outfit that you are a cowboy,"
   These words he did say as I boldly stepped by.
   "Come sit down beside me and hear my sad story,
   I'm shot in the breast and I'm going to die."

3. "Now once in the saddle I used to go dashing,
   Yes, once in the saddle I used to be gay,
   I'd dress myself up and go down to the card-house,
   I got myself shot and I'm dying today."

4. "Get six husky cowboys to carry my coffin,
   Get ten lovely maidens to sing me a song,
   And beat the drum slowly and play the fife lowly,
   For I'm a young cowboy who knows he was wrong."

5. "Oh, please go and bring me a cup of cold water
   To cool my parched lips, they are burning," he said.
   Before I could get it, his soul had departed
   And gone to its Maker, the cowboy was dead.

6. We beat the drum slowly and played the fife lowly
   And wept in our grief as we bore him along,
   For we loved the cowboy, so brave and so handsome,
   We loved that young cowboy although he'd done wrong.

Theme
Concerto in D for Violin and Orchestra

Ludwig van Beethoven

Cancan
Orpheus in Hades

Jacques Offenbach

The following compositions do not have any keyboard fingerings indicated. Use this opportunity to find your own finger patterns to perform them. Write the finger numbers above the staff. Remember that any of the following techniques that you have learned may be used:

Keeping a fixed position over a group of five keys.
Stretching the fingers or thumb.
Contracting the fingers or thumb.
Lifting the hand and placing it in a new position.
Passing the fingers over the thumb.
Passing the thumb under the fingers.

The resulting fingerings often will be a matter of personal preference depending on the size, shape, coordination, and dexterity of your thumb, fingers, and hand. Experiment with various patterns until you find the fingerings with which you are comfortable.

Sinner Man

United States

1. Oh,   sin - ner   man,   where   you   gon - na   run   ·to?

Oh, sin - ner man, where you gon - na run to? Oh, sin - ner man,

where you gon - na run to, All on that day?

2. <u>Run</u> to the rock, <u>rock</u> it was a'melting. . .

3. <u>Run</u> to the sea, <u>sea</u> it was a'raging. . .

4. <u>Run</u> to the trees, <u>trees</u> they were a'swaying. . .

5. <u>Fall</u> to the earth, <u>earth</u> it was a'rolling. . .

6. <u>Run</u> to the Devil, <u>Devil</u> stood a'waiting. . .

7. <u>Oh</u>, sinner man <u>should</u> a' been a'praying. . .

8. <u>Oh</u>, sinner man, <u>where</u> you gonna run to?

9. <u>Run</u> to the Lord, "<u>Lordie</u>, won't you hide me?". . .

Pomp and Circumstance
Military March No. 1

Edward Elgar

Tzena, Tzena

G. Wachhaus

Israel

1. Tze - na, tze - na, tze - na, tze - na, Can't you hear the laugh - ing of the peo - ple in the square? Tze - na, tze - na, tze - na, tze - na, Can't you hear the rhy - thm of the peo - ple danc - ing there?

Tze - na, tze - na, danc - ing in the sun - shine, Won't you join us in the cel - e - bra - tion? Tze - na, tze - na, laugh - ing in the sun - shine, Join the danc - ing in the square?

The following may be played as a third section to this round's music and sung with the word "Tzena" repeated.

2. Tzena, tzena, tzena, tzena,
Don't you hear the sighing of the sweethearts in the square?
Tzena, tzena, tzena, tzena,
Don't you hear the beating of their hearts together there?
Tzena, tzena, dancing in the moonlight,
Come and join us, what a great sensation!
Tzena, tzena, meet us in the starlight,
Join your sweetheart in the square.

Early One Morning

England

2. Then as she went to wash, she came a-strolling o'er the hill.
Squirrels, chipmunks, cats, and dogs all joined her by the mill.
Chorus

3. Bright are the roses near the gardens which are newly sown.
She skips along the scented fields freshly mown.
Chorus

4. When evening comes along and darkness follows all around,
Still, the maid sings her song, a happy little sound.
Chorus

CHAPTER NINE
Understanding Lead Sheet Notation

CHAPTER NINE
Understanding
Lead Sheet Notation

In Chapter 1 you learned to read rhythm. In Chapter 2 you learned to read pitch. Chapters 10, 12, and 13 will introduce you to instruments on which you can play chordal accompaniments for songs. You will learn techniques for playing chords on the autoharp, keyboard instruments, and guitar. Before you begin playing those instruments, you need to learn one more aspect of music notation: the chord symbols that are placed above the staff.

Lead sheet notation (pronounced leed) is the practice of notating the melody, chords, and words of a song on a single staff. A large number of songbooks, including basal series music texts, use this style of notation.

Based on your study of Chapters 1 and 2 you should be able to read the rhythm and pitch of a song's melody. You will learn how to play chords on autoharp, keyboard, and guitar in succeeding chapters. Information on how chords are constructed is presented in Chapter 11.

The purpose of this chapter is to teach you how to play chords for the proper rhythmic durations in a given song. Chord symbols alone do not contain any clues to chord duration: it is their placement above the staff that signifies when one chord changes to another. Most chords change at the beginning of a measure, some change halfway through a measure, and still others change on or within single beats of a measure. Careful attention to the meter of the song and the placement of the chord symbol above the melody is usually all that is needed to "chord a melody."

A *chord* is the simultaneous sounding of three or more tones. Chords are indicated by a capital letter that may be followed by one or more symbols. The symbols always include a capital letter, and they also may include a sharp sign (♯), a flat sign (♭), a small letter "m," or a number.

A capital letter, with or without a sharp or flat, stands for the name of the chord. If it includes no more symbols, then it refers to a *major chord*. The following are all major chords: C, D, E♭, F♯, and B♭. When you say the names of these chords, they are pronounced "C major," "D major," "E-flat major," "F-sharp major," and "B-flat major."

A capital letter with or without a sharp or flat *plus* a small letter "m" signifies a *minor chord*. The following chords are all minor chords: Cm, Dm, E♭m, F♯m, and B♭m. Pronounce them "C minor," "D minor," "E-flat minor," "F-sharp minor," and "B-flat minor."

The addition of the number seven to a capital letter with or without an added sharp or flat denotes a *dominant seventh chord:* C7, D7, E♭7, F♯7, and B♭7 are all seventh chords. The names of these chords are pronounced "C seven," "D seven," "E-flat seven," "F-sharp seven," and "B-flat seven."

In lead sheet notation, chord symbols are placed above the five-line staff. In order to introduce you to playing chord rhythm, we shall use the two-line staff previously seen in Chapter 1. The beat-note again will be placed on the lower line, one note for each beat. The chords to be strummed on each beat are symbolized on the upper staff line.

Study the song "Melody" and compare it to the two-line staff which follows to see how to play the chord rhythm. Sing the name of the chord you will play on each beat. The same chord is played until a different letter is given in a new chord symbol. The same chord is retained even if that means playing the same chord for several measures.

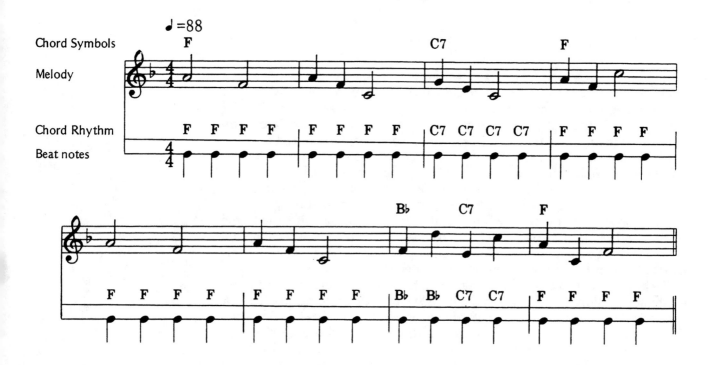

Study the following exercise. Sing the note that is the name of the chord on each beat, and clap to be sure that you maintain a steady beat. Notice carefully the tempo and the number of beats per measure. Be aware of when the chord changes.

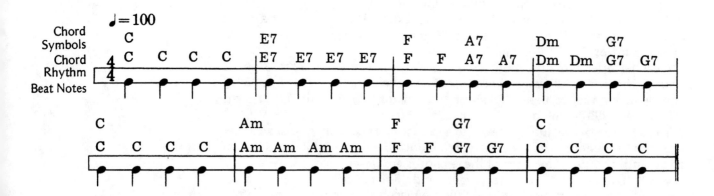

The melody of "Go Tell Aunt Rhody" below is juxtaposed with a two-line staff that indicates the beat notes and how many times each chord is to be strummed. Study this example carefully. Sing the note that is the name of the chord on each beat, and clap to be sure that you maintain a steady beat.

Go Tell Aunt Rhody

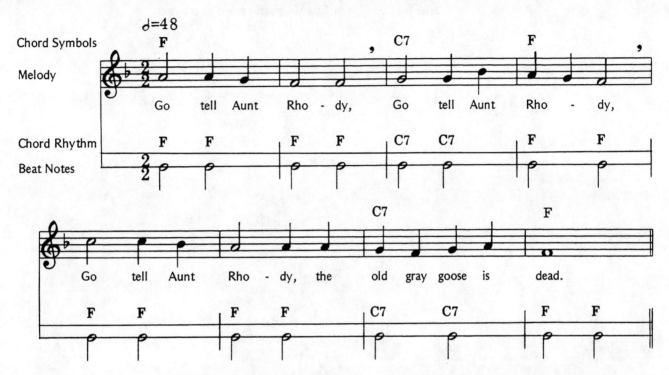

Write in the correct chord symbol on the two-line staff, indicating the number of times each chord should be played in the chorus of "Bile Them Cabbage Down."

Bile Them Cabbage Down

As an assignment, turn to "Amazing Grace" (page 249) and prepare a chart of the number of beats each chord should be played. Use a two-line staff and fill in the tempo, the meter signature, the notes that depict the beat, the chord symbols, and the number of beats each chord is played.

CHAPTER TEN
Playing Accompaniments and Melodies on Autoharp

CHAPTER TEN
Playing Accompaniments and Melodies on Autoharp

The autoharp*is perhaps the most rewarding of the easy-to-play instruments. It is versatile in that it can play harmonic accompaniments for songs and, with practice, can even be used to play melody with harmony. The autoharp is small and easily carried, making it ideal for use in classrooms, on field trips, for camping and vacations, or wherever groups of people are inclined to make their own music.

Table position

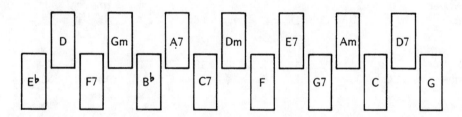

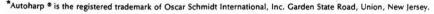

Autoharp Keyboard

*Autoharp ® is the registered trademark of Oscar Schmidt International, Inc. Garden State Road, Union, New Jersey.

Pictured above is the keyboard of a fifteen-bar autoharp. Each bar bears a chord name. If you have access to a twelve-bar autoharp, you will notice that the keyboard is identical, except that the E♯, D, and F7 chords do not appear on that instrument. Recent instruments can have twenty-one or more chord bars.

When you press a chord bar, some of the strings are blocked from sounding. The pitches of the strings that are free to sound all belong in the chord named on the bar. By pressing bars and strumming the strings you can produce the chords that provide the harmony part for songs.

Before you try to play a song, just experiment with the autoharp. Lay it flat on a table in front of you with the longest strings closest to you. You might prefer to hold it in your lap. Then press the C chord bar with your left-hand index finger, cross your right arm over your left, and strum your pick across the strings from low to high (that is, away from you) keeping time with the beat of the music. Hold the pick loosely between your thumb and index finger.

Strumming with pick

Determine how hard you must press the chord bar to produce a clear sound. Strum quickly and evenly, keeping a steady beat. Keep strumming and switch to an F chord, back to C, to G7, and then back to C again. In this position you will play the F chord with your ring finger and the G7 chord with your middle finger. When playing a song you will change chords each time a new chord is written above the staff (Chapter 9).

For different sound qualities you may want to experiment with picks made from different materials. Plastic for a bright sound and felt for a more somber, subdued sound tend to work well. Credit cards, coins, blackboard erasers,

Lap position

paper clips, and crumpled paper produce distinct sound qualities when used to strum the autoharp.

Songs are often begun with a short instrumental introduction. You can play a short introduction to "Reuben's Train" by strumming C three times before you begin singing. These strums will set the tempo of the song and help you begin singing on the correct pitch.

To find your beginning singing pitch, first strum the strings slowly while pressing the C chord. After you have the C-chord sound in mind, look at the right-hand end of your autoharp, and you will find the names of all the notes and a picture of a piano keyboard. Find the beginning note of the song and pluck it. In "Reuben's Train" the first melody note is middle C. Hum that tone, play the introduction, and begin singing along.

If your autoharp is a model that does not have the names of the strings pictured on the body of the instrument, then you can count the strings according to the following information.

Autoharp String Numbers and Pitches*

Low Strings

Number	1	2	3	4	5	6	7	8	9	10	11	12
Name	F_2	G_2	C_3	D_3	E_3	F_3	$F\sharp_3$	G_3	A_3	$A\sharp_3$	B_3	C_4

Middle Strings

Number	13	14	15	16	17	18	19	20	21	22	23	24
Name	$C\sharp_4$	D_4	$D\sharp_4$	E_4	F_4	$F\sharp_4$	G_4	$G\sharp_4$	A_4	$A\sharp_4$	B_4	C_5

High Strings

Number	25	26	27	28	29	30	31	32	33	34	35	36
Name	$C\sharp_5$	D_5	$D\sharp_5$	E_5	F_5	$F\sharp_5$	G_5	$G\sharp_5$	A_5	$A\sharp_5$	B_5	C_6

---

*C_4 is middle C; C_5 is one octave above middle C.

To find the opening pitch for "Reuben's Train," pluck the twelfth string, counting from the longest to the shortest strings. It will be middle C. Match that pitch with your voice, strum the introduction, and start singing. Play the harmonic accompaniment for "Reuben's Train" while you or your classmates sing the melody.

In the music printed on the following pages, strums are represented by capital letters and slashes (╱). Strum once for each capital letter or slash.

Reuben's Train

United States

1. Reu - ben's com - ing down the track, If he's

pulled the throt - tle back Then the rails will a car - ry him_ from home._____

2. If the <u>boil</u>er won't <u>bust</u>,
   It's all <u>eat</u>en with <u>rust</u>,
   He will <u>soon</u> be a <u>long</u> ways from <u>home</u>.

3. If you <u>don't</u> think I'm <u>gone</u>,
   You can <u>look</u> for the train I'm <u>on</u>;
   You can <u>hear</u> the whistle <u>blow</u> a hundred <u>miles</u>.

4. Well the <u>train</u> was rollin' <u>fast</u>,
   'Till I <u>knowed</u> it wouldn't <u>last</u>;
   For the <u>wheels</u> was a-<u>firing</u> near the <u>track</u>.

5. When old <u>Reu</u>ben went <u>crash</u>,
   And the <u>en</u>gine went <u>splash</u>;
   The old <u>tres</u>tle went a-<u>fallin'</u> into the <u>stream</u>.

6. Now you <u>ought</u> to've been in <u>town</u>
   When old <u>Reu</u>ben's train went <u>down</u>;
   That old <u>whis</u>tle was <u>heard</u> near and <u>far</u>.

7. Well old <u>Reu</u>ben's still <u>around</u>
   Never <u>hit</u> the <u>ground</u>,
   He is <u>still</u> pullin' that <u>throt</u>tle toward his <u>home</u>.

There are two chords, F and C7, in "Go Tell Aunt Rhody." You must synchronize the chord changes with the melody and the words. Play the following progression as an introduction:

F / C7 / F / / /

Strum the indicated chord once for each slash until a different chord is given. Begin singing with the chordal accompaniment after the introduction. Be sure to press and hold the chord bars hard and long enough to maintain a clear tone.

Go Tell Aunt Rhody

United States

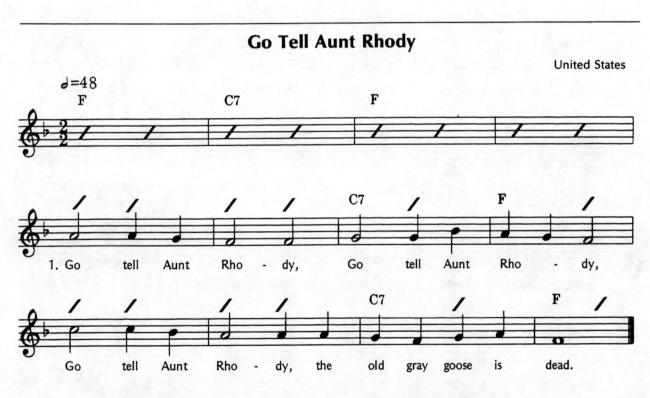

2. The <u>one</u> she was <u>saving</u>, *(3 times)*
   To <u>make</u> a feather <u>bed</u>.

3. She <u>died</u> in the <u>mill</u> pond, *(3 times)*
   A-<u>standin'</u> on her <u>head</u>.

4. The goslings are <u>crying</u>, *(3 times)*
   Be<u>cause</u> their mother's <u>dead</u>.

5. The gander is weeping, *(3 times)*
   Be<u>cause</u> his wife is <u>dead</u>.

Low strings

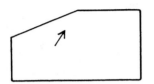

Higher strings

In "Polly Wolly Doodle" try strumming low strings on the accented beats (1 and 3) and higher strings on the unaccented beats (2 and 4).

This type of strum is indicated with a flag on the slash. A flag on the bottom of the slash tells you to play on the low strings (**⌐**), and a flag at the top of the slash tells you to strum higher strings (**⌐**).

If you do not have a D chord on your autoharp, you will have to transpose this song to the key of C or F. (See Chapter 14, "Understanding Transposition.") The term "simile" means to continue the same strum throughout the piece. You can provide an introduction by playing two complete measures of the first chord. Begin singing on the fourth beat of the introduction's second measure.

Polly Wolly Doodle

United States

2. Oh, my <u>Sal</u>, she is a <u>mai</u>den fair. . .
With <u>cur</u>ly eyes and <u>laugh</u>ing hair. . .
Chorus

4. Oh, I <u>went</u> to bed, but it <u>was</u>n't no use. . .
My <u>feet</u> stuck out for a <u>chick</u>en roost. . .
Chorus

3. Oh, a <u>grass</u>hopper sittin' on a <u>rail</u>road track. . .
A-<u>pick</u>in' his teeth with a <u>car</u>pet tack. . .
Chorus

5. Be<u>hind</u> the barn, down <u>on</u> my knees. . .
I <u>thought</u> I heard a <u>chick</u>en sneeze. . .
Chorus

6. He <u>sneezed</u> so hard with the <u>whoop</u>ing cough. . .
He <u>sneezed</u> his head and <u>tail</u> right off. . .
Chorus

Try the following strum in "Skip to My Lou."

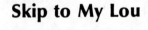

Strum low strings on the accented beats (1 and 3) and play two even strokes on
the middle strings — one away from you and then one stroke toward you —
during the unaccented beats (2 and 4).

Skip to My Lou

United States

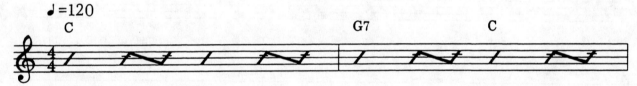

1. <u>Fly</u> in the buttermilk, <u>shoo</u> fly shoo *(3 times)*
<u>Skip</u> to my Lou, my <u>dar</u>ling.
Chorus

3. <u>I'll</u> get another one, <u>pret</u>tier than you. *(3 times)*
<u>Skip</u> to my Lou, my <u>dar</u>ling.
Chorus

2. <u>Lost</u> my partner, <u>what'll</u> I do? *(3 times)*
<u>Skip</u> to my Lou, my <u>dar</u>ling.
Chorus

4. <u>Can't</u> get a red bird, a <u>blue</u> bird'll do. *(3 times)*
<u>Skip</u> to my Lou, my <u>dar</u>ling.
Chorus

5. <u>Lit</u>tle red wagon, <u>paint</u>ed blue. *(3 times)*
<u>Skip</u> to my Lou, my <u>dar</u>ling.
Chorus

Three beats are grouped together in each measure of the song "Clementine." In order to emphasize the stress on the first beat of each measure, try strumming the autoharp in three different ranges: low, middle, then high strings. The flag in the middle of the slash means middle strumming range.

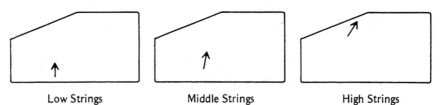

Low Strings   Middle Strings   High Strings

You can produce different tone qualities by strumming in the middle of the strings or strumming near the tuning pegs.

Clementine

United States

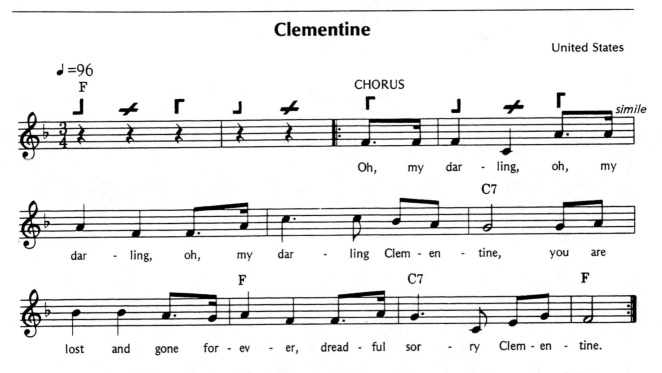

1. In a cavern, in a canyon, excavating for a mine,
   Dwelt a miner, forty-niner, and his daughter, Clementine.
   Chorus

2. Light she was, and like a fairy, and her shoes were number nine,
   Herring boxes, without topses, sandals were for Clementine.
   Chorus

3. Drove she ducklings to the water, every morning just at nine,
   Hit her foot against a splinter, fell into the foaming brine.
   Chorus

4. Ruby lips above the water, blowing bubbles soft and fine;
   As for me, I was no swimmer, and I lost my Clementine.
   Chorus

5. How I missed her, how I missed her, how I missed my Clementine,
   Till I kissed her little sister, and forgot my Clementine.
   Chorus

Use the techniques you have learned so far to play the next six songs. No special autoharp strums are indicated so that you may choose an appropriate strum for each song. You may create your own introductions. Sing out as you play!

Bile Them Cabbage Down

Harvey Reid

United States

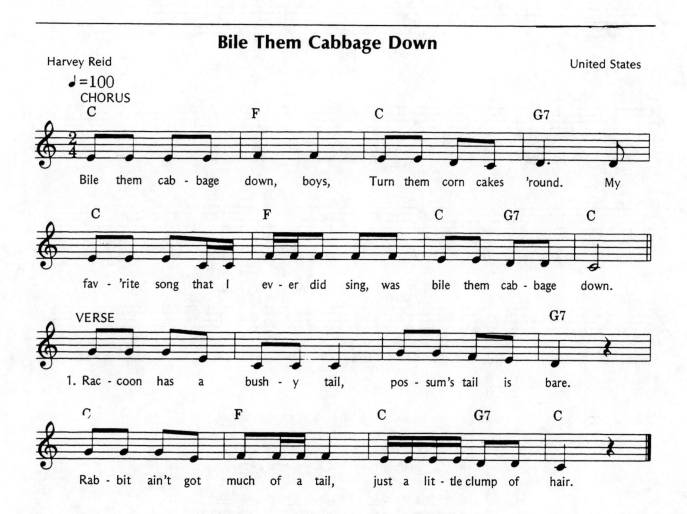

Bile them cab - bage down, boys, Turn them corn cakes 'round. My

fav - 'rite song that I ev - er did sing, was bile them cab - bage down.

1. Rac - coon has a bush - y tail, pos - sum's tail is bare.

Rab - bit ain't got much of a tail, just a lit - tle clump of hair.

2. I'll <u>eat</u> my cabbage <u>cold</u> boys, And I <u>like</u> it steamin' <u>hot</u>,
   <u>Served</u> up every <u>evenin'</u> In <u>Mammy's</u> great big <u>pot</u>.
   Chorus

3. I got a four-string <u>fiddle</u>, But I <u>got</u> a two-string <u>bow</u>,
   I'll <u>scrape</u> you a tune by the <u>light</u> of the moon,
   But there's <u>on</u>ly one tune I <u>know</u>.
   Chorus

4. <u>Kick</u> your heels up <u>high</u>, Sal, And <u>turn</u> the lamp down <u>low</u>,
   Ring, ring that <u>old</u> five-string, And '<u>round</u> and 'round we'll <u>go</u>.
   Chorus

5. <u>Revenue</u> men got my <u>still</u> now, <u>Poured</u> my likker on the <u>ground</u>.
   We'll <u>sing</u> this song from <u>dusk</u> to dawn,
   And <u>bile</u> them cabbage <u>down</u>.
   Chorus

Wildwood Flower

United States

♩=66

1. I will tie up my ring - lets of wav - ing black

hair With some ro - ses of red and some li - lies so

fair, And the myr - tle so green casts its em - er - ald

hue, And the pale li - lacs laced 'round sad eyes of faint blue.

2. I will dance, I will sing, and my laugh shall be gay,
   I will charm every heart, all the crowds I will sway,
   But I woke from my dream, and my idol was clay,
   The old passions of love had all gone far away.

3. Oh, he told me he loved me, he called me his flower,
   I was bloomin' to cheer him through life's dreary hour,
   Now I am broken-hearted in this lonely hour,
   When he's gone and forgotten this pale wildwood flower.

4. But he told me he loved me, he promised to care,
   Through our days and our trials all our lives we would share.
   Oh, he said he would keep me so near his warm heart,
   That he could never bear, should we be far apart.

5. I will dance, I will sing, and my life shall be gay,
   I will cry no more now, turn all nights into day,
   But I wake from my dreamin' my idol's away,
   And my visions of love have all faded away.

6. Can this man who deceived me be worth my great woe,
   Should he take all my joys and should I sit here so?
   No, he won't be the end of my life or my show,
   But a flower that is trampled can no longer grow.

Oh, Susanna

Stephen Foster

2. I had a dream the other night, when ev'rything was still;
   I thought I saw Susanna dear, a-coming down the hill.
   The buckwheat cake was in her mouth, the tear was in her eye,
   I says, "I'm coming from the south, Susanna don't you cry."
   Chorus

3. I soon will be in New Orleans, and then I'll look around,
   And when I find Susanna, I'll fall upon the ground.
   And if I do not find her, then I will surely die,
   And when I'm dead and buried, Susanna don't you cry.
   Chorus

Bingo

Scotland

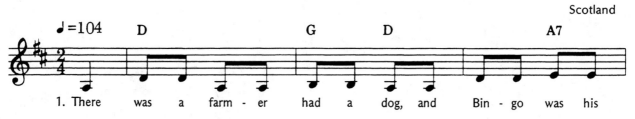

1. There was a farm - er had a dog, and Bin - go was his

name - o. B - i - n - g - o, B - i - n - g - o,

B - i - n - g - o, and Bin - go was his name - o.

2. The farmer had an awful cold, and couldn't even sing-o.
S - i - n - g - o, s - i - n - g - o, s - i - n - g - o,
He couldn't even sing-o.

3. The farmer loved a sweet young thing, and bought a wedding ring-o.
R - i - n - g - o, r - i - n - g - o, r - i - n - g - o,
He bought a wedding ring-o.

4. Now, wasn't this a lovely song? It surely is, by jing-o.
J - i - n - g - o, j - i - n - g - o, j - i - n - g - o,
It surely is, by jing-o.

Old Joe Clark

United States

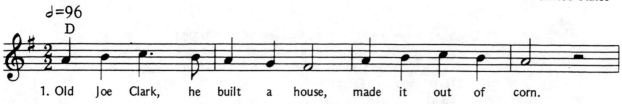

1. Old Joe Clark, he built a house, made it out of corn.

Ev - 'ry night he goes to sleep, snores and eats 'till morn.

CHORUS

'Round   and 'round,   Old   Joe   Clark,   'round   and 'round   I   say,

'Round   and 'round,   Old   Joe   Clark,   I   don't have   long   to   stay.

2. Old Joe Clark, he had a house, twenty stories long,
   Ev'ry story in that house, was sung to a little song.
   Chorus

3. When Joe was a little boy, used to want a knife,
   Now he is a bigger boy, now he wants a wife.
   Chorus

4. Joe wouldn't marry no city gal, tell you the reason why,
   Blew her nose in old cornbread, and called it pumpkin pie.
   Chorus

5. Joe Clark lived on the mountain top, lived there all his life,
   Only time he went to town, brought him back a wife.
   Chorus

6. Old Joe had a muley cow, knew it when she's born,
   Took a jaybird half a year, to fly from horn to horn.
   Chorus

7. Old Joe Clark he had a cat, not like any you've seen,
   Carried off that muley cow, my that cat was mean.
   Chorus

8. Joe Clark had an old black cat, 'twas his lucky charm.
   Crossed in front of ev'rything, wrecked his whole durn farm.
   Chorus

9. I wish I was a flying bird, I'd fly up high and low,
   Ev'ry time old Joe came out, I'd give him a little show.
   Chorus

10. Joe Clark had a violin, played it all the day,
    Never did he fiddle around, all he'd do is play.
    Chorus

Ev'rything's Alright with Me

Words and music
by Jewel Mayo

♩=114

This is my left hand, this is my right.   I   have two eyes to

see   the sight.   La,   da, da, da, _____ da,   la,   da, da, dee;

Ev - 'ry - thing's al - right with me!   And these   are   my   lips (smack),   and

these   are   my   hips (boom, boom). My   ears   are cute as can be;   to

lis - ten to what you tell me.   La,   da, da, da, _____ da,

la,   da, da, dee;   Ev - 'ry - thing's al - right with me!

This is my nose, my nos - trils two, that I might smell, and sniff,

it's true! La, da, da, da, ___ da, la, da, da, dee;

Ev - 'ry - thing's al - right with me! Let's move right a - long; I

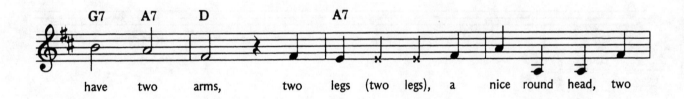

have two arms, two legs (two legs), a nice round head, two

feet (that's neat), I'm quite a treat! La, da, da, da, ___ da,

la, da, da, dee; Ev - 'ry - thing's al - right with me!

The "Drunken Sailor" is played with a chord progression based on Dm and C. Pressing Dm and D7 at the same time produces a stark, open sound that fits this song well. These two chords played as a single chord can be used in this song alternating with the C chord. See if you can capture the spirit of the sailors who are working and feeling the lack of help from their shipmates who are not working due to overindulgence. You might also try "Reuben's Train" with the Dm + D7 combination.

Drunken Sailor

United States

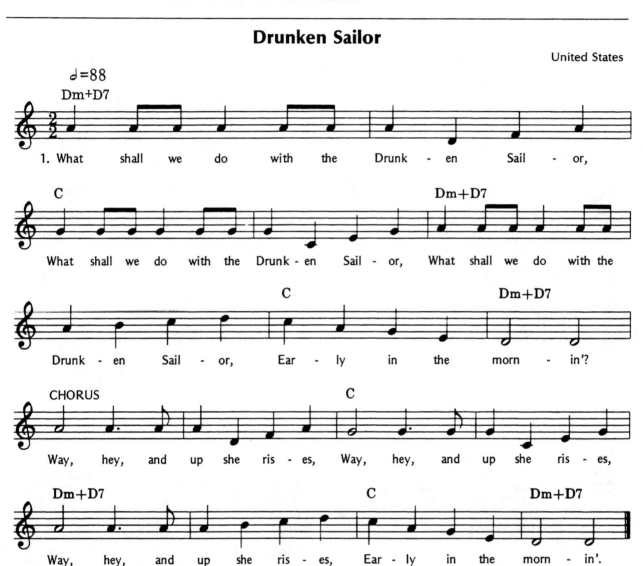

2. Pull out the plug and wet him all over...
   Chorus

3. Put him in the scuppers with the hose pipe on him...
   Chorus

4. Put him in a leaky boat and make him bale her...
   Chorus

5. Heave him by the leg in a running bowline...
   Chorus .

6. Tie him to the topmast when she's under...
   Chorus

7. Keel haul him until he's sober...
   Chorus

8. Shave his belly with a rusty razor...
   Chorus

9. Make him swab the deck with a soapy toothbrush...
   Chorus

10. <u>Make</u> him peel potatoes with a <u>tiny</u> toothpick. . .
Chorus

11. <u>Peter</u> Piper picked a peck of <u>pickled</u> peppers. . .
Chorus

PLAYING MELODIES

In addition to providing a harmonic background, the autoharp can be used as a solo instrument playing both the melody and harmony of a song. The autoharp was not originally intended to be used as a melody instrument by its inventor, Charles Zimmerman (1881); but many folk performers, notably Maybelle Carter, Kilby Snow, Mike Seeger, and Harvey Reid, have developed sophisticated melody techniques. Solo technique on autoharp requires a more complete understanding of how the instrument functions, and it also requires a more facile finger movement — both on the chord bars, and in the right hand.

To learn the basics of this *Appalachian style* of playing, hold the back of the autoharp against your chest and wrap your arms around it. Observe the picture on page 175 for an example of this position. You will need a plastic or metal thumb pick and usually two metal finger picks for your right hand. Some people use only one, while others use as many as three or four finger picks. Metal finger picks from .015 to .025 gauge thickness work well. Different thicknesses produce slightly different sounds. Metal picks, being adjustable, are preferable to plastic picks.

Thumb and finger picks

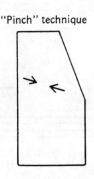

"Pinch" technique

In this section three basic right-hand motions will be explained. The first motion is the *pinch* technique (notated ^m_p), in which the right-hand thumb (p) and middle finger (m) literally pinch at the same time. The thumb and middle finger are held in a spread-out fashion, and they "claw" at the strings, the thumb playing a few bass strings and the middle finger playing the melody tones. As the chord bar felts stop all but the chord tones from sounding, it is necessary only to be close to the correct string. Avoid strumming strings pitched higher than the melody tone.

Brush technique

The next right-hand motion to be learned is the *brush* (notated *l*). The brush is played with the thumb strumming several strings in the range between the bass and melody tones.

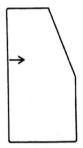

Thumb on bass strings

The last strum we will consider in this section is playing with the thumb alone on just a few bass strings to emphasize the heavy beat (p). The thumb has a very important role in keeping both bass notes and the rhythmic accompaniment of the song moving.

To get started, try the song "Go Tell Aunt Rhody." This song uses just two of the right-hand strums discussed above, the pinch (^m_p) and the brush (*l*). These marks are given below the staff. Above the staff are given the chord bars that must be depressed in order to sound the melody notes of the song.

When the F chord bar is pressed, all the F, A, and C strings are allowed to vibrate and produce tones. When the C7 chord bar is pressed, all the C, E, G, and Bb strings produce tones. (The pitches in chords are discussed in Chapter 11.) In order to play the melody you will press whichever chord bar allows the melody note to sound. You can develop a feeling for where to strum with your right hand by doing a few pinch strums over the entire range of the autoharp; after that, narrow your experimentation until your middle finger can play the notes F, A, C, A, F. Then locate the "A" string by sight and by sound. "Claw" at the strings with a fairly exaggerated motion, letting your ear give you cues to your accuracy. You will notice that many more chord changes are required when you play the melody.

As you practice the following songs you will learn that the autoharp is a "forgiving" instrument. Even mistakes can sound musical on this instrument. You will also learn that varying tone qualities can be produced by playing at different places on the strings.

Go Tell Aunt Rhody

United States

Wildwood Flower

Try playing the C-major scale by using just the C, G7, and F chord bars as follows:

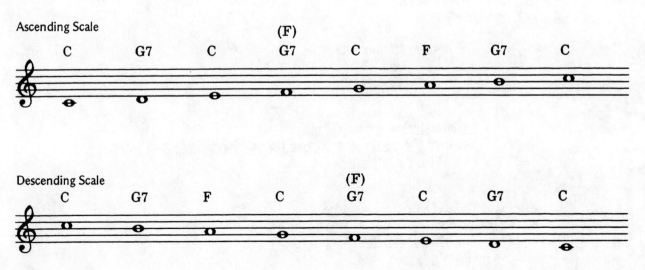

The F chord can be used on the fourth scale degree; however, the alternation between C and G7 in the scale degrees one through five is mechanically easier. As you develop facility in playing scales, you will be able to start picking songs out by ear because many songs will use only the tones in a scale. Use of only three chord bars will also facilitate transposition, inasmuch as the function of each chord can be assumed by another chord in the new key.

"Billy Boy" and "Railroad Bill" use all three types of strums. Watch the chords!

Railroad Bill

United States

Rail - road Bill, Rail - road Bill, He nev - er

worked and__ he nev - er will, And it's ride, ride, ride. ___

1. Railroad Bill's a mighty vicious man,
   Shot the light from a brakeman's hand,
   And it's ride, ride, ride.
   Chorus

2. Railroad Bill is so bad
   Shot at his Ma and he hit his Dad,
   And it's ride, ride, ride.
   Chorus

3. Railroad Bill, took my wife,
   Said if I didn't like it he would take my life,
   And it's ride, ride, ride.
   Chorus

4. Kill me a chicken, get me a wing,
   You think I'm workin' when I haven't done a thing,
   And it's ride, ride, ride.
   Chorus

5. Railroad Bill, strung me along,
   Stole my wallet, then he sang this here song,
   And it's ride, ride, ride.
   Chorus

Billy Boy

United States

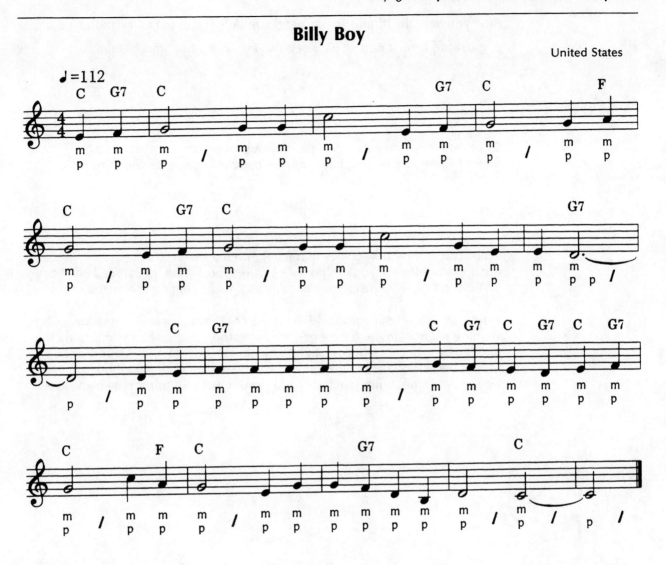

If you're looking for a real challenge in playing the autoharp, then try the following guitar-style pattern pick in which the index finger (i) of the right hand is used also.

		m						
Finger:	P		P	i	P	m	P	
Counting:	1	+	2	+	3	+	4	+

Start learning this pick by playing the thumb on all four beats, alternating between low and low-middle strings. Play lower strings on the first and third beats, and play higher strings on the second and fourth beats. You should be playing four steady beats with the thumb, going low-higher-low-higher.

	P		P
P		P	

After you have the thumb going, add the middle finger (m) to the thumb on the first beat to form a pinch (^m_P). Keep playing. Zing, two, three, four . . .

```
        P         P
   m
     P        P
```

Once you have mastered the picking described above, then add the index finger (i) after the second beat and the middle finger after the third beat.

```
      P    i        m    P
   m
     P            P
```

Keep it slow until it becomes automatic, then allow it to speed up. What an exciting sound! Now you can go back to "Reuben's Train," "Railroad Bill," and "Wildwood Flower," using this pattern pick while singing the melody.

A note on tuning your autoharp: The strings of the autoharp are tuned by using a tuning wrench on the tuning peg for each string. Exercise care in turning the tuning pegs, because only a slight adjustment (1/16 of a revolution or so) is usually necessary. For the inexperienced, the easiest tuning method is to use a well-tuned piano, tuning each string to the pitch of the appropriate piano key.

CHAPTER ELEVEN
Understanding Intervals and Chords

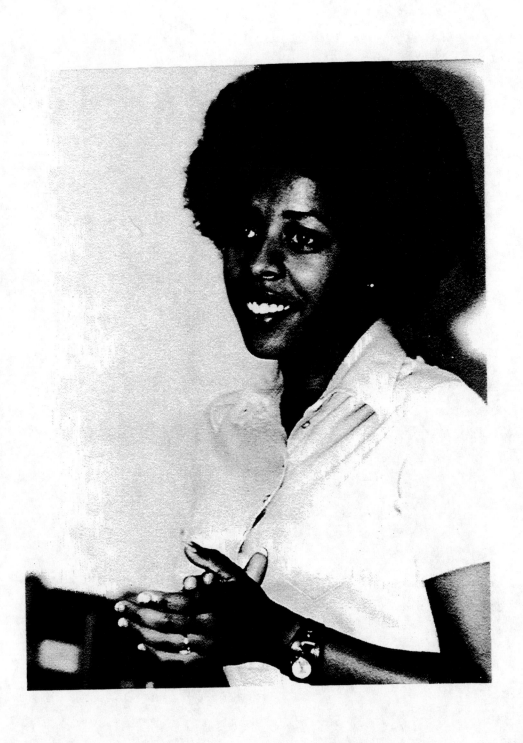

CHAPTER ELEVEN
Understanding Intervals and Chords

INTERVALS

An *interval* is the distance between two pitches. Intervals are identified in two steps: first they are named, and then they are classified. Intervals are named by counting the letter names that occur between the two pitches. Intervals are classified by counting the number of half steps between the two pitches.

Naming Intervals

The name of an interval is the number of letter names included between two pitches. From C up to E is a third, because three letter names are included (C, D, and E). From E down to B is a fourth because four letter names are included (E, D, C, and B). Name the following intervals:

G up to C	=	fourth	A down to F	=	third
F down to B	=	fifth	D up to C	=	seventh
E up to E	=	octave	B up to G	=	sixth
C down to B	=	second			

Classifying Intervals

After intervals are named, they are classified by counting the number of half steps between the two tones. For instance, a third always contains three letter names (G, A, and B). A *major* third encompasses *four* half steps, whereas a *minor* third encompasses *three* half steps. The following example shows how to name and classify intervals through this two-step process. Step 1 is to determine the name of the interval by counting the number of letter names included, and step 2 is to classify the interval by counting the number of half steps encompassed by the two notes. A third step merely combines those two pieces of information in order to label the interval. Study the two examples carefully. The example on the left is a minor third and the example on the right is a major third.

Naming and Classifying Minor and Major Thirds

(1) Three letter names included on staff (G, A, and B). The interval is a third.
(2) Three half steps counted on keyboard (G to G♯, G♯ to A, and A to B♭). The interval is minor.
(3) The interval is a minor third.

(1) Three letter names included on staff (G, A, and B). The interval is a third.
(2) Four half steps counted on keyboard (G to G♯, G♯ to A, A to A♯, and A♯ to B). The interval is major.
(3) The interval is a major third.

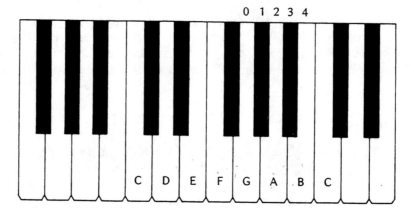

Here is a chart of some of the intervals found within one octave.

Name of Interval	Letter Names Included	Half Steps Contained	Example G up to	Example G down to
Unison	1	0	G	G
Minor Second	2	1	A♭	F♯
Major Second	2	2	A	F
Minor Third	3	3	B♭	E
Major Third	3	4	B	E♭
Perfect Fourth	4	5	C	D
Augmented Fourth	4	6	C♯	D♭
Diminished Fifth	5	6	D♭	C♯
Perfect Fifth	5	7	D	C
Minor Sixth	6	8	E♭	B
Major Sixth	6	9	E	B♭
Minor Seventh	7	10	F	A
Major Seventh	7	11	F♯	A♭
Octave	8	12	G	G

In counting the number of letter names included, start counting with number "one" on the first letter name. In counting the number of half steps included on the keyboard, begin counting with "zero" on the first key.

Intervals over one octave in size are identified in the same way; however, counting the half steps to determine the type of interval is easier if first you move one of the tones one octave closer to the other tone. Be careful not to move the tone past the pitch of the other tone. Here is an example to clarify this point. In counting the number of letter names included in the following interval you would obtain the number 10 (A-B-C-D-E-F-G-A-B-C).

Hypothetically move the lower tone one octave higher and then count the number of half steps. You should count three letter names and three half steps (A to A♯, A♯ to B, and B to C), indicating a minor third. The name of this interval, therefore, is a minor tenth.

Write the name and classification of the interval between each successive pair of tones in the round "Dona Nobis Pacem."

CHORDS

Chords are three or more different pitches played or sung simultaneously. You can define any chord in terms of the intervals between the pitches. The chords you will study in this text are limited to major, minor, and seventh chords. These three types of chords are illustrated below, all built from the same root, G.

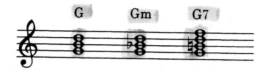

Notice that when a set of pitches is to be performed simultaneously, the notes are written one above the other.

Chords support and enrich both the melody and rhythm of the song to which they are assigned. In turn, the construction and performance of chords derive from the melody and rhythm of the song itself. The instruments on which you will perform the chords explained here are the autoharp, piano, and guitar. Specific techniques for playing chords on each of these instruments are described in Chapters 10, 12, and 13, respectively. People who sing or play melody instruments (Chapters 3, 5, 7, and 8) also can form chords by performing together, each taking one pitch from the chord. Go back to "Dona Nobis Pacem" and sing or play it with two classmates as a three-part round. Stop at those points where there is a total of three different pitches, one in each part (for example, the first measure, second and third beats of each of the three parts). Together you will be performing a chord.

The chords that you will find most frequently in the songs in this text are major chords. Some primary examples are D, G, C, F, and Bb major. Chords are referred to as *triads* when they include three different pitches. They always are spelled in thirds (that is, in ascending order, using every other letter name: C-E-G, D-F-A, E-G-B, F-A-C, G-B-D, A-C-E, B-D-F). A *major chord* always contains the chord name (the "root"), a second pitch that is a major third above the chord name (the "third"), and a third pitch that is a perfect fifth above the root and a minor third above the second pitch (the "fifth"). Therefore, a major chord always contains two thirds, a major third on the bottom and a minor third on top. The C-major chord contains the notes C, E, and G.

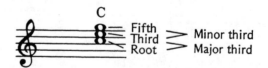

A *minor chord* always contains the chord name (the "root"), a second pitch that is a minor third above the chord name (the "third"), and a third pitch that is a perfect fifth above the first pitch and a major third above the second pitch (the "fifth"). A small letter "m" after the name of the root indicates a minor chord. For example, Cm indicates that a performer should play a C-minor chord containing the tones C (the root), Eb (the note a minor third above C), and G (the note a major third above Eb).

Major and minor chords always have three different pitches. Once you have found each of the three different pitches you may rearrange the order of these pitches to suit the song you wish to accompany or to facilitate your playing technique on an accompanying instrument. Chord tones may be either inverted (reading from the bottom to the top: C-E-G, E-G-C, G-C-E, E-C-G) or doubled (C-E-G-C-E) depending on the instrument you are using and the techniques you learn on that instrument. As long as the C, E, and G tones are sounding, you are playing a C-major chord.

C major chords

Chords that have the number "7" to the right of the capital letter are called seventh chords. These chords have the same three pitches as major chords with the same root, and one additional tone, which is called the seventh. Any seventh chord may have as many as four different pitches. Sometimes the fifth of a seventh chord is omitted and there are only three different pitches sounding.

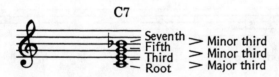

The C7 chord is formed from the three pitches that make up the C-major chord (C, E, and G) plus one different pitch, B♭. The B♭ is called the seventh because it is seven letters away from the name of the chord (1-C, 2-D, 3-E, 4-F, 5-G, 6-A, 7-B♭). The seventh is also a minor third above the fifth of a major chord. For example, C, E, and G are the pitches used in a C-major chord. Count up a minor third from G (three half steps) to find B♭, the seventh of the C7 chord.

Once you have learned to name the three or four tones associated with major, minor, and seventh chords you can learn to play them in a manner appropriate to the instrument you are using and the character of the song. In general you should begin by playing one chord for each beat of the song.

Using the "Hippopotamus" song, review the content of this chapter by naming and classifying each successive interval formed by the melody notes. Then name all of the pitches in each of the chords of the song, filling in the following chart.

Seventh	___	___	___	___	___
Fifth	___	___	___	___	___
Third	___	___	___	___	___
Root	___	___	___	___	___
Chord Symbol	D	A7	Bm	E	G

Hippopotamus

John Hooley/Terry Lee Kuhn

Terry Lee Kuhn

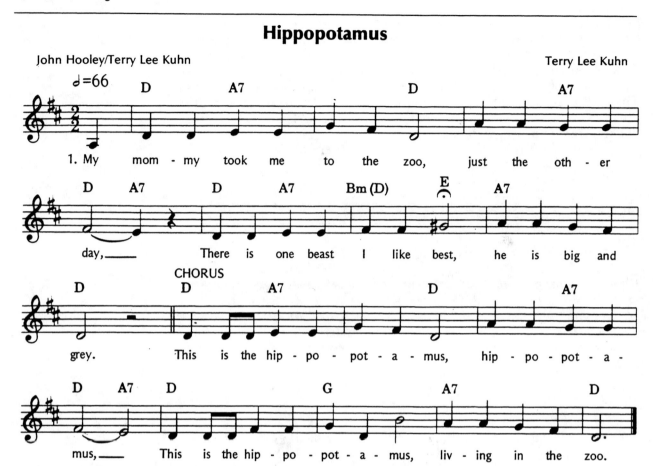

2. I brought some peanuts for my friend, threw them in his mouth,
   He closed it up with a great big crunch, spit the shells right out.
   Chorus

3. Sloppy hippopotamus, now it's time to play,
   You're a hippopota-MESS, rolls in mud all day.
   Chorus

4. He has a great big swimming pool, right there in his pen,
   Jumps in with a great big splash, now he's clean again.
   Chorus

5. See him open his big mouth, see his teeth so white,
   He is tired and has to yawn, time to say good night.
   Chorus

October 11, 1996

WORKSHEET

(1) Name the following intervals:

Eb up to G	= 3rd	C up to B	= 7 9th	
F# down to C#	= 5 4th	D down to G	= 5th	
Bb up to D	= 4 3rd	G up to E	= 6th	
Ab down to Gb	= 8 2nd	C up to C	= 8 (octave)	

(2) How many half steps does each of the following intervals contain? (Assume that the first pitch is lower than the second.)

Eb to G	= 4	A to F#	= 11 9	
F# to C#	= 7	C to F	= 5	
B to D	= 3	G to Bb	= 3	
D to Eb	= 1	F to A	= 4	

(3) Indicate how many letter names and half steps each of the following intervals contains.

	Letter Names	Half Steps
Minor Third	3	3
Perfect Fifth	5	7
Major Second	2	2
Unison	1	0
Minor Second	2	1
Major Third	3	4

(4) Write on the staff the note that is a major third above each of the printed notes.

(5) Write on the staff the note that is a major second above each of the printed notes.

(6) Write on the staff the note that is a minor second above each of the printed notes.

Double Flat

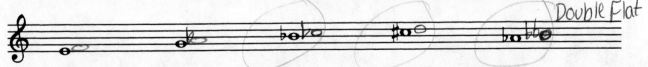

(7) Write on the staff the note that is a minor third above each of the printed notes.

(8) Chords contain three or four different tones (a root, third, fifth, and sometimes a seventh at intervals of thirds. Label these thirds for each type of chord listed below.

Major Chord	Minor Chord	Seventh Chord
		seventh ⟩ ———
fifth ⟩	fifth ⟩	fifth ⟩
third ⟨ ———	third ⟨ ———	third ⟨ ———
root ⟩ ———	root ⟩ ———	root ⟩ ———

(9) Write the names of the following chords:

(10) Write the notes contained in the following chords:

Cm   G   D7   B♭m   F7   A

CHAPTER TWELVE
Playing Accompaniments on Keyboard Instruments

CHAPTER TWELVE
Playing Accompaniments on Keyboard Instruments

Acquiring the ability to play accompaniments on a keyboard instrument is very rewarding and has many applications. Chords played on these instruments provide both rhythmic and harmonic support to solo and group singing or instrumental performance, and may be used along with guitar and autoharp accompaniments in many musical activities.

The skills to be learned in this chapter augment material presented earlier in this text. If you have not already done so, you should read Chapter 9, "Understanding Lead Sheet Notation," Chapter 8, "Playing Melodies on Keyboard Instruments," and Chapter 11, "Understanding Intervals and Chords." Three types of chords — major, minor, and seventh — will be used to play accompaniments. They were introduced in Chapter 11.

The left hand is preferred for playing accompaniments; it traditionally is used to support the performance of melodies played by the right hand. The sound of chords played in the same area of the keyboard by either hand is exactly the same, but the fingering is different. The materials in this chapter will be directed toward the use of the left hand.

The fingers of the left hand are numbered in the same way as those of the right hand: The thumb is 1, the index finger is 2, the middle finger is 3, the ring finger is 4, and the little finger is 5. When you play triads in root position (C-E-G, for example), the root (C) is played by the little finger, the third (E) is played by the middle finger, and the fifth (G) is played by the thumb.

Study the figure of the left hand playing a C-major triad. Notice that the tips of the fifth and middle fingers and the right edge of the thumb touch the keys. The middle finger is curved and the second and fourth fingers are raised slightly. You will find it most comfortable to allow your unused second and fourth fingers to remain suspended above the keyboard. Always extend your unused fingers rather than curling them into your palm.

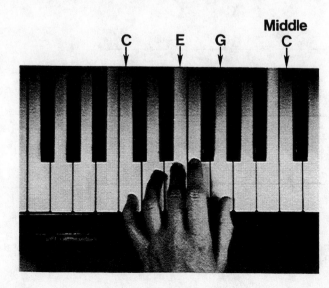

Figure 12.1. C-major triad

Figure 12.2 and the figures that follow in this chapter show which keys are to be depressed and which fingers of the left hand are used to depress the keys. In addition, the letter names of each of the three different chord tones are given.

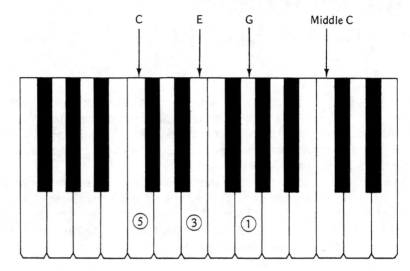

Figure 12.2. C-major chord fingering, root position

Place your left hand over the keys which form a C-major chord as shown in Figure 12.2. Use the area of the keyboard one octave below middle C. Now try the practice exercise. Press the keys down together firmly on beat 1 and raise your hand slightly on beat 2. Continue doing this pattern until you have played the C-major chord eight times.

Practice Exercise

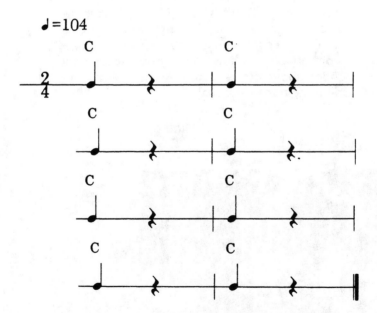

Accompany the following song by playing the C-major chord a total of eight times, once at the beginning of each measure.

Frère Jacques
Round

France

♩=104

① C

Frè - re   Jac - ques!   Frè - re   Jac - ques!

②

Dor - mez - vous?   Dor - mez - vous?

③

Son - nez les ma - ti - nes,   Son - nez les ma - ti - nes,

④

Din,   din,   don!   Din,   din,   don!

Are You Sleeping?

Are you sleeping, are you sleeping?
Brother John, Brother John?
Morning bells are ringing, morning bells are ringing,
Ding, ding, dong! Ding, ding, dong!

Music Teacher

⹀ – – –, ⹀ – – –*
Is your name, is your name.
You will teach us music, you will teach us music,
Day by day, day by day.

* Insert the name of your music teacher. For example, "Doc-tor Wach-haus, Doc-tor Wach-haus."

The next song, "Little Tom Tinker," is to be accompanied by an A-major chord. Study the figure of the A-major triad, which shows the fingers and chord tones used.

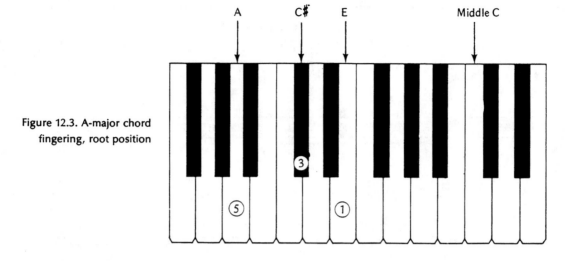

Figure 12.3. A-major chord
fingering, root position

Notice that the little finger is placed over the white key, A. The middle finger extends over the black key, C♯, and the thumb plays the white key, E. Practice pressing these keys down together as you count two steady beats per measure.

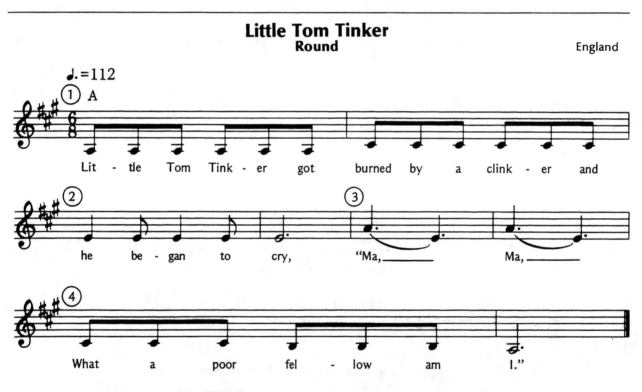

Little Tom Tinker
Round

England

♩.=112

① A

Lit - tle   Tom   Tink - er   got   burned   by   a   clink - er   and

② he   be - gan   to   cry,   ③ "Ma,_____   Ma,_____

④ What   a   poor   fel - low   am   I."

KEY CHORDS

You can find the key chord, or tonic chord, for a song written in a major key by counting the half steps that appear on the keyboard between the pitches of the triad. First, name the key in which the song you want to accompany is written. Next, locate a key on the keyboard with the same name as the key of the song. Call that key "zero" and place your little finger on it. Count up the chromatic scale (to the right) four consecutive keys from that pitch and place your middle finger on that key. Then count up three consecutive keys from your middle finger and place your thumb on that key.

The key chord for a song written in the key of F major contains F (zero), A (four half steps above F), and C (three half steps above A). Place your fingers and thumb over those three keys and play F-major triads on the first beat of every measure of the following song, beginning with the first complete measure. Hold each chord for two beats and release the chord on beat 3.

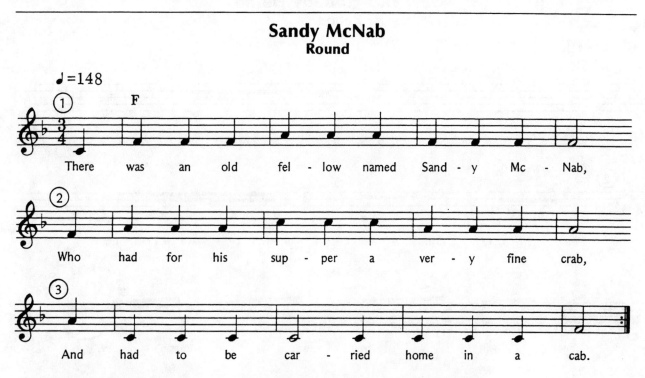

Sandy McNab
Round

The key chord or tonic chord for songs written in minor keys is found by counting on the keyboard the number of half steps between the pitches of a minor tonic triad. Place the little finger of your left hand on the key that corresponds to the name of the key of the song. Call that key "zero," count up to the right three consecutive keys, and place your middle finger on that key. Then count up four consecutive keys from your middle finger and place your thumb on that key.

The key chord for D minor is D (zero), F (three half steps above D), and A (four half steps above F). Place your fingers and thumb over the keys as shown in Figure 12.4.

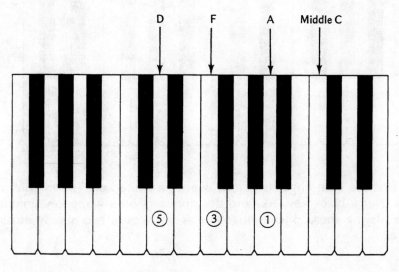

Figure 12.4. D-minor chord fingering, root position

Play D-minor chords on the first beat of every measure of the following song. Hold each chord until the second beat and then release it.

Hey, Ho! Nobody Home
Round

England

The next song, "Zum Gali, Gali," is to be accompanied by an F-minor chord. Study the figure of the F-minor triad before attempting to play it.

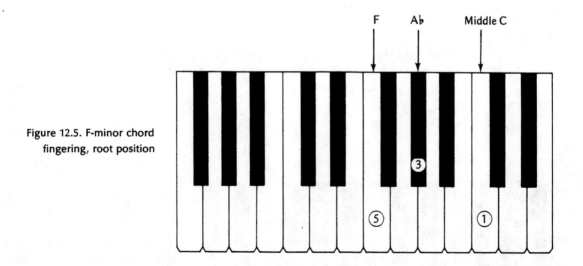

Figure 12.5. F-minor chord fingering, root position

Notice that the little finger is placed over F, a white key. The middle finger extends over a black key, A♭, and the thumb is on a white key, middle C. Practice playing these pitches together as you count two steady beats per measure.

Zum Gali, Gali

♩=66

CHORUS

Fm

Israel

Zum ga - li, ga - li, ga - li, zum ga - li, ga - li.

1. He - cha - lutz le 'man a - vo - dah; A - vo - dah le 'man he - cha - lutz.

2. Avodah le 'man hechalutz;
Hechalutz le 'man avodah.
Chorus

3. Hechalutz le 'man hab'tulah;
Hab'tulah le 'man hechalutz.
Chorus

4. Hashalom le 'man ha'amim;
Ha'amim le 'man hashalom.
Chorus

"Old House" is written in the key of B minor. The B-minor chord is played with the little finger on B, the middle finger on D, and the thumb extended over the black key, F♯. The B-minor triad position is shown in Figure 12.6.

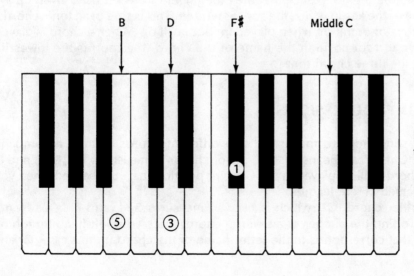

Figure 12.6. B-minor chord fingering, root position

Old House
Round

United States

♩=114

① Bm   ②

1. Old   house. (Tear it   down!) Who's goin' to help   me? (Tear it   down!)

③   ④

Bring   me a ham-mer. (Tear it   down!) Bring   me a saw.___ (Tear it   down!)

⑤   ⑥

Next thing you bring me, (Tear it   down!) Is   a wreck-ing ma-chine. (Tear it   down!)

2. New house. (Build it up!)
   Who's going to help me? (Build it up!)
   Bring me a hammer. (Build it up!)
   Bring me a saw. (Build it up!)
   Next thing you bring me, (Build it up!)
   Is a carpenter man. (Build it up!)

Up to this point you have been playing key chords, also known as tonic chords, to accompany songs. The major chords and keys were C, F, and A; and the minor chords and keys were Dm, Fm, and Bm. These chords were all formed in a similar fashion. If the song was in a major key there was a major third (four half steps) between the fifth and third fingers, and a minor third (three half steps) between the third finger and the thumb. If the song was written in a minor key, the two intervals were reversed. There was a minor third between the fifth and third fingers and a major third between the third finger and the thumb. Notice that the little finger of the left hand always plays the name of the key in which the song is written. This is true of all tonic chords, whether major or minor, when played in root position. When a chord is played or written in root position the name of the chord (the root) is the lowest in pitch of the three chord tones.

CHORD PROGRESSIONS

Some songs require the use of two different chords in their accompaniments. "Oats, Peas, Beans" uses C-major chords in measures 1, 2, 5, 6, and 8. These chords will be played in the C-major position that you learned when you accompanied "Frère Jacques."

The other chord, G7, which is used in measures 3, 4, and 7, is a seventh chord. To find the pitches of a seventh chord, place your left-hand thumb on the key that corresponds to the letter name of the chord (in this case, G) and call that pitch "zero." Count down (to the left) two half steps (the distance of a major second) and place your index finger on that key (F). Count down again six half steps (the distance of two minor thirds) and place your little finger on that key (B).

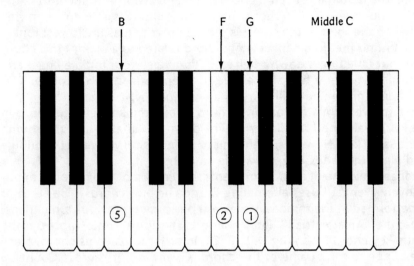

Figure 12.7 G7 chord fingering, first inversion

Notice in figure 12.7 that the left-hand thumb is on G, the index finger is on F, and the little finger is on B, all white keys. Practice playing C major and G7, holding each chord for one beat and releasing at beat 2. Shift smoothly from one chord to the other when the chord symbols change.

Oats, Peas, Beans

2. First the farmer sows his seed
   Then he stands and takes his ease;
   He stamps his foot and claps his hands,
   And turns around to view his lands.

3. Waiting for a partner,
   Waiting for a partner,
   Open the ring and take one in
   While we join hands and sing again.

Chords that succeed one another form a *progression*. The progression from the C to the G7 chord is known as I–V7, or tonic to dominant seventh. A dominant seventh chord is built on the fifth pitch in the scale of the tonic chord. You have learned to play this progression with the tonic chord in root position and the dominant seventh chord in first inversion with the fifth of the chord (D in the case of a G7 chord) omitted. A chord is said to be in *first inversion* when the third of the chord is played or written as the lowest tone.

One way to find the dominant seventh chord related to a major tonic chord is to move your little finger down a half step, then raise your middle finger and place your index finger a half step above it. Keep your thumb in place. This pattern of finger movement will work in any major key.

When you move from a minor tonic chord to a dominant seventh chord in the same key, again the little finger moves down a half step and the thumb stays on the same key. However, in the minor progression you raise the middle finger and place the index finger a whole step above it.

Some songs make use of accompaniments that consist of two major or minor triads. "Lovely Evening" uses alternating D and G-major chords. The D-major chord is performed in the same way that you performed previous tonic triads. Notice that the G-major triad's letter name is the fourth letter up from the name of the key chord (counting D, E, F, G). In order to play this chord, place your index finger on the name of the chord, G, and call it "zero." Count up four half steps (a major third) and place your thumb on B. Next, place your little finger on D, the name of the key of this song. This is not the same G-major chord that is used as a tonic chord for songs written in the key of G-major. This chord is inverted; that is, the letter names of pitches are the same but the root of the chord is not the lowest tone. Such a chord, in which the fifth (D) is the lowest note played, is said to be in *second inversion*.

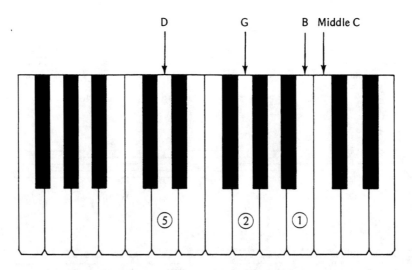

Figure 12.8. G-major chord fingering, second inversion

Inverting the G-major chord simplifies finger movement in the accompaniment to "Lovely Evening." With the use of this inversion only two fingers move a small distance, whereas all three fingers would have to move a greater distance if a root position G-major chord were used.

Lovely Evening
Round

Germany

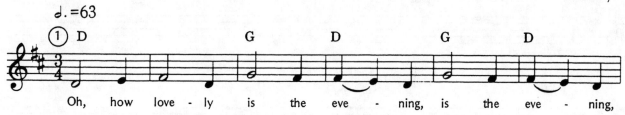

Oh, how love - ly is the eve - ning, is the eve - ning,

When the bells are sweet - ly ring - ing, sweet - ly ring - ing,

Ding, dong, ding, dong, ding, dong.

The chord progression used in "Lovely Evening" is known as a I–IV, or tonic to subdominant progression. The tonic or key chord is D, and the subdominant chord is G. A *subdominant chord* is built on the fourth pitch in the scale of the tonic; in this case, G is the fourth pitch in the scale of D major. When you move your fingers from a tonic chord to a subdominant chord in a major key, notice that the little finger stays on the same key, the middle finger is raised away from the key it played, and the index finger is placed a half step above the middle finger's former position. The thumb moves up a whole step.

The accompaniment for "Wayfaring Stranger" makes use of alternating B-minor and E-minor chords. The B-minor chord is performed like the minor chords you have already learned. Notice that the E-minor triad's letter name is the fourth letter up from the name of the key chord, so E-minor is the subdominant. In order to play this chord, place your index finger on the name of the chord, E, and call it "zero." Count up three half steps (a minor third) and place your thumb on G. Next, place your little finger on B, the name of the key of this song. When moving from a minor tonic chord to a minor subdominant chord (as in "Wayfaring Stranger"), notice that the little finger stays on the same key, the index finger is placed a whole step above the raised third finger, and the thumb moves up a half step.

Wayfaring Stranger

United States

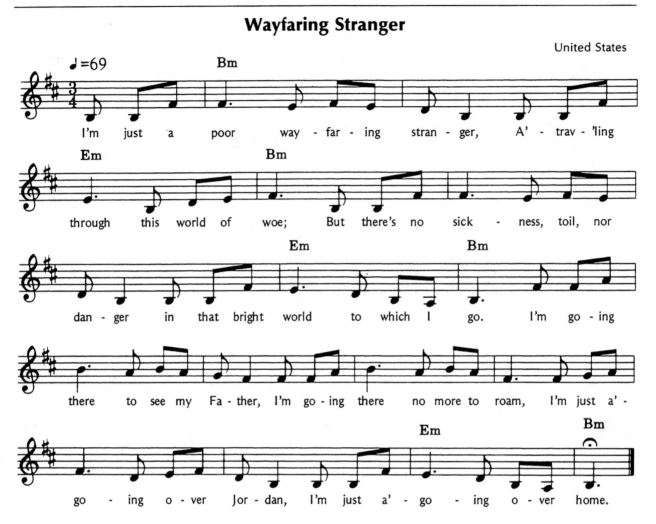

♩=69

Bm

I'm just a poor way - far - ing stran - ger, A' - trav - 'ling

Em   **Bm**

through this world of woe; But there's no sick - ness, toil, nor

Em   **Bm**

dan - ger in that bright world to which I go. I'm go - ing

there to see my Fa - ther, I'm go - ing there no more to roam, I'm just a' -

Em   **Bm**

go - ing o - ver Jor - dan, I'm just a' - go - ing o - ver home.

The chords for the accompaniment to "Rattler" are F major and C7. Notice in Figure 12.9 that the C7 chord is played by placing the thumb on C, the index finger on B♭ and, the little finger on E. When you move from F to C7, the little finger always moves down a half step, the index finger is placed a half step above the raised middle finger, and the thumb remains on the same key.

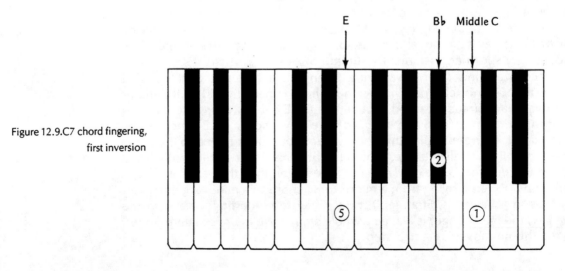

Figure 12.9. C7 chord fingering,
first inversion

Rattler

United States

♩=96

1. Rat - tler was a fine old dog, fine as he could be.

Ev - 'ry night at sup - per - time I paid that dog a fee.

CHORUS

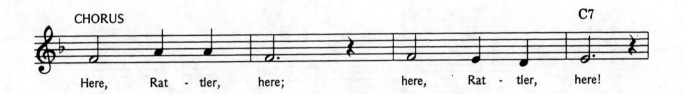

Here, Rat - tler, here; here, Rat - tler, here!

Call Rat - tler from the barn. Here, Rat - tler, here!

2. Once I had a settin' hen, set her as you know,
Set her on a hundred eggs and hatched out one old crow.
Chorus

3. Once I had a muley cow, muley when she was born,
Took two jaybirds forty years to fly from horn to horn.
Chorus

4. Rattler's dead and Rattler's gone, gone where good dogs go.
Watch out and don't be mean or you'll get yours, I know.
Chorus

Use the same pattern of finger motion to accompany "London Bridge" that you used to accompany "Rattler." The chord tones and fingers used to perform the E7 chord are shown in Figure 12.10. Notice that one black key, G♯, and two white keys, D and E, are used.

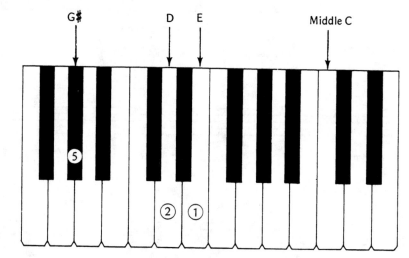

Figure 12.10. E7 chord fingering,
first inversion

London Bridge

England

1. Lon - don bridge is fall - ing down, fall - ing down, fall - ing down.

Lon - don bridge is fall - ing down, my fair la - dy.

2. Build it up with iron bars, iron bars, iron bars,
   Build it up with iron bars, my fair lady.

3. Iron bars will rust and break, rust and break, rust and break.
   Iron bars will rust and break, my fair lady.

4. Build it up with sticks and stones, sticks and stones, sticks and stones.
   Build it up with sticks and stones, my fair lady.

5. Sticks and stones will tumble down, tumble down, tumble down.
   Sticks and stones will tumble down, my fair lady.

6. Here's a prisoner I have found, I have found, I have found.
   Here's a prisoner I have found, my fair lady.

7. Off to prison you must go, you must go, you must go.
   Off to prison you must go, my fair lady.

8. Have the jailer lock him up, lock him up, lock him up,
   Have the jailer lock him up, my fair lady.

The next melody, "Minka," has two chords, D minor and A seven, in its accompaniment. When you move from any minor tonic chord to the dominant seventh chord the thumb remains on the same key, the index finger is placed one whole step above the raised middle finger, and the little finger moves down one half step.

Minka

G. Wachhaus

Russia

1. Shiv - er, shiv - er, when it's snow - ing, Shiv - er, when the wind is blow - ing,

Stay here where the fire is glow - ing, Come, sit clos - er, Mink - a.

In the win - ter, when it's freez - ing, If the chill wind starts you sneez - ing,

Don't be shy. Come, stop your teas - ing. Come, sit close to me, dear.

2. If you want me for a lover
   Come, sit closer and discover,
   That we do not need a cover,
   Come, sit closer, Minka.
   Kisses for you I have plenty,
   Maybe even ten or twenty,
   Even if you accidently
   Were to sit by me, dear.

"Home on the Range" has three primary chords in its accompaniment: D major, G major, and A7. To play these chords, use the patterns of finger movement previously studied. (G is the subdominant; A7 the dominant seventh.) Alternate secondary chords, E7 and E minor, are indicated in parentheses. Choose positions for these chords that keep your fingers closest to the keys in the chords that precede and follow.

Home on the Range

United States

♪=98

1. Oh, give me a home where the buf - fa - lo roam, Where the deer and the an - te - lope play; _____ Where sel - dom is heard a dis - cour - ag-ing word, And the skies are not cloud - y all day. _____

CHORUS
Home, home on the range, _____ Where the deer and the an - te - lope play; _____ Where sel - dom is heard a dis - cour - ag - ing word, And the skies are not cloud - y all day. _____

2. How often at night when the heavens are bright
From the light of the glittering stars
Have I stood there, amazed, and asked as I gazed
If their glory exceeds that of ours.
Chorus

3. Where the air is so pure and the zephyrs so free;
And the breezes so balmy and light,
Oh, I would not exchange my home on the range
For the glittering cities so bright.
Chorus

4. Oh, give me the land where the bright diamond sand
Flows leisurely down with the stream,
Where the graceful, white swan glides slowly along
Like a maid in a heavenly dream.
Chorus

PATTERNS OF ACCOMPANIMENT

The songs at the end of this chapter are harmonized with combinations of major, minor, and seventh chords. Play the chords according to the patterns of finger and hand movement we have suggested. Chords may be played on the accented first beat of each measure, or if the tempo is slow enough, on the primary and secondary accented beats of each measure.

The individual pitches of each chord may be played separately instead of together, and individual chord tones may be repeated or played in pairs on the unaccented beats. Simple chord patterns make interesting accompaniments for songs. After you can maintain a steady beat while changing chords during the performance of a song, try to incorporate one of the following patterns into your accompaniment. The patterns in $\frac{2}{4}$ meter may also be used to accompany songs written in $\frac{2}{2}$, ¢ , or slow $\frac{6}{8}$ (♩.).

Major or Minor Tonic Chord Accompaniment Patterns

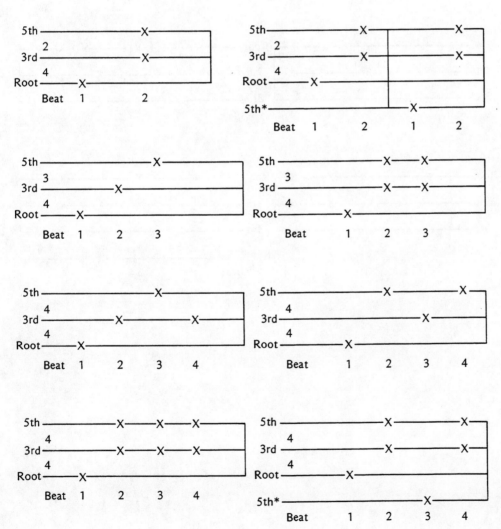

*Below the root.

Dominant Seventh Chord (First Inversion) Accompaniment Patterns

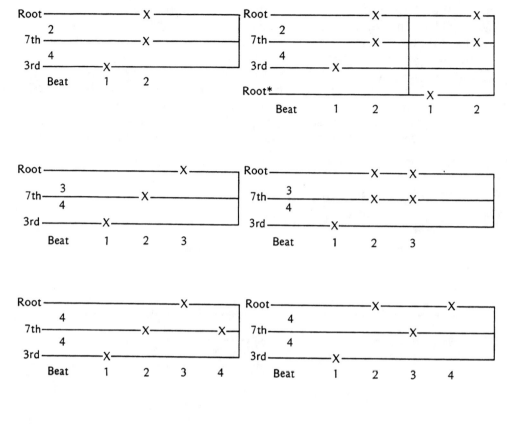

*Below the third.

Subdominant Chord (Second Inversion) Accompaniment Patterns

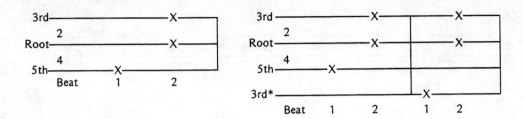

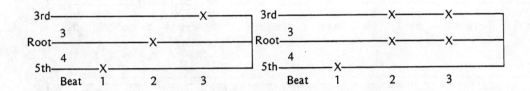

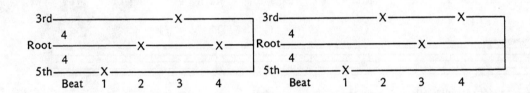

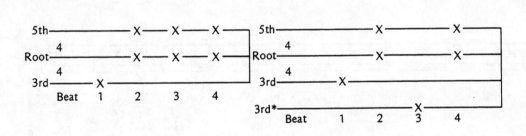

*Below the fifth.

The Battle Hymn of the Republic

Julia Ward Howe

William Steffe

1. Mine eyes have seen the glo - ry of the com - ing of the Lord; He is tram - pling out the vin - tage where the grapes of wrath are stored; He hath loosed the fate - ful light - ning of His ter - ri - ble swift sword; His truth is march - ing on.

CHORUS

Glo - ry, glo - ry hal - le - lu - jah! Glo - ry, glo - ry hal - le - lu - jah! Glo - ry, glo - ry hal - le - lu - jah! His truth is march - ing on.

2. I have seen Him in the watch-fires of a hundred circling camps,
They have builded Him an altar in the evening dews and damps;
I can read His righteous sentence by the dim and flaring lamps,
His day is marching on.
Chorus

3. He has sounded forth the trumpet that shall never call retreat,
He is sifting out the hearts of men before His judgment seat,
Oh, be swift, my soul, to answer Him! Be jubilant, my feet,
Our God is marching on.
Chorus

4. I have <u>read</u> a fiery gospel, writ in <u>bur</u>nished rows of steel:
   "As ye <u>deal</u> with my condemners, so with <u>you</u> my grace shall deal;
   Let the <u>He</u>ro, born of woman, crush the serpent with His heel,
   Since <u>God</u> is marching <u>on</u>."
   Chorus

5. In the <u>beau</u>ty of the lilies Christ was <u>born</u> across the sea,
   With a <u>glo</u>ry in His bosom that trans<u>fig</u>ures you and me;
   As He <u>died</u> to make men holy, let us <u>die</u> to make men free,
   While <u>God</u> is marching <u>on</u>.
   Chorus

6. He is <u>com</u>ing like the glory of the <u>morn</u>ing on the wave,
   He is <u>wis</u>dom to the mighty, He is <u>hon</u>or to the brave,
   So the <u>world</u> shall be His footstool, and the <u>soul</u> of wrong His slave,
   Our <u>God</u> is marching <u>on</u>!
   Chorus

I Love the Mountains
Round

United States

Descant for Melody Instruments or Voices

Lullaby

Johannes Brahms

1. Lul - la - by and good - night with __ ro - ses be - dight, __ With __ down o - ver __ spread is __ ba - by's wee bed; Lay thee down now and rest, may thy slum - bers be blest, Lay thee down now and rest, may thy slum - bers be blest.

2. Lullaby and good night, thy mother's delight,
Bright angels beside my darling abide.
They will guard thee at rest, thou shalt wake on my breast,
They will guard thee at rest, thou shalt wake on my breast.

Wiegenlied

1. Guten Abend, gut' Nacht, mit Rosen bedacht,
Mit Näglein besteckt, schlüpf' unter die Deck':
Morgen früh, wenn Gott will, wirst du wieder geweckt,
Morgen früh, wenn Gott will, wirst du wieder geweckt.

2. Guten Abend, gut' Nacht, von Eng'lein Bewacht,
Die zeigen im Traum dir Christkindlein's Baum;
Schlaf'nun selig und süss, schau' im Traum's Paradies,
Schlaf'nun selig und süss, schau'im Traum's Paradies.

River Theme
The Moldau

Bedrich Smetana

Tum Balalaika

Russia

♩.=53

Gm   **D7**

1. On the Don when once I was young, This, the

Gm

song I once used to strum. Sing - ing of love and

Cm   **D7**   **Gm**

what it might bring. This was the song I once used to sing:

CHORUS   **D7**

"Tum ba - la, tum ba - la, tum ba - la - lai - ka, Tum ba - la,

Gm

tum ba - la, tum ba - la - lai - ka, Tum ba - la - lai - ka,

Cm   **D7**   **Gm**

tum ba - la - lai - ka, Tum ba - la - lai - ka, tum ba - la - lai."

2. Love is shy, but it can be bold,
   Love has moods which are thousand-fold.
   Love has so many beautiful shapes,
   You think you've caught it, then it escapes.
   Chorus

Was an Old Woman

Words and music
by G. Wachhaus

Was an old wom - an, wom - an, wom - an, Lived in a

shoe, shoe, shoe, Had so man - y chil - dren,

chil - dren, chil - dren, She knew what to do, do, do.

Gave them some ice cream, ice cream, ice cream, Chick - en and

bread, bread, bread, Hugged them and kissed them, kissed them,

kissed them, And tucked them in bed, bed, bed.

CHAPTER THIRTEEN
Playing Accompaniments on Guitar

CHAPTER THIRTEEN
Playing Accompaniments on Guitar

The accessibility and widespread use of the guitar in our society makes an introduction to the instrument superfluous. This chapter will acquaint you with basic right- and left-hand skills that will enable you to perform chordal accompaniments for songs. Keep in mind that as you find songs you'd like to play, many will be published in keys awkward for the guitar; however, it is likely that these songs can be transposed into a key that will enable you to play them with relative ease (see Chapter 14).

This chapter stresses the learning of five chords and four right-hand strumming techniques. The materials accommodate several ability levels. Students who are playing guitar for the first time will probably find it easier to use a pick or just their thumb in strumming chords. Students who have previous guitar-playing experience can play the same songs, but use the finger-picking patterns for the right hand given at the end of this chapter.

Blind students and some handicapped students may find that the open D

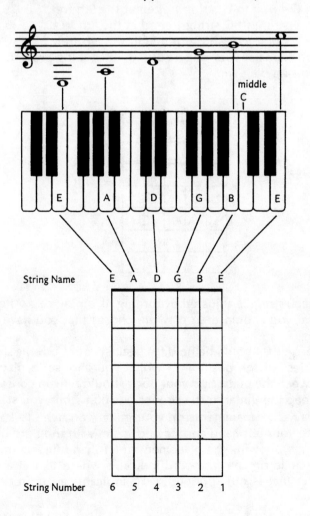

tuning, which is explained near the end of this chapter, can facilitate their guitar playing. All the songs in this chapter that do not contain minor chords can be played in this tuning. Small children can use the guitar to strum chords in this tuning. Because their fingers are often not strong enough to press all six strings simultaneously, children can use a device called a bottleneck or slide to good advantage.

Tune the open (unfretted) strings of your guitar to a piano as shown in the following diagram. You will notice that the strings are numbered from the highest, pitched as "1," through the lowest, pitched as "6." It is also important to be aware that guitar strings are notated one octave higher than they actually sound.

You may also tune the strings of your guitar to each other by fretting a lower-pitched string so that it sounds the pitch of the next highest unfretted string. To "fret" a string is to press it with a finger so that it makes contact with one of the raised metal strips that is attached across the fingerboard. These metal strips are called frets. Shortening the length of a string by one fret raises its pitch one half step. Raising the pitch of a lower string the proper number of half steps will produce the pitch of the adjacent higher string. This procedure is accomplished one string at a time, from low to higher-pitched strings, as follows:

(1) Tune low E string to piano, pitch pipe, or tuning fork.
(2) Tune open A string to E string fretted at the 5th fret.
(3) Tune open D string to A string fretted at the 5th fret.
(4) Tune open G string to D string fretted at the 5th fret.
(5) Tune open B string to G string fretted at the 4th fret.
(6) Tune open E string to B string fretted at the 5th fret.

The successive positions of your fingers during this tuning procedure are indicated in the following diagram.

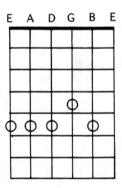

The pitch of each string is adjusted by turning its tuning peg. After you have tuned your guitar you should then play the chords that you have learned to check the tuning.

The back of the guitar should be held flat against your body, as shown in the pictures. Regardless of the position in which you choose to play, the basic relationship between the guitar and your body should remain constant. A neck strap helps to keep the guitar in the proper position while you stand.

In order to play accompaniments on your guitar you need to know how to form chords with your left hand and how to strum with the right hand. In the following diagrams, showing the placement of left-hand fingers for the D and A7 chords, the circle on the fretboard indicates where to fret a string, "X" indicates a string that is not sounded, "0" indicates an unfretted or open

Classical style position

Folk style position

Standing position

string, and the numbering indicates which finger should press the string. Left-hand fingers are identified as follows:

> 1 = index finger
> 2 = middle finger
> 3 = ring finger
> 4 = little finger

Notice that these numbers are different from the finger numbers used for piano. The left thumb is not normally used in playing guitar. The fingertips of your left hand should press the strings down with sufficient pressure to obtain a clear sound. They should be close above the frets that stop the strings, but not touch the frets. Here are the D and A7 chord diagrams:

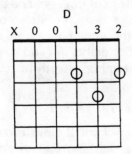

D
X 0 0 1 3 2

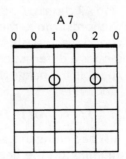

A 7
0 0 1 0 2 0

Keep your left thumb near the middle of the back of the fingerboard. Do not let it wrap around the fingerboard so that it can be seen from the front. Likewise, keep the palm of your left hand from touching the side of the fingerboard. The root of the D chord is the fourth string, and the root of the A7 chord is the fifth string. Begin strumming on those strings for an optimal sound.

D-major chord

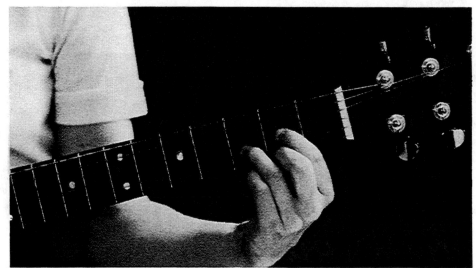

Use your right thumb (P) to strum across the four highest-pitched strings while you finger the D chord with the left hand. Strum the five highest-pitched strings while fingering the A7 chord. Strum near the sound hole, in a downward motion toward the floor. This *downstroke* will cause the strings to sound from lower through higher pitches. You might prefer to use a pick rather than your thumb. Hold a flatpick loosely between your right index finger and thumb, as shown in the picture.

Strumming with thumb

Strumming with pick

Practice the following chord progression to develop facility in changing between the D and A7 chords. Notice the similar pattern of fingers 1 and 2 in both the D and A7 chords. Move these fingers together as a unit. Strum once for each chord and for each slash. Keep strumming the same chord until a different letter indicates a different chord: Play eight Ds, eight A7s, and so on. It is important to be able to change the chords while keeping a steady beat with the strumming hand.

D/// //// A7/// //// D/// //// A7/// ////

If you are just beginning to learn the guitar, you will find it most rewarding to continue strumming on the beat. As you acquire skill, more involved strumming and picking patterns should be attempted. Some of these patterns are shown at the end of the chapter. Now play "Tom Dooley" using the D and A7 chords, strumming once for each beat.

Tom Dooley

United States

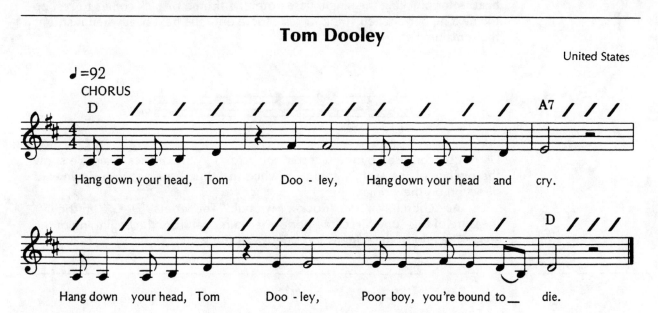

Hang down your head, Tom Doo - ley, Hang down your head and cry.

Hang down your head, Tom Doo - ley, Poor boy, you're bound to＿ die.

1. <u>Hand</u> me down my <u>banjo</u>, I'<u>ll</u> pick hit on my <u>knee</u>,
<u>This</u> time tomorrow <u>night</u>, <u>It</u>'ll be no use to <u>me</u>.
Chorus

2. <u>I</u> met her on the <u>mountain</u>, <u>I</u> swore she'd be my <u>wife</u>.
<u>I</u> met her on the <u>mountain</u>, <u>An</u>' I stabbed her with my <u>knife</u>.
Chorus

3. <u>This</u> time to<u>morrow</u>, <u>Reck</u>on where I'll <u>be</u>,
<u>Down</u> in some lonesome <u>valley</u>, <u>Hangin</u>' on a white oak <u>tree</u>.
Chorus

4. <u>I</u> had my trial at <u>Wilkesboro</u>, <u>And</u> what you reckon they <u>done</u>?
<u>They</u> bound me over to <u>States</u>ville, <u>And</u> that's where I'll be <u>hung</u>.
Chorus

5. <u>The</u> limb a-bein' <u>oak</u>, boys, <u>The</u> rope a-bein' <u>strong</u>.
<u>Bow</u> down your head, Tom Dooley, <u>You</u> know you're gonna be <u>hung</u>.
Chorus

In order to learn to play any instrument it is necessary to practice, and this is particularly true in the case of the guitar. Work on the chord changes until you can switch chords precisely in rhythm, then sing the songs. When you first start practicing, you may find that your muscles grow tense; stop playing and relax when that happens. Recheck your sitting and hand positions to be sure that they are enhancing the sound you produce and are permitting you to play with a minimum of muscle fatigue. You eventually will acquire calluses on your fingertips, which will mitigate the soreness. In addition, the strength in your fingers will increase, so that you will not tire so easily. In this initial stage of playing, remember that it is possible to play meaningful and lovely music with a minimum of technique, especially by accompanying a singing voice or another instrument. That, precisely, is the goal of this chapter.

Although it is relatively easy to play, the plain brush stroke is repetitious and quickly loses musical interest; therefore, try the following "church lick" style. An underlined chord letter or slash denotes a single plucked bass note on that beat. After plucking the single bass note, the thumb or pick comes to rest on the next higher-pitched string. It rests there until the next beat when it strums the remaining strings.

Do not be confused by the fact that the arrows in the musical example show the pitches of the strings going up while the thumb moves in a downward direction on the strings.

Try the "church lick" on "Rock-a My Soul." The letters "D. C." on the last measure of this song direct the performer to repeat from the beginning of the song. The end of the song is indicated with the word "Fine."

Rock-a My Soul*

United States

Rock - a my soul ___ in the bos - om of A - bra - ham,

Rock-a my soul ___ in the bos-om of A - bra - ham, Rock-a my soul ___ in the

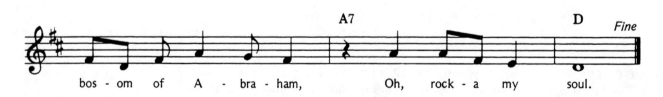

bos - om of A - bra - ham, Oh, rock - a my soul.

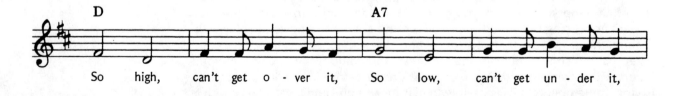

So high, can't get o - ver it, So low, can't get un - der it,

*Partner Song: "He's Got the Whole World in His Hands" (p. 117) can be performed simultaneously with "Rock-a My Soul."

So wide, can't go a - round it, Must go in at the door.

Six Little Ducks

United States

1. Six lit - tle ducks that I once knew, Fat ones, skin - ny ones,

fair ones too, But the one lit - tle duck with a feath-er on his back,

He ruled the oth - ers with his "Quack, quack, quack!" "Quack, quack, quack,

quack, quack, quack!" He ruled the oth - ers with his "Quack, quack, quack!"

2. <u>Down</u> to the river <u>they</u> would go,
   <u>Wi</u>bble, wobble, wibble, wobble, <u>to</u> and fro,
   But the <u>one</u> little duck with a <u>fea</u>ther on his back,
   <u>He</u> ruled the others with his "<u>Quack</u>, quack, quack!"
   "<u>Quack</u>, quack, quack, <u>quack</u>, quack, quack!"
   <u>He</u> ruled the others with his "<u>Quack</u>, quack, quack!"

3. <u>Home</u> from the river <u>they</u> would come,
   <u>Wi</u>bble, wobble, wibble, wobble, <u>ho</u> hum hum,
   But the <u>one</u> little duck with a <u>fea</u>ther on his back,
   <u>He</u> ruled the others with his "<u>Quack</u>, quack, quack!"
   "<u>Quack</u>, quack, quack, <u>quack</u>, quack, quack!"
   <u>He</u> ruled the others with his "<u>Quack</u>, quack, quack!"

Use a similar strum for "Down in the Valley," but play two brushstrokes following the plucked bass. This technique will provide a three-beat strum appropriate for $\frac{3}{4}$ meters. Play the following progression until it is smooth and then go on to "Down in the Valley."

Down in the Valley

United States

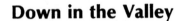

1. Down in the val - ley, val - ley so low,_____
Hang your head o - ver, hear the wind blow._____

2. Hear the wind <u>blow</u>, love, hear the wind <u>blow</u>,
   Hang your head <u>over</u>, hear the wind <u>blow</u>.

3. If you don't <u>love</u> me, love whom you <u>please</u>,
   Throw your arms '<u>round</u> me, give my heart <u>ease</u>.

4. Give my heart <u>ease</u>, love, give my heart <u>ease</u>,
   Throw your arms '<u>round</u> me, give my heart <u>ease</u>.

5. Write me a <u>letter</u>, send it by <u>mail</u>,
   Send it in <u>care</u> of Birmingham <u>Jail</u>.

6. Birmingham <u>Jail</u>, love, Birmingham <u>Jail</u>,
   Send it in <u>care</u> of Birmingham <u>Jail</u>.

7. Build me a <u>castle</u>, forty feet <u>high</u>,
   So I can <u>see</u> her, as she rides <u>by</u>.

8. As she rides <u>by</u>, love, as she rides <u>by</u>,
   So I can <u>see</u> her, as she rides <u>by</u>.

9. Roses love <u>sun</u>shine, violets love <u>dew</u>,
   Angels in <u>hea</u>ven, know I love <u>you</u>.

10. Know I love <u>you</u>, dear, know I love <u>you</u>,
    Angels in <u>hea</u>ven, know I love <u>you</u>.

Recorder Descant

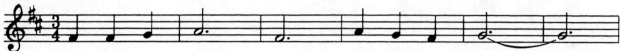

The G chord is required to play "Polly Wolly Doodle." Spend some time practicing the change in left-hand position from G to D before attempting to play the song. When playing the G chord, pluck the sixth string on the accented beats in the "church lick" strum.

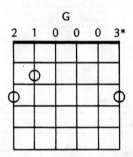

*Some people prefer to use the little finger (4) instead of the ring finger (3).

Sometimes a simpler G chord is played with just the third finger. In this version of the G chord, only the four treble strings are sounded. This chord fingering is used as a substitute for the regular G chord only in order to facilitate steady rhythm for beginning guitarists. You should continue to practice the full G chord until you can perform it with rhythmic accuracy.

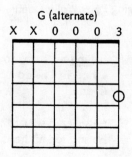

Polly Wolly Doodle

United States

1. Oh, I went down South for to see my Sal, Sing - in'

Pol - ly Wol - ly Doo - dle all the day, For my Sal she is a

spun - ky gal, Sing - in' Pol - ly Wol - ly Doo - dle all the day.

CHORUS

Fare thee well, fare thee well, fare thee well my fai - ry

fay; For I'm goin' to Lou' - si - an - a, for to

see my Su - si - an - a, Sing - in' Pol - ly Wol - ly Doo - dle all the day.

2. Oh, my Sal, she is a maiden fair, Singin', Polly Wolly Doodle all the day,
With curly eyes and laughing hair, Singin', Polly Wolly Doodle all the day.
Chorus

3. Oh, a grasshopper sittin' on a railroad track, . . .
A pickin' his teeth with a carpet tack.
Chorus

4. Oh, I went to bed, but it wasn't no use, . . .
My feet stuck out for a chicken roost.
Chorus

5. Behind the barn, down on my knees, . . .
I thought I heard a chicken sneeze.
Chorus

6. He sneezed so hard with the whooping cough, . . .
He sneezed his head and tail right off.
Chorus

Try a "pluck-scratch" strum on "The Yellow Rose of Texas." In the "pluck-scratch" strum the thumb plucks the D string; then the index finger scratches the third, second, and first strings in a downstroke and immediately scratches back upward across the first string. The scratch consists of two motions in the time of one beat. Notice that the arrows in the example below show the pitch direction of the strings, *not* the direction in which the index finger moves.

If you are strumming with a pick you can use the same basic motions to play this song.

The Yellow Rose of Texas

United States

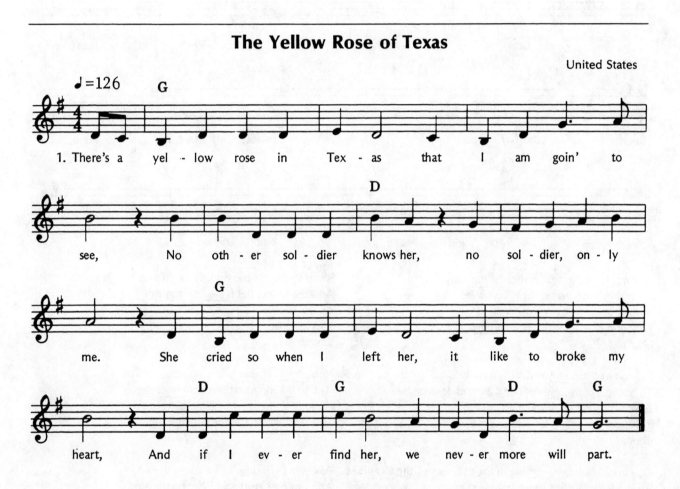

CHORUS
She's the sweetest rose of color this soldier ever knew,
Her eyes are bright as diamonds, they sparkle like the dew;
You may talk about your dearest May and sing of Aura Lea,
But the Yellow Rose of Texas beats the belles of Tennessee.

2. Where the Rio Grande is flowing and the starry skies are bright,
She walks along the river in the quiet summer night:
She thinks if I remember, when we parted long ago,
I promised to come back again and not to leave her so.
Chorus

3. Oh, now I'm going to find her, for my heart is full of woe,
And we'll sing the song together, that we sung so long ago;
We'll play the banjo gaily, and we'll sing the songs of yore,
And the Yellow Rose of Texas shall be mine forevermore.
Chorus

This Land Is Your Land

Words and music by
Woody Guthrie

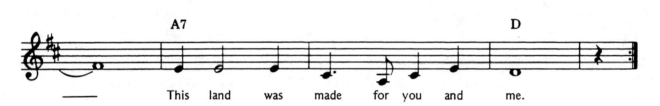

1. As I was walking, that ribbon of highway,
   I saw above me that endless skyway;
   I saw below me that golden valley;
   This land was made for you and me.
   Chorus

2. I've roamed and rambled and I followed my footsteps
   To the sparkling sands of her diamond deserts;
   And all around me a voice was sounding;
   This land was made for you and me.
   Chorus

3. One bright Sunday morning in the shadows of the steeple
   By the Relief Office I seen my people;
   As they stood there hungry, I stood there whistling;
   This land was made for you and me.
   Chorus

4. When the sun came shining, and I was strolling,
   And the wheat fields waving and the dust clouds rolling,
   As the fog was lifting a voice was chanting;
   This land was made for you and me.
   Chorus

5. Nobody living can ever stop me,
   As I go walking that freedom highway;
   Nobody living can make me turn back,
   This land was made for you and me.
   Chorus

6. As I went walking, I saw a sign there,
   And on the sign it said "No Trespassing,"
   But on the other side it didn't say nothing,
   That side was made for you and me.
   Chorus

Try the "church lick" with alternating bass notes. Particular bass notes are written with the chord over a slash and the note under the slash. For instance, D/A means to finger a D chord and to play the note A in the bass. When alternating bass notes in $\frac{4}{4}$ meter, it is usual to play the root of the chord on the first beat of a measure and move to an adjacent string on the third beat. The table and examples below present the usual root and alternating bass notes for the D, A7, and G chords.

Chord	Root and String	Fret	Alternating Bass Note	Fret
D	D	/ Open	A	/ Open
A7	A	/ Open	D	/ 2
G	E	3	D	/ Open

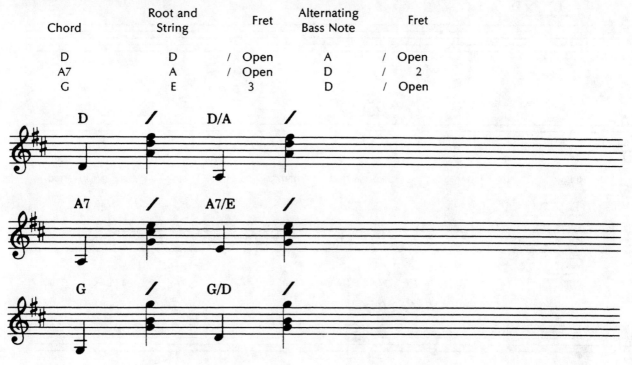

Since I Laid My Burden Down

United States

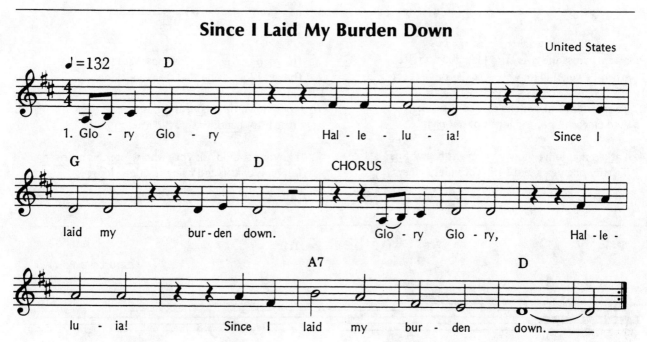

2. No more sickness, no more sorrow,
Since I laid my burden down.
Chorus

3. I'm goin' home to live with Jesus,
Since I laid my burden down.
Chorus

4. Burden down, Lord, Burden down, Lord,
Since I laid my burden down.
Chorus

5. Glory, glory, halleluia,
Since I laid my burden down.
Chorus

Worried Man Blues

United States

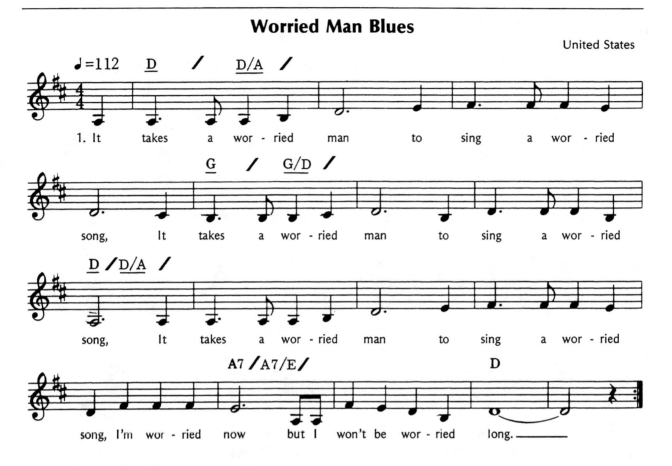

♩=112 D / D/A /

1. It takes a wor - ried man to sing a wor - ried

G / G/D /

song, It takes a wor - ried man to sing a wor - ried

D / D/A /

song, It takes a wor - ried man to sing a wor - ried

A7 / A7/E /   D

song, I'm wor - ried now but I won't be wor - ried long. _____

2. I <u>went</u> across the <u>river</u>, and I <u>lay</u> down to <u>sleep</u>,
When I <u>awoke</u>, there were <u>shackles</u> on my <u>feet</u>.

3. <u>Twenty-nine</u> links of <u>chain</u>, <u>around</u> my <u>leg</u>,
And on each <u>link</u>, and ini<u>tial</u> of my <u>name</u>.

4. I <u>asked</u> that <u>judge</u>, now <u>what</u> might be my <u>fine</u>?
Twenty-one <u>years</u>, but I <u>still</u> got ninety-<u>nine</u>.

5. The <u>train</u> arrived, eigh<u>teen</u> coaches <u>long</u>,
The girl I <u>love</u>, is <u>on</u> that train and <u>gone</u>.

6. I <u>look</u> down the <u>track</u>, as <u>far</u> as I could <u>see</u>,
Little bitty <u>hand</u>, was <u>wavin'</u> after <u>me</u>.

7. If <u>anyone</u> should ask <u>you</u>, who <u>wrote</u> this here song,
Tell him 'twas <u>I</u>, and I <u>sing</u> it all day <u>long</u>.

The Bear Song

Source Unknown

♩=100   D

1. The oth - er day I saw a bear, Up in a

A7   D

tree A - way up there. The oth - er day I saw a

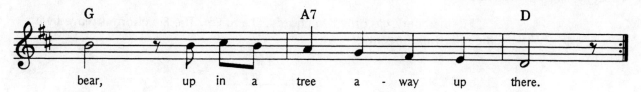

bear,   up in a tree a - way up there.

2. He looked at me, I looked at him,
   He sized me up, I sized up him. . .

3. He said to me, "Why don't you run?
   I see you don't, have any gun.". . .

4. And so I ran, away from there,
   But right behind, me came that bear. . .

5. And then I saw, ahead of me,
   A great big tree, oh, my, oh me. . .

6. The nearest branch, was ten feet up,
   I'd have to jump, and trust to luck. . .

7. And so I jumped, into the air,
   But I missed that branch, away up there. . .

8. Now don't you fret, now don't you frown,
   'Cause I caught that branch, on my way down. . .

9. That's all there is, this is the end,
   Unless I make, that bear a friend. . .

10. The moral of, this story is,
    Don't talk to bears, in tennis shoes. . .

11. The end, the end, the end, the end,
    The end, the end, the end, the end. . .

Amazing Grace

United States

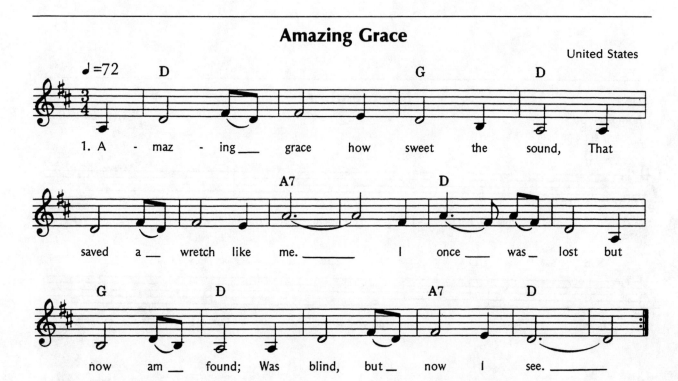

1. A - maz - ing___ grace how sweet the sound, That saved a___ wretch like me.___ I once___ was___ lost but now am___ found; Was blind, but___ now I see.___

2. 'Twas grace that taught my heart to fear,
   And grace my fears relieved.
   How precious did that grace appear;
   The hour I first believed.

3. Through many dangers, toils and snares,
   I have already come.
   'Tis grace hath brought me safe thus far,
   And grace will lead me home.

4. When we've been there ten thousand years,
   Bright shining as the sun.
   We've no less days to sing God's praise,
   Than when we first begun.

"I Remember" has only two chords, D and Em. The Em chord is played with the following fingering:

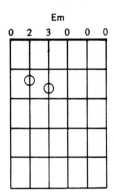

The root of the Em chord can be played on either the sixth string or on the fourth string. Practice the following progression until you can move from D to Em back to D without any rhythmic hesitation. Once you master this progression, play "I Remember."

Am / / / / /   G / / / / /   Am / / / / /
D   / / / / /   Am / / / / /   G / / / / /

I Remember

Thomas Hood

Terry Lee Kuhn

♩=110

2. I remember, I remember,
   The roses, red and white,
   The vi'lets, and the lily-cups--
   Those flowers made of light!
   The lilacs where the robin built,
   And where my brother set
   The laburnum on his birthday,--
   The tree is living yet!

3. I remember, I remember,
   Where I was used to swing,
   And thought the air must rush as fresh
   To swallows on the wing;
   My spirit flew in feathers then,
   That is so heavy now,
   The summer pools could hardly cool
   The fever on my brow!

4. I remember, I remember,
   The fir-trees dark and high;
   I used to think their slender tops
   Were close against the sky:
   It was a childish ignorance,
   But now 'tis little joy
   To know I'm farther off from Heaven
   Than when I was a boy.

Stewball

Robert Yellin, John Herald, & Ralph Rinzler

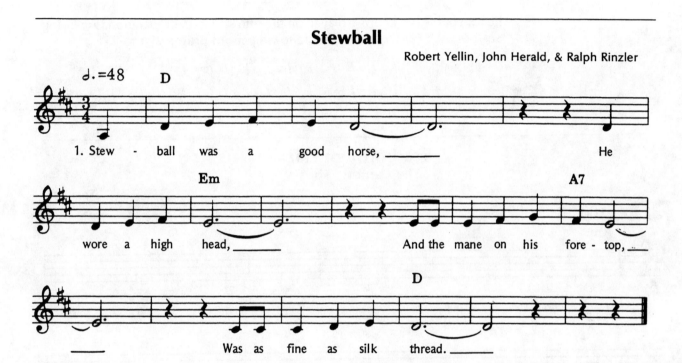

1. Stew - ball was a good horse, _____ He wore a high head, _____ And the mane on his fore - top, ___ ___ Was as fine as silk thread. _____

2. I rode him in England,   I rode him in Spain,
   And I never did lose, boys,   I always did gain.

3. So come all you gamblers,   Wherever you are,
   And don't bet your money,   On that little gray mare.

4. Most likely she'll stumble,   Most likely she'll fall,
   But you never will lose, boys,   On my noble Stewball.

5. As they were a riding,   'Bout halfway 'round.
   That gray mare she stumbled,   And fell on the ground.

6. And way over yonder.   Ahead of them all,
   Came a-prancing and dancing,   My noble Stewball.

Another useful minor chord is Am, which is played with the following fingering:

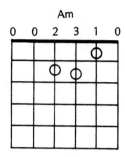

The root of the Am chord is played on the fifth string. In preparation for playing "Scarborough Fair," practice the following chord progression:

‖: Am / / / / / G / / / / / Am / / / / /
D / / / / / Am / / / / / G / / / / / :‖

Scarborough Fair
The Cambric Shirt

England

2. <u>Tell</u> her to <u>make</u> me a <u>cambric shirt, Parsley, sage</u>, rosemary, and <u>thyme</u>;
   With<u>out</u> any <u>seam</u> or <u>fine</u> needle<u>work</u>, And <u>then</u> she'll <u>be</u> a <u>true</u> love of <u>mine</u>.

3. <u>Tell</u> her to <u>wash</u> it in <u>yonder</u> dry <u>well</u>, . . .
   Where <u>water</u> ne'er <u>ran</u>, nor <u>rain</u> never <u>fell</u>, . . .

4. <u>Tell</u> her to <u>dry</u> it on yonder sharp <u>thorn</u>, . . .
   Which <u>never</u> bore <u>blossom</u> since <u>Adam</u> was <u>born</u>, . . .

5. <u>Said</u> that one <u>from</u> the <u>faraway town, Parsley, sage</u>, rose<u>mary</u>, and <u>thyme</u>;
   <u>Words</u> that <u>go</u> around and <u>around</u>, So he could <u>be</u> a <u>true</u> love in <u>time</u>.

6. Tell him to clear me an acre of land, Parsley, sage, rosemary, and thyme.
   Between the sea foam and the sea sand, Then he shall be a true love of mine.

7. Tell him to plough with a curly ram's horn, . . .
   Sow it all over with one grain of corn, . . .

8. Tell him to reap with a sickle of leather, . . .
   Tie it all up with an old peacock's feather, . . .

9. When he has done and finished this work, Parsley, sage, rosemary, and thyme;
   Send him to me for his cambric shirt, For then he shall be a true love of mine.

Roll On, Columbia, Roll On

Woody Guthrie

♩.=60
CHORUS

1. Green Douglas firs where the waters cut through,
   Down her wild mountains and canyons she flew.
   Canadian Northwest to the ocean, so blue,
   Roll on, Columbia, roll on!
   Chorus

2. Other great rivers add power to you,
   Yakima, Snake and the Klickitat too,
   Sandy, Willamette and Hood River too,
   Roll on, Columbia, roll on.
   Chorus

3. Tom Jefferson's vision would not let him rest,
   An empire he saw in the Pacific Northwest.
   Sent Lewis and Clark and they did the rest,
   Roll on, Columbia, roll on.
   Chorus

4. It's there on your banks that we fought many a fight,
   Sheridan's boys in the blockhouse that night,
   They saw us in death but never in flight,
   Roll on, Columbia, roll on.
   Chorus

5. At Bonneville now there are ships in the locks,
   The waters have risen and cleared all the rocks,
   Shiploads of plenty will steam past the docks, so
   Roll on, Columbia, roll on.
   Chorus

6. And on up the river is Grand Coulee Dam,
   The mightiest thing ever built by a man,
   To run the great factories and water the land, it's
   Roll on, Columbia, roll on.
   Chorus

7. These mighty men labored by day and by night,
   Matching their strength 'gainst the river's wild flight,
   Through rapids and falls they won the hard fight,
   Roll on, Columbia, roll on.
   Chorus

OPEN D TUNING

Alternative tunings for guitar strings may be used for variety or for classes that cannot devote time to mastering the skill of changing the fingering of left-hand chords in rhythm. The open D tuning is shown below:

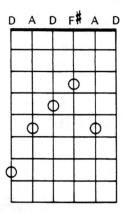

The D-major chord can be played in this tuning by merely strumming the open strings. Other major chords can be played by forming a bar with the left index finger and pressing all six strings simultaneously. Each successive fret raises the pitch one half step; therefore, a G chord is played at the fifth fret, an A chord at the seventh fret, and so on. Notice that major chords (D) must be substituted for seventh chords (D7) and that no minor chords are available in this tuning.

FRET:	0	1	2	3	4	5	6	7	8	9	10
CHORD:	D	D♯/E♭	E	F	F♯/G♭	G	G♯/A♭	A	A♯/B♭	B	C

Caution: When experimenting with different tunings, always *lower* the pitch of the string(s). This practice will avoid putting undue pressure on the neck of the guitar.

Miss Lucy Long

United States

take your time, Miss Lu - cy,   Take your time, Miss Lu - cy   Long.

2. I asked her for to marry, She hadn't much to say,
    But said she'd rather tarry, So I let her have her way.
    Chorus

3. We went down near the river, and there she said to me,
    "If I consent to marry, no longer I'll be free."
    Chorus

Once I Was a Poor Lost Soul

Susan C. Rogers

1. Once I was a poor lost soul, did - n't know right from wrong.___ Then you came in - to my life, showed me where I be - long, I be - long.___ How I feel the chang - es as my life it re - ar - rang - es, In the cir - cle of your car - ing ev - 'ry - where, ev - 'ry - where.___

2. Patiently you spend your time,
    Showing me a better way,
    Confident your heart was mine,
    Knowing love's here to stay, here to stay.
    Chorus

3. In this world of changes,
    We never are alone,
    Strength eternal in our souls,
    We're always close to home, close to home.
    Chorus

Old Rosin, the Beau

England

♩.=50 D

1. I live for the good of my na - tion And my sons are

G   A7   D

all grow - ing low, But I hope that my next gen - er -

G   D   A7   D

a - tion Will re - sem - ble old Ros - in, the beau._____ I've

G   D

trav - el'd this coun - try all o - ver, And_____ now to the

G   A7   D

next I will go, For I know that good quar - ters a -

G   D   A7   D

wait me To wel - come old Ros - in, the beau._____

2. In the gay round of pleasure I've traveled, Nor will I behind leave a foe;
   And when my companions are jovial, They will drink to old Rosin, the beau.
   But my life is now drawn to a closing, And all will at last be so:
   So we'll take a full bumper at parting, To the name of old Rosin, the beau.

3. When I'm dead and laid out on the counter, The people all making a show,
   Just sprinkle plain whiskey and water, On the corpse of old Rosin, the beau.
   I'll have to be buried, I reckon, And the ladies will all want to know,
   And they'll lift up the lid of my coffin, Saying, "Here lies old Rosin, the beau."

4. Oh! when to my grave I am going, The children will all want to go;
   They'll run to the doors and the windows, Saying, "There goes old Rosin, the beau."
   Then pick me out six trusty fellows, And let them all stand in a row,
   And dig a big hole in a circle, And in it toss Rosin, the beau.

5. Then shape me out two little donochs, Place one at my head and my toe,
   And do not forget to scratch on it, The name of old Rosin, the beau.
   Then let those six trusty good fellows, Oh! let them all stand in a row,
   And take down that big-bellied bottle, And drink to old Rosin, the beau.

The Miller of the Dee

England

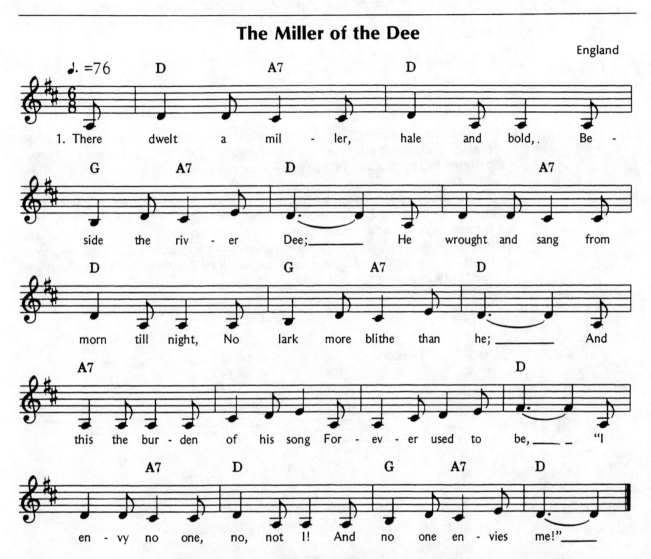

2. "Thou'rt wrong, my friend!" said old King Hal, "As wrong as wrong can be;
   For could my heart be light as thine, I'd gladly change with thee.
   And tell me now what makes thee sing, With voice so loud and free,
   While I am sad, tho' I'm the King, Beside the river Dee?"

3. The miller smiled and doff'd his cap: "I earn my bread" quoth he;
   "I love my wife, I love my friend, I love my children three.
   I owe no debt I cannot pay, I thank the river Dee,
   That turns the mill that grinds the corn to feed my babes and me."

4. "Good friend," said Hal, and sigh'd the while, "Farewell and happy be;
   But say no more, if thou'dst be true, That no one envies thee;
   Thy mealy cap is worth my crown; Thy mill my kingdom's fee!
   Such men as thou are England's boast, O miller of the Dee!"

Right-Hand Finger Picking

Finger-picking patterns with simple chords can provide a beautiful guitar accompaniment. Each finger plucks a single string of a chord in rhythmic succession. We show these patterns both in guitar tablature and in musical notation so that the strings and fingers can be clearly represented along with the musical pitches and rhythms. The right-hand fingers are identified with the following letters:

P = thumb
i = index finger
m = middle finger
a = ring finger

In *tablature notation* each string is represented by a horizontal line. The tuning of each string is given at the beginning of the set of six lines. In these patterns the thumb always plays downstrokes and the fingers always play upstrokes.

Nine picking patterns are given below for songs in this chapter. Practice each pattern until you can play it fluently from memory. After you can play the pattern with rhythmic stability, sing the suggested song for each pattern. Do not be in a hurry to learn all of these patterns in a short period of time. Some of them are mastered easily, but others require long practice. Any pattern can be used with any song that has a similar meter.

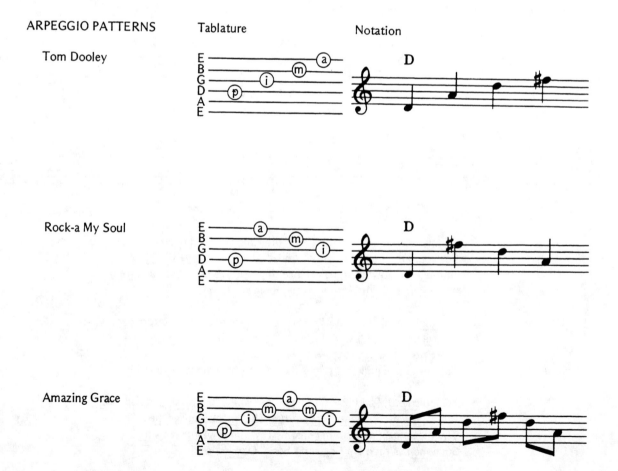

ARPEGGIO PATTERNS   Tablature   Notation

Tom Dooley

Rock-a My Soul

Amazing Grace

ROLL PATTERNS
Once I Was a
Poor Lost Soul

Polly Wolly Doodle

PINCH PATTERNS*
Down in the Valley

Since I Laid My
Burden Down

Worried Man Blues

The Yellow Rose
of Texas

*The pinch is a simultaneous pluck of two strings by the thumb and one other finger, usually ⓜ
or ⓐ. The thumb plucks a low string and the finger plucks a high string.

COMMON GUITAR CHORDS

There are hundreds of possible chord fingerings for the guitar. The following chart presents some of those chords in a suggested learning sequence. Judicious choice of key, transposing, and use of a capo (Chapter 14) will permit a guitarist knowing only these chords to perform most songs at any pitch level.

D	A7	G	Am	Em	D7
X 0 0 1 3 2	0 0 1 0 2 0	2 1 0 0 0 4	0 0 2 3 1 0	0 2 3 0 0 0	X 0 0 2 1 3

   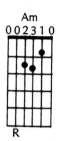 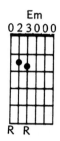 

A	E	E7	B7	C	G7
0 0 2 1 3 0	0 2 3 1 0 0	0 2 0 1 0 0	X 2 1 3 0 4	3 4 2 0 1 0	3 2 0 0 0 1

  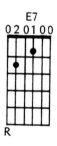   

Dm	F# m	Bm
X 0 0 2 3 1	X X X 1 1 1	X X 0 3 2 1

 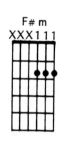 

Symbols:
X — String not played
0 — open string
1 — left index finger
2 — left middle finger
3 — left ring finger
4 — left little finger
R — root of chord

CHAPTER FOURTEEN
Understanding Transposition

CHAPTER FOURTEEN
Understanding Transposition

When a song is transposed, its pitch level is moved to a higher or to a lower level. Songs can be transposed in order to make them easier to sing or easier to play on instruments. When transposing songs for elementary school students, try to keep the extremes of the high and low terminal pitches of the songs within the following range of notes:

In deciding whether or not the pitch level of a song needs to be transposed, employ the following three checks:

(1) Find the highest note in the song.
(2) Find the lowest note in the song.
(3) Find where most of the notes lie: are they in the upper, middle, or lower end of the prescribed vocal range.

You should have an idea at this time as to how far the pitch level can, or should, be moved. Measure that distance on the chromatic scale in number of half steps.

Chromatic Scale

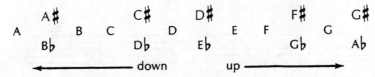

Find the number of half steps in the following intervals

B up to E	_____	F down to D	_____
G up to B♭	_____	E♭ down to C	_____
F♯ up to A	_____	B♭ down to F	_____
B♭ up to F	_____	A down to D	_____

Examine the following phrase:

Notice the following information:
(1) Highest note is fourth line E (pretty high for singing).
(2) Lowest note is second line G♯ (this note is in the middle of the prescribed vocal range, leaving plenty of room for transposing the song lower).
(3) Most of the notes are in the upper middle range, again suggesting that the pitch level could be lowered.

If one wanted this phrase to be easily singable, then a good high note might be third line Bb. The distance from fourth space E down to Bb is six half steps (count: E=0, Eb=1, D=2, Db=3, C=4, B=5, Bb=6). The next step is to move every reference to *pitch* down six half steps: this will include both notes and chords. Do not alter the rhythm or the rests.

Chord symbols should be observed with special care. A capital letter alone indicates a major chord, a capital letter with a lower case "m" indicates a minor chord, and a capital letter with a "7" indicates a seventh chord. These chord qualities—major, minor, and seventh—must remain constant in the transposition. Sharps and flats attached to capital letters are part of the pitch identification of the chord.

Transposing the previous phrase down six half steps would give the following result:

If you noticed that the old key was "A major," you might have deduced that the new key is six half steps lower in "Eb major" and you might have written the above transposition as follows using the key signature for Eb major rather than accidentals.

Assume that some sixth-grade boys still complained that the phrase was too high. Transpose it from the preceding example to a lower key.

TRANSPOSING WITH A CAPO

The use of the capo on guitar is a special instance of transposing. The *capo* is an elastic strap or a clamping device that fits around the neck and frets all six strings at the same fret, thereby raising the pitches of all the strings an equal amount. In fingering chords the capo is considered the end of the string; therefore, chords are fingered as if the capoed fret is the nut. All the strings sound higher than they normally do by an interval equal to one half step for each fret the capo is placed from the nut.

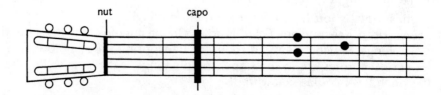

Thus, if you were to finger a D chord above the capo with the capo placed on the second fret as shown, then all the strings would sound a whole step higher; the chord that would sound would be an E-major chord rather than a D-major chord. The capo has "transposed" the fingering one whole step higher. If the capo were placed at the first fret and a G chord were fretted above the capo, it would produce an A♭ chord, since the pitch of all the tones would be raised one half step.

This easy method of transposing is very important when teaching children. You have probably noticed that many of the songs in Chapter 14 were pitched in a key that is easy for the guitar, but that may be too low for the characteristic range and timbre of young voices. For instance, the first phrase of "The Miller of the Dee" is given in the key of D as follows:

If you placed a capo at the third fret and continued to finger the chords in the key of D, the resulting chords and melody would be in the key of F.

Being able to transpose songs to different keys will permit you to pitch songs in comfortable keys or to play them in easier keys. It is also possible that you will be able to do both, through the use of the capo on guitar. Test your ability to transpose by working the following exercises.

WORKSHEET

(1) Transpose each of the following notes the distance given:

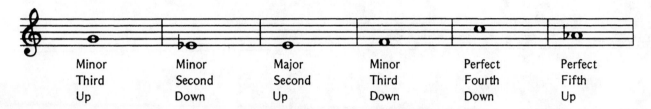

Minor	Minor	Major	Minor	Perfect	Perfect
Third	Second	Second	Third	Fourth	Fifth
Up	Down	Up	Down	Down	Up

(2) Transpose the following song to the key of G:

(3) Transpose the following song to the key of F:

(4) Transpose the following song to the key of D minor:

(5) Transpose the following song to a singable key that can be accompanied by the autoharp:

CHAPTER FIFTEEN
Playing Rhythms on Percussion Instruments

CHAPTER FIFTEEN
Playing Rhythms on Percussion Instruments

Percussion instruments are different from the melodic and harmonic instruments that you have studied. They usually play a repetitive rhythmic pattern rather than melodies or chords. "Percussion" may be defined as a way of performing; hitting, rather than pressing or strumming, only one surface of the instrument meets the hand. Compare the dexterity needed to play the recorder with that required to play the triangle.

Classroom percussion instruments are similar in construction to those used in marching bands and symphony orchestras, but they are used in different ways for different purposes. They are usually inexpensive, easy to hold and play, and of indefinite pitch. Their purpose is to accompany group singing, instrumental performances, and folk dancing. The materials from which they are generally made are wood, plastic, or metal. As a rule, the larger the instrument the lower the pitch, and the smaller the instrument the higher the pitch.

Following are brief descriptions of ten common percussion instruments used in classrooms, with accompanying photographs. Three typical rhythm patterns are given for each instrument in each of two meters, $\frac{2}{4}$ and $\frac{3}{4}$. The patterns may be adapted for other meters by adding beats or rests to each measure. Play these patterns at appropriate tempos to accompany songs you learned in previous chapters. The volume of sound can be controlled by using more or less force when playing the instruments.

LOW DRUMS

Drums of low pitch, such as tympani, bass drums, or tub drums, usually play the heavy rhythm of the accented beat. The drum pictured here is a conga

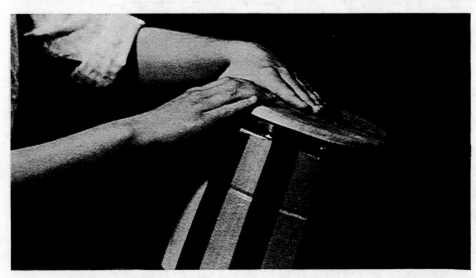

Conga drum

drum, often associated with Latin-American music. The drum may be placed on the floor between the knees of the player or suspended from a shoulder by means of a strap. Make sure that the open end of the drum is not covered, so that the sound will not be muffled. Keep your fingers together and strike the center of the drum head to produce a deep tone. Striking the edge, or rim of the drum will produce a higher pitch.

Low Drums

HIGH DRUMS

High-pitched drums such as snare drums, bongos, timbales, and tambours often play the unaccented beats or after-beats. The drum in the picture is a mano drum, which consists of a tightly stretched piece of plastic or animal skin fastened inside a round frame. The pitch of the head may be changed by adjusting the bolts on the perimeter of the drum.

Mano drum

High Drums

TRIANGLES

Triangles are always made of metal bent into a three-sided shape, leaving one corner open for resonance. They are played by suspending a closed corner from a holder with an attached knob. A metal beater is used to tap or roll rhythms on a side or in the other closed corner of the triangle. In order to observe a rest, stop the vibrations by placing your fingers lightly on the metal.

Triangles

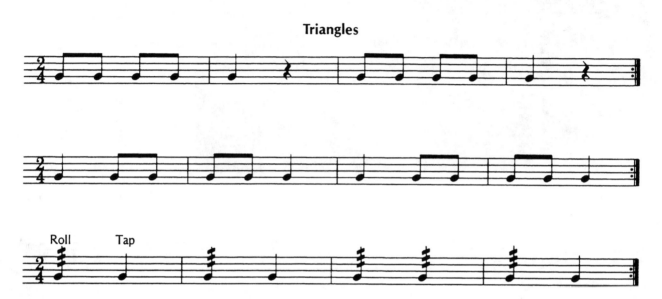

Triangle

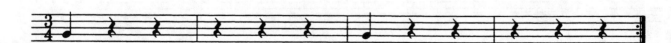

JINGLES

The term "jingles" is used here to denote any instrument that consists of small pieces of metal attached to a frame or handle. They include jingle bells, jingle clogs, and wrist bells.

Jingles are played by shaking them with one hand, or by holding them in one hand and striking the frame against the heel of the other hand. They are suitable for accompanying winter or Christmas music.

Jingles

Jingles

FINGER CYMBALS

Finger cymbals that are made from brass of good quality will add much to music of a subdued nature. They consist of two plates held in the hands by means of attached elastic thongs. They are played by tapping the edges together at an angle. After tapping the edges, hold the cymbals apart to allow them to ring. Do not clap the cymbals directly together; they will not vibrate.

Finger cymbals

Finger Cymbals

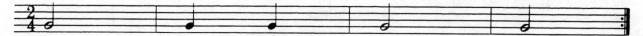

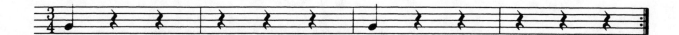

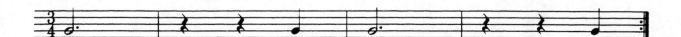

TAMBOURINES

A tambourine is really a one-headed drum with jingles around the rim. It is held by grasping the wooden rim with one hand at an open spot where there are no jingles. Play it by shaking the rim or by striking the head with the fingers of your opposite hand.

Tambourine

Tambourines

WOOD BLOCKS

Wood blocks are simply hollowed-out pieces of hard, resonant wood. A tone block is a cylindrical piece of wood with an attached handle, which may have ridges on its outer surface. Chinese temple blocks are matched sets of five different-sized wooden chambers that produce five different pitches when struck. A hard rubber or wooden mallet is used to strike the center or tap on the edge of these instruments.

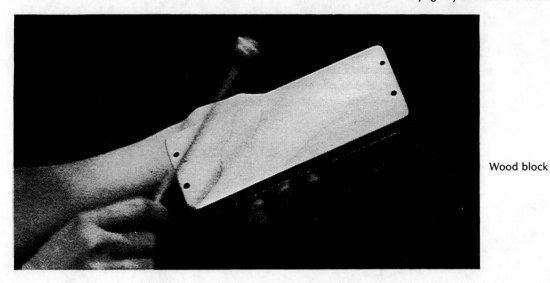

Wood block

Wood Blocks

RHYTHM STICKS

Rhythm sticks are usually made from foot-long lengths of dowel rod that may or may not be painted. One stick is held in each hand so that the two can be tapped together. If one of the sticks is notched, you can produce a scratching sound by rubbing the smooth stick across the notches.

Rhythm Sticks

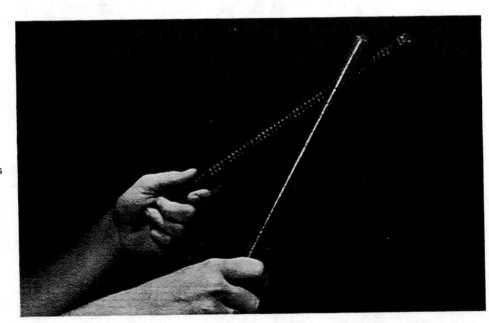

Rhythm sticks

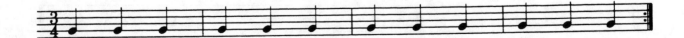

CLAVES

Claves (pronounced *clah*-vays) are cylindrical hardwood blocks first used in Cuba and the Antilles. They are generally about six inches in length, one inch in diameter, and made from resonant material such as Brazilian rosewood. One clave should be balanced between the heel of the hand and the fingertips so that there is air space in the palm of the hand. A second clave, held in the fingers of the other hand, is used to tap a rhythm against the first.

Claves

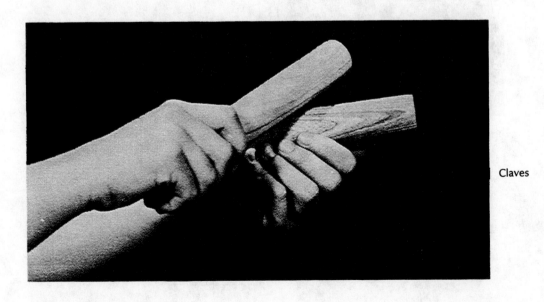

Claves

MARACAS

Maracas were made originally by hollowing out gourds, drying them, placing seeds or pebbles inside, then attaching handles and painting them. Today maracas are made from wood or plastic and are used to accompany Latin-American music. A pair may be held by the handles and shaken together. Usually they are played alternately by placing the index fingers on top of each maraca to lightly tap or shake the rhythm.

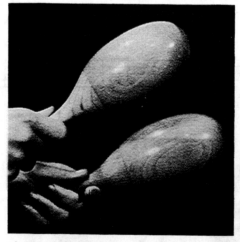

Maracas, position 1

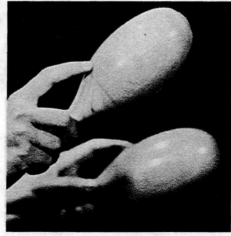

Maracas, position 2

Maracas

PERCUSSION SCORES

We conclude this chapter with two arrangements for accompanying songs on percussion instruments. Both "Sweet Betsy" and "Pawpaw Patch" may be accompanied by several combinations of percussion instruments—especially those constructed from skin (low pitch), wood (medium pitch), and metal (high pitch).

Notice that three separate parts for rhythm instruments are connected in these arrangements. The metallic instruments play the rhythms on the upper line, the wooden instruments play the rhythms on the center line, and drums or tambourines play the rhythms on the lowest of the three lines.

Metallic instruments of high pitch are the jingles, cymbals, and triangles. Wooden instruments of medium pitch include maracas, rhythm sticks, claves, wood blocks, and tone blocks. Low-pitched instruments whose resonators are made from animal skin or plastic include conga, bongo, mano, and tub drums, as well as tambourines and tom-toms. Use one or more groups of these instruments to accompany the singing and playing of the following songs.

Sweet Betsy

United States

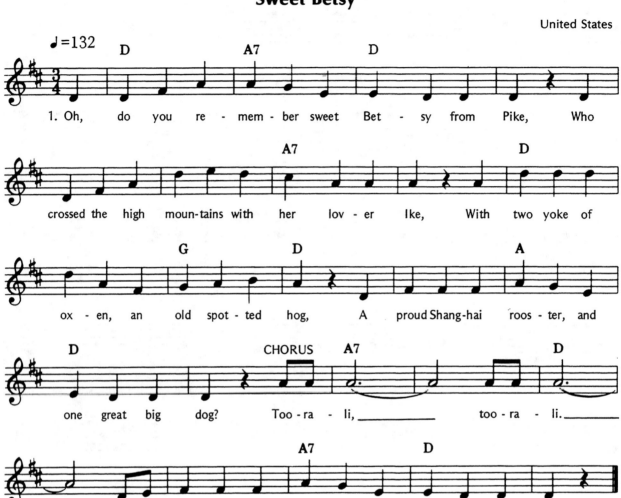

♩=132

1. Oh, do you re - mem - ber sweet Bet - sy from Pike, Who crossed the high moun-tains with her lov - er Ike, With two yoke of ox - en, an old spot - ted hog, A proud Shang-hai roos - ter, and one great big dog? Too - ra - li, _____ too - ra - li. _____ Sing - ing too - ra - li, too - ra - li, too - ra - li - aye.

2. They swam the wild rivers and climbed the high peaks
And camped on the prairie for weeks upon weeks;
They fought off the Indians with musket and ball,
And said they would get there if they had to crawl.
Chorus

3. They soon reached the desert, where Betsy gave out,
And down on the ground she was rolling about.
Old Ike wasn't worried, he swatted some flies,
Saying, "Betsy, get up, you'll get sand in your eyes."
Chorus

4. The wagon wheel fell off one dark stormy day,
It rolled down the valley a long ways away.
And Ike brought it back and he made a repair:
It held on just fine with a nail and a prayer.
Chorus

5. The wind always blowing was much to despair:
When they would breath in they'd get sand with their air.
'Twas seventeen miles on the trail each day,
Walking closer and-closer in spite of delay.
Chorus

6. The wagons were passing the mountains of snow,
All eyes there saw old California below,
They all started shouting, they gave a big cheer,
They all thought they'd soon be a rich millionaire.
Chorus

7. I've sung you this song and it's soon to be done,
About our sweet Betsy and Ike, how they've come,
A long ways from Pike from their comfort and home
Across the hot deserts and mountains to roam.
Chorus

Percussion Score

Arranged by G. Wachhaus

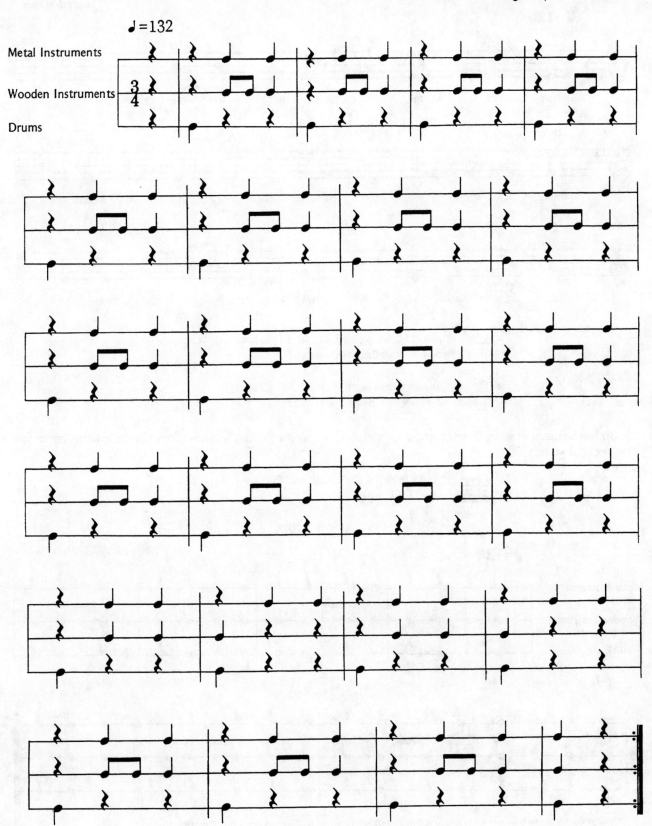

Pawpaw Patch*

United States

2. <u>Come</u> on, boys (girls), <u>we</u> will look and find her (his), *(3 times)*
<u>Way</u> down yonder in the <u>paw</u>paw patch.

3. <u>Picking</u> pawpaws, <u>in</u>to her (his) pockets, *(3 times)*
<u>Way</u> down yonder in the <u>paw</u>paw patch.

If you are using this song to encourage participation you might like to substitute the following verse for the second stanza.

(2) <u>Come</u> on, boys (girls), <u>we</u> will look and find her (him), *(3 times)*
<u>There</u> she (he) is hiding <u>over</u> there.

Percussion Score

Arranged by G. Wachhaus

*This song must be transposed if it is used as a partner song with "Skip to My Lou,"' p. 181.

CHAPTER SIXTEEN
Developing Listening Skills with Instruments

CHAPTER SIXTEEN
Developing Listening Skills with Instruments

The purpose of the preceding chapters has been to help you acquire the musical performance skills and knowledge that you need to function in the classroom or in any informal music-making situation. Once you have learned to use instruments to support and enrich song-oriented activity, you may use them in the acquisition of another dimension of musical awareness, commonly known as "music appreciation."

The listening skills to be acquired in this chapter center around the performance of themes from selected compositions. The purpose of this chapter is to increase your enjoyment and knowledge of music literature and to cultivate the art of listening through performance on classroom music instruments. The analyses deal with the music itself, not with such peripheral material as biographical anecdotes or pictorial allusions. It is assumed that active, rather than passive, listening will lead to musical understanding and result in appreciation. A specific activity for each composition will help you follow the musical ideas.

Recommended recordings are cited. Reference to the *Schwann-1 Record & Tape Guide,* published monthly, will assist the teacher and student to select alternate versions.

The phonograph or component system used for reproduction of recordings should be of the highest fidelity obtainable. One essential feature of any such sound-reproduction system is a variable speed control. This device will allow the pitch of the recorded sound to be manipulated to the pretuned pitch level of resonator bells, pianos, and autoharps. Guitars and recorders, as well as voices, may be tuned more readily to phonographs that do not have such an accessory.

CANON IN D MAJOR FOR STRINGS AND CONTINUO BY JOHANN PACHELBEL

Johann Pachelbel (1653–1706) is a representative composer of the Baroque period of music history (1600–1750). Besides being one of the most notable organ virtuosos of his day, Pachelbel was an important influence on Johann Sebastian Bach in the writing of music for organ. He also composed suites, fantasias, and variations for harpsichord as well as various instrumental combinations.

Pachelbel's *Canon* was originally composed for three violins and continuo consisting of cello and harpsichord. A *canon,* like a round, is a contrapuntal compositional technique in which every voice or part imitates exactly the melody presented by the first voice or part. The canon composed by Pachelbel features the use of *básso ostináto,* or ground bass, in which a short melodic phrase of four measures is repeated a total of 28 times as a bass line, with variations in the upper parts based on the repetitive harmony.

First, listen to a recording of the composition while following one or more of the instrumental lines. Next, study and perform the individual melody or harmony parts slowly on the instrument of your choice. Third, play an instrumental part while listening to the recording. Repeated listening to the recording while performing different instrumental parts will help you to acquire skill in musical performance and understanding. Finally, combine two, three, or more different instrumental lines while listening to the recording. You should be aware of increasingly complex variations over the repeated figure in the bass line as you listen and play.

The following instrumental parts may be played on guitar, piano, soprano recorder, or resonator bells. The easy bell part may be played on a diatonic bell set, while the moderate and advanced parts may be played on any chromatic bell set.

Recommended Recording: Jean-François Paillard Chamber Orchestra
12″ LP   #MHS 1060   Time = 7:09
The Musical Heritage Society, Inc.
1991 Broadway
New York, NY 10023

Canon

Johann Pachelbel

Recorder, Piano, Bells, or Guitar (Basso Ostinato Melody)

Piano

Recorder or Bells — Easy

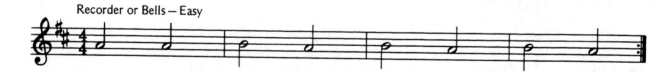

Recorder or Bells — Moderate

Recorder or Bells — Advanced

TWELVE VARIATIONS ON "AH!, VOUS DIRAI-JE, MAMAN," K. 265, BY WOLFGANG AMADEUS MOZART

The compositions of Wolfgang Amadeus Mozart (1756–1791) represent the finest aspects of vocal and instrumental music written during the Classical period (1750–1825). He is noted for the operas *Cosi Fan Tutte, Don Giovanni, The Magic Flute,* and *The Marriage of Figaro.* In addition, he composed forty-one symphonies, numerous concertos, trios, quartets, quintets, and sonatas, as well as serenades, divertimentos, and nocturnes.

Compared to the elaborate variation techniques employed during the Baroque period, Mozart's variations for keyboard are fairly simple. One of his most straightforward compositions in this form is the *Variations* on "Ah!, vous dirai-je, Maman" (1778), a theme probably written by Nicholas Dezede but better known by children as "The Alphabet Song" or "Twinkle, Twinkle, Little Star." Mozart probably wrote the *Variations* for one of his pupils, since they explore the techniques of playing scales, arpeggios, and ornaments necessary for mastery of a keyboard instrument.

The theme and the twelve variations that follow may be hummed, sung with the words given in Chapter 8, or played on the piano or bells. The chords may be played on either twelve-bar or fifteen-bar autoharps as well as the piano. Play the theme along with any of the variations except number 8, which changes mode. Notice the primary compositional technique used in each variation to modify either the melody, rhythm, tempo, or harmony of the theme.

Recommended Recording: Igor Kipnis, Harpsichord

12" LP   #Y-30289   Time = 9:46
Odyssey Records

Photograph by Russell Dian

Twelve Variations on "Ah!, Vous Dirai-Je, Maman," K. 265

Wolfgang Amadeus Mozart

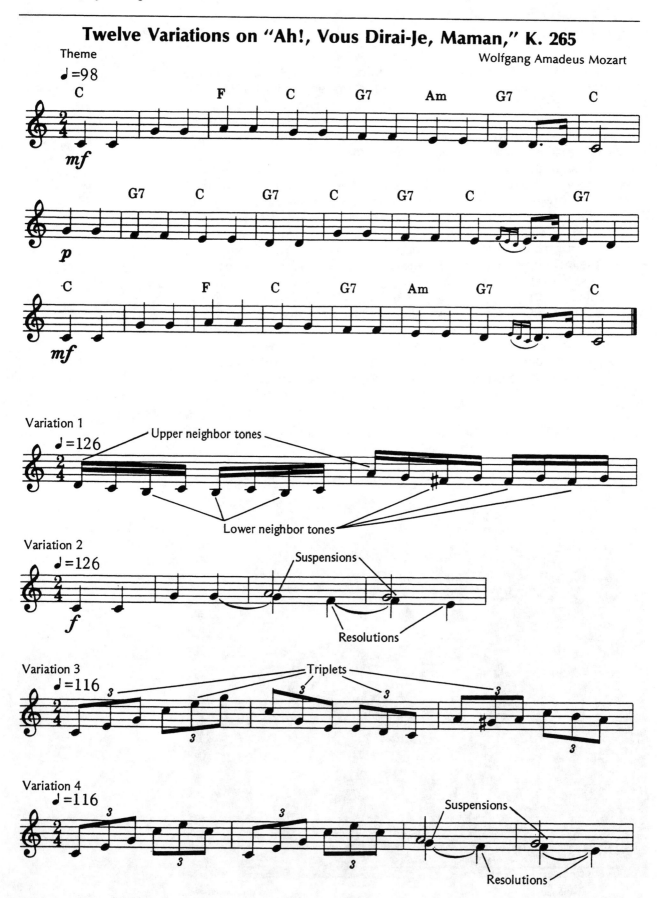

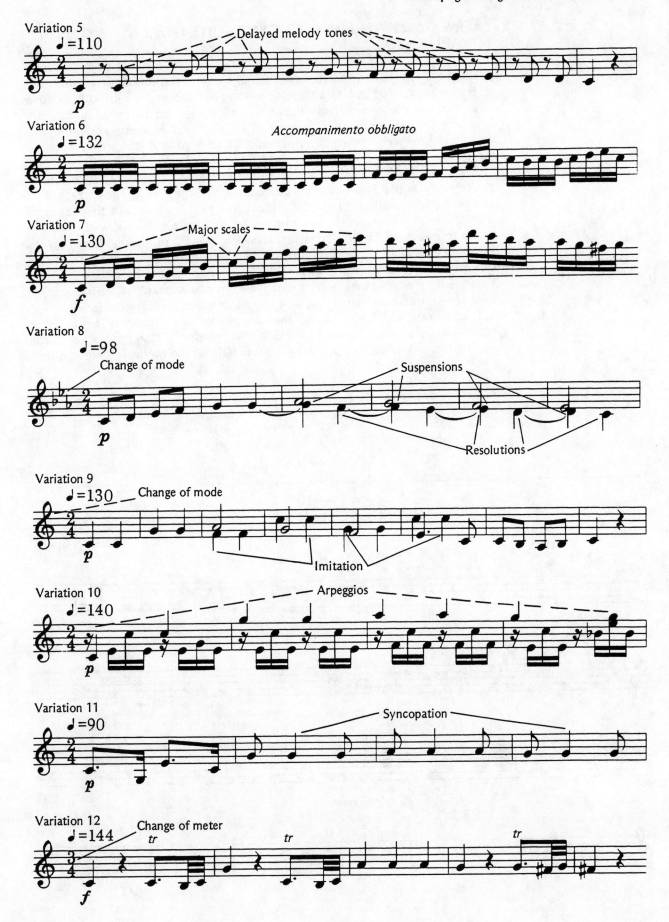

"ASE'S DEATH" FROM PEER GYNT SUITE NO. I BY EDVARD GRIEG

Edvard Grieg (1843–1907) represents one trend of the Romantic period, that of Nationalism; that is, his compositions tend to express the spirit of his native land, Norway. He incorporated the native folk songs and dances of his country into his works either literally, or more often, in free elaboration and imitation. Another of his well-known compositions is *Concerto in A minor for Piano and Orchestra*.

The music for *Peer Gynt* was written for a theatrical production that relates the adventures of a Scandinavian "Sinbad" who, though inherently lazy, has an overactive imagination. One of the most touching moments in this series of musical daydreams is the scene where Peer returns to his widowed mother's home to find her lying in bed. Peer, knowing that his mother is dying, makes her believe that they are on a journey to a beautiful castle that sparkles and gleams and is blazing with light. Outside the door of the castle stands Saint Peter, who welcomes Ase. Peer had taken her to a beautiful land of make-believe—in much the same way she took him when he was young.

The melody of "Ase's Death" may be played on a piano or on a set of resonator bells which contains the B below middle C. Carefully observe the key signature and the accidentals used throughout the melody. Sixteen different pitches are used.

Recommended Recording: English Chamber Orchestra
Raymond Leppard, Conductor
12" LP   #9500 106   Time = 4:08
Philips Records

"Ase's Death"
Peer Gynt Suite No. 1

Edvard Grieg

SYMPHONY NO. 7 IN A MAJOR, OP. 92, MOVEMENT II, BY LUDWIG VAN BEETHOVEN

Ludwig Van Beethoven (1770–1827) simultaneously represents the end of the Classical period and the beginning of the Romantic period (1825–1900). Beethoven expanded many aspects of symphonic composition and developed musical material in a more dramatic fashion than did earlier composers. His advances in the use of soloists and chorus in symphonic writing paved the way for other composers of the nineteenth century. His best-known compositions include nine symphonies, five piano concertos, thirty-two sonatas for piano, and a large body of chamber music.

Beethoven's Symphony No. 7 is in four movements and was composed during the years 1811 and 1812. The second movement (called "Allegretto") is scored for pairs of flutes, oboes, clarinets, bassoons, horns, and trumpets, plus tympani and string orchestra. Play through the principal theme of the Allegretto. How many times is the ♩♫ | ♩ ♩♩ rhythm presented in this theme?

Your major task in this composition will be to determine how many times that theme is presented completely and to identify entrances of portions of that theme. Sing through it to be sure that you are completely familiar with the theme. Accompany it with the indicated chords.

Distribute the E, F♯, G, G♯, A, and B bells from one set of resonator bells to six students. More sets of resonator bells may be used to accommodate more students in the class. Students with bells will play all the pitches of the theme that correspond to the particular bells that they were given. The resonator bells make a particularly pleasing sound with the recording, and giving each student only one bell will make the performance of the theme a challenge. After trying the movement once while humming and once with bells, try it one more time and see if you can also follow the "Listening Guide" from beginning to end.

Recommended Recording: London Symphony Orchestra
Colin Davis, Conductor
12" LP   #9500 219   Time = 9:33
Philips Records

Allegretto
Symphony No. 7 in A Major, Op. 92

Ludwig van Beethoven

Listening Guide
Allegretto from Symphony No. 7 in A Major, Op. 92
(Numbers indicate the entries of the principal theme.)

Section A, Principal Theme (minor key)
(1) Viola
(2) Second Violins
(3) First Violins
(4) Woodwinds and French Horns
Section B (major key)
Many triplets, new melody in clarinets, rhythmic motive ♩ ♫ | ♩ ♩ | underpinning the structure.
Section A (minor key)
(5) Violin
Imitative section, ends with crescendo.
(6) Brass instruments play shortened version of the theme.
Section B (major key)
Melody in clarinet again, hints at principal theme, section ends with big, full chords.
Section A (minor key)
(7) Theme begins in the flutes and then portions of the melody alternate among other instruments. The second line of the theme is not repeated at the end of the movement, but there is an overlapping of entrances to bring the movement to a close.

"GALLOP" FROM *THE COMEDIANS,* OP. 26, BY DMITRI KABALEVSKY

Originally written in 1938 as incidental music for a children's play, the suite *The Comedians* is probably the best known work of the twentieth-century composer Dmitri Kabalevsky (born 1904). Kabalevsky is of the same generation as such other Soviet composers as Shostakovitch, Prokofiev, and Khachaturian. Music for children has long been a major preoccupation with Kabalevsky, who has said that such music should be tested by playing it to audiences of youngsters.

The inspiration for this music was the play "Inventor and Comedian" by Daniel, which concerns a group of wandering comedians and their experiences as they travel from town to town performing at fairs and in public squares. The suite which accompanies the play has ten sections, the second of which is the "Gallop." A xylophone hammers incisively with articulated brass and woodwind passages, suggesting an entertaining troupe of jugglers and acrobats at their agile work.

The eight-note theme of the "Gallop" contains the five pitches of the F-major pentatonic scale: F, G, A, C, and D. These pitches can be played on the soprano recorder and piano as well as diatonic or chromatic resonator bell sets.

The measures that have no pitches indicated and have numbers written above them are extended rests. They indicate that more than one measure of silence is to be observed. Count them by saying the number of the measure on the accented beat and then saying the number of the following beat; for example, "1 2, 2 2, 3 2," and so on.

Recommended Recording: Vienna State Opera Orchestra
Vladimir Golschmann, Conductor
12" LP   #SRV-207 SD   Time = 1:36
Vanguard Records

"Gallop"
The Comedians, Op. 26

Dmitri Kabalevsky

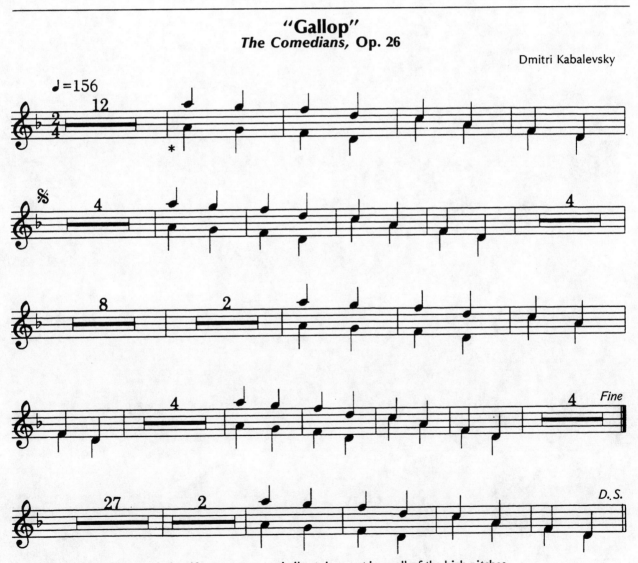

* Use the alternate lower pitches if your resonator bell set does not have all of the high pitches.

Appendixes

APPENDIX A
Definitions of Common Musical Terms

A cappella: Sung without accompaniment.

Accelerando: Gradually becoming faster.

Accent: (1) A stress, usually with dynamics, and sometimes with time, in which case it is called an agogic accent. An agogic accent emphasizes a note by slightly elongating it. (2) A beat which receives an accent. Accents are indicated with an accent mark (> or ∧) placed over or under a note.

Accidentals: The symbols of chromatic alteration. A sharp (♯), flat (♭), or natural (♮) is placed before a note for the purpose of altering the pitch one half step.

Accompaniment: The background part for a more important melody. The accompaniment is designed to enhance the general effect of a piece of music.

Adagio: Slowly.

Aeolian mode: The same pattern of whole and half steps as a minor scale.

Al Fine: Literally, "to the end." This term indicates the repetition of the first part of a movement either from the beginning (D. C.) or from a sign (D. S.) to the place marked by the term "Fine."

Alla breve: Literally, "in shortness." Sometimes written ¢ and referred to as "cut time." A meter signature indicating two beats per measure with a half note (♩) receiving one beat.

Allegro: Literally, "cheerful." Quick, light, lively.

Alternate chords: Chords in parentheses that may be substituted for the regular chords given or may be omitted.

Alto: The lower female voice.

Anacrusis: Incomplete measure of one or more notes that begins a song. Sometimes called an "upbeat." To maintain the symmetry of the total song, the last measure supplies the beats needed to make a complete measure when added to the beats in the anacrusis.

Andante: Literally, "walking." Moving at a moderate pace.

Antecedent (phrase): Used with the term "consequent" to describe pairs of musical phrases that are complementary in that they begin in the same way but end differently. The antecedent phrase has a partial cadence and the consequent phrase usually has a complete cadence. In some cases the consequent phrase may change keys and require further development.

Appalachian style: A manner of playing autoharp in which it is held upright and finger picks are used on the right hand to play melodies.

Arpeggio: Literally, "to play upon a harp." Playing the notes of a chord in succession rather than simultaneously; sometimes called a broken chord.

Art song: A composed song, as opposed to a folk song. See *song*.

A tempo: Literally, "in time." Return to the original speed after an alteration of the pace.

Augmented interval: A perfect or major interval expanded by a chromatic semitone; an interval one half step larger than a perfect fourth: C up to F♯.

Autoharp: An easy-to-play instrument designed to produce chords. When a chord bar is pressed, it damps all the strings except those contained in a particular chord.

Ballad: A narrative song of several stanzas, sometimes with a refrain.

Bar: (1) A guitar technique in which all six strings are fretted simultaneously at the same fret with the index finger. (2) See *Chord bar* and *Bar line*.

Bar line: A vertical line touching all five staff lines, which groups beats and divides the staff into measures.

Baroque fingering: Sometimes referred to as the English fingering system for recorder, a system that utilizes the historical fingerings. See *German fingering.*

Bass:ʾ(1) The lower male voice. (2) The lowest in a group of notes or tones, as a bass note or a bass string.

Basso ostinato: A bass line that is continually repeated throughout a composition. Various melodic and harmonic variations occur in the upper parts throughout the composition.

Bass clef: Also called the F clef (𝄢). Used to indicate that the fourth line of the staff is the first F below middle C.

Baton: A thin, tapered piece of wood or fiberglass used by conductors to beat time.

Beam: A thick, solid line that connects the ends of the stems of notes, making them into eighth notes. Two beams make sixteenth notes, and so on. Identical in function to flags on note stems.

Beat: The underlying pulse that forms the temporal unit of a composition. A single beat consists of a point in time and a duration to the next point. The beat is often identified by a physical motion such as foot tapping, clapping, or swaying.

Bird's eye: See *Fermata.*

Blue notes: (1) Tones created by simultaneously playing both the natural and the flatted third, seventh, or fifth scale degrees. (2) A flatted note in blues style.

Bottleneck: A device used on guitar to stop a string without fretting. It is usually a cylindrical pipe made of metal or ceramic, which is worn on the ring or little finger of the left hand. When touched to the string it forms a movable fret.

Breath mark: A comma placed above the staff to indicate that a singer or wind instrument player should breathe at that point.

Bridge: (1) A transition leading from one theme or section of a song to another. Sometimes used to return to the beginning of a song. (2) A thin piece of plastic set upright on the body of a guitar to raise and stretch the strings above the body and to transfer the string vibrations for resonance.

Brushstroke: A sweeping motion with the thumb or a pick across the strings of a guitar or autoharp.

Cadence: A point of rest or relaxation marking the end of a phrase. The cadence can be partial, requiring another phrase for a sense of completeness; or a cadence can be complete, in which case the music bears a sense of finality.

Canon: See *Round.*

Capo: A device used on a guitar to shorten all six strings simultaneously at the same fret. The effect of using a capo is to transpose the notes fingered to a higher pitch level.

Chest voice: The lowest vocal register, the resonance for which is thought to be produced in the chest.

Chord: (1) The simultaneous occurrence of three or more tones, spelled in thirds (CEG, DFA, EGB, and so on). (2) A letter used to identify chords in written music. The letter is placed above the staff approximately where the chord is to sound.

Chord bar: Autoharp device pressed in order to produce the tones in specified chords.

Chord rhythm: See *Harmonic rhythm.*

Chorus: A regularly recurring section of a song that is sung after each verse. Both the words and the music are identical on each repetition.

Chromatic: (1) A scale made entirely of half step intervals. (2) Tones not in the given major or minor scale of a song.

Circle of fifths: A diagram that depicts a succession of tones spaced the interval of a fifth apart that eventually lead back to the initial tone.

Clef: A symbol placed on the staff to indicate the pitch names of the lines and spaces. The treble and bass clefs are most common.

Coda: Literally, "the tail." An added section that serves as a conclusion to a piece of music.

Common meter: A term used to indicate that each beat subdivides into two. For instance, $\frac{3}{4}$ would be interpreted as three beats per measure, each beat having two subdivisions. A common meter of $\frac{4}{4}$ would be interpreted as four beats per measure, each beat having two subdivisions.

Common time: Name for $\frac{4}{4}$ meter. Indicated with a **C** for the meter signature.

Composition: (1) A general name for a piece of music. (2) The process of writing a piece of music.

Compound meter: A term used to indicate that each beat subdivides into three. For instance, $\frac{6}{8}$ would be interpreted as two beats per measure, each beat of which has three subdivisions.

Con: With.

Conducting: The art of directing the simultaneous performance of several singers and/or instrumentalists by the use of bodily motions, facial expressions, and so on.

Consequent (phrase):; See *Antecedent*.

Continuo: A term that refers to the simultaneous performance of the bass line by a keyboard instrument together with a cello or bassoon. In addition to playing the bass line the keyboard also fills in chords above the bass line.

Crescendo: A gradual increase in the dynamic level, or loudness of a phrase. Abbreviated "cresc." and sometimes indicated with the symbol

Cut time: See *Alla breve*.

Da Capo: Repeat "from the beginning." Usually written D.C. al Fine, meaning to repeat from the beginning and end at "Fine."

D.C.: Abbreviation for Da Capo.

Dal Segno: Repeat from the sign. Usually written D. S. al Fine, meaning to repeat from the sign and end at "Fine."

Decrescendo: A gradual decrease in the dynamic level, or loudness of a phrase. Abbreviated "dim." or "decresc." and sometimes indicated with the symbol

Degrees: The eight consecutive tones in diatonic scales. Degrees are always counted from low to high beginning on the key note as the first degree.

Descant: A melodic accompaniment line that harmonizes with the melody and chords of a song.

Design: See *Form*.

Diatonic: (1) Stepwise movement within a major or minor scale. (2) Music that uses the tones of a major or minor scale and includes no chromatic alterations.

Diminished fifth: A perfect or minor interval contracted by a chromatic semitone; an interval one half step smaller than a perfect fifth, such as C up to G♭.

Diminuendo: See *Decrescendo*.

Dissonant: A term that refers to a combination of tones that are unstable and require resolution.

Dolce: Sweetly and softly.

Dominant: (1) Fifth degree of a scale. (2) The chord built on the fifth scale degree.

Dorian mode: A scale pattern similar to minor, but with a raised sixth scale degree. The notes D, E, F, G, A, B, C, D form a D dorian scale.

Dot: (1) A dot placed after a note or rest increases its duration by one half. (2) A dot placed above or below a note indicates that it is to be performed staccato.

Double bar: A pair of bar lines drawn closely parallel to indicate a main or sectional division in a piece of music. The end of a song is always marked with a double bar.

Double flat: A symbol (♭♭) placed before a note to designate that a tone be lowered two half steps.

Double sharp: A symbol (𝄪) placed before a note to designate that a tone be raised two half steps.

Downbeat: The indication for the first beat of a measure in a conducting pattern. It is usually a forceful downward movement in the center of the body.

D.S.: Abbreviation for Dal Segno.

Duet: A composition for two voices or instruments.

Duple: Meter consisting of two beats per measure.

Duplet: A group of two notes that are played in the duration usually occupied by three notes.

Duration: The length of time a tone is sustained.

Dynamics: The relative loudness of musical tones. Dynamic levels are indicated with various symbols, including p, f, $>$, $<$, and so on.

Eighth note: A note (♪) equal to two sixteenth notes (♫) in duration.

Eighth rest: A symbol (𝄾) that indicates a duration of silence equal to the duration of an eighth note.

Embouchure: The formation of the lips, cheeks, and tongue in playing a wind instrument.

Enharmonic: A term used to identify two names for the same pitch; such as, F♯ and G♭.

f: Abbreviation for forte; loud.

Falsetto: An artificial method of tone production used to reach pitches above the normal range of a male voice.

Fermata: A pause or hold identified by the symbol ⌢; a momentary interruption of the rhythmic flow of beats. The note under which the fermata occurs should be held for approximately double its normal duration.

ff: Abbreviation for fortissimo; as loud as possible.

Fifth: (1) An interval that contains five diatonic letters. (2) The note in a chord that is five diatonic letters above the root.

Fine: The end.

Fingerboard: A thin, narrow strip of hardwood glued to the top of the neck of a guitar, above which the strings are stretched for playing upon by the fingers. The fingerboard of the guitar has frets on it.

Flag: One or more curved lines placed on the stem opposite the note head to alter the duration of a note. One flag indicates an eighth note, ♪.

Flat: (1) The symbol ♭ that indicates the lowering of the pitch of a note by one half step. (2) A tone that is lower in pitch than a comparison tone.

Folk song: Originally, music passed on through oral tradition. More recently, any music that expresses the feelings and concerns of the common man.

Form: Organization of a song that outlines the repetition and contrast of melodies, motives, rhythms, and/or harmonies.

Forte: Loud.

Fret: A raised metal strip attached across the fingerboard of the guitar, which stops a pressed string. Frets are arranged so that they produce a succession of half steps on each string.

Fretboard: See *Fingerboard.*

Fundamental: (1) Bass tone of a chord in root position. (2) The main pitch from which overtones are produced. (3) The first partial or the first harmonic.

G clef: See *Treble clef.*

German fingering system: A simplified fingering system for recorder.

Glissando: Production of a rapid series of tones by a sliding movement.

Grand staff: The combined treble and bass clefs connected by common bar lines.

Grave: Very slowly and solemnly.

Ground bass: See *Basso ostinato.*

Half note: A note (♩) equal in duration to two quarter notes (♩♩).

Half rest: A symbol (▬) that indicates a duration of silence equal to the duration of a half note.

Half step: The pitch distance between two adjacent keys on the keyboard. E up to F, A up to B♭, and D down to C♯ are all half steps.

Harmonic rhythm: The rhythm created by chord changes.

Harmony: The chordal structure of music, taking into consideration successions of chords and the functional relationships among chords.

Head voice: A higher vocal register, the resonance for which is thought to be produced in the head.

Hold: See *Fermata.*

Homophonic texture: A style of music in which a single melody is supported by a chordal accompaniment.

Imitation: The restatement in close succession of a melody in different parts of a contrapuntal texture, as in a round.

Imitative section: A portion of a longer piece of music in which imitative compositional techniques predominate.

Interval: The pitch distance between two notes or tones.

Intonation: The pitch accuracy of a voice or an instrument.

Introduction: A preliminary phrase or section that occurs before the melody of a song.

Inversion: The tones of a chord played so that the root of the chord sounds above either the third, or the fifth, or both.

Inverted chord: A chord with the root sounding above the third and/or the fifth.

Key: (1) The tone on which the scale is built, and the series of melodic and harmonic relationships that provide a gravitational "pull" toward the "key tone" at the final cadence of a song. (2) A digital, or finger, lever on a keyboard instrument that sounds a tone when pressed.

Key chord: See *Tonic*.

Key signature: The sharp(s) or flat(s) given at the beginning of each staff of a song.

Largo: A very slow tempo.

Leading tone: The seventh degree of the major, harmonic minor, and melodic minor scales. It is called the "leading tone" because of its tendency to move to the tonic.

Lead sheet: Single staff notation with only the melody, text, and chord symbols placed on, below, and above the staff.

Leap: See *Skip*.

Ledger lines: Short lines drawn through the stem and/or the head of a note that is too high or too low to be represented on the staff. They extend the pitch range of the staff.

Legato: Smooth, sustained movement from one tone to another. Legato is often indicated by slurs or dashes placed either above or below the notes.

Lento: Slowly.

Listening: An active perceptual process in which a person's attention is focused on the musical elements of a composition.

Lyrics: The text of a song.

m: Abbreviation for mezzo, meaning moderately, medium, or half. Most often used to modify other dynamic symbols, such as mp or mf.

Major chord: A chord with a major third between the root and the third, and a minor third between the third and the fifth.

Major key: A key based on a major scale.

Major scale: A scale of eight degrees consisting of whole steps except between the third and fourth scale degrees and between the seventh and eighth scale degrees — both of which are half steps. The notes C, D, E, F, G, A, B, and C form a major scale.

Marcato: Literally, "marked"; with emphasis.

Measure: The metric unit used in musical notation to represent a group of beats. Also, the number of beats contained between two bar lines. Regularity of accent is provided through the use of measures, because the first beat of every measure is usually accented.

Mediant: The third scale degree.

Melodic rhythm: The rhythmic element of the single tones of a song's melody.

Melody: A progression of single musical tones that express a unified idea and assume an identity. A tune. The tones of a melody possess the qualities of pitch, rhythm, tone color, and dynamics.

Meno: Less.

Meter: The grouping of beats into measures in a piece of music, with an implied accent on the first beat of each measure.

Meter signature: Two numbers at the beginning of the first staff of a song, the upper of which indicates the number of beats in a measure, and the lower of which specifies the note value that receives one beat.

Metronome: A mechanical instrument calibrated to produce any given tempo in beats-per-minute.

Mezzo: (1) Half, moderately. Abbreviated "m," and used to modify other symbols such as mp or mf. (2) A medium female voice range; mezzo soprano.

Middle C: The C key that is located nearest the center of the keyboard on a full-sized piano. Middle C is written on the first ledger line below the treble staff.

Minor chord: A chord with a minor third between the root and the third, and a major third between the third and the fifth.

Minor key: A key based on a minor scale.

Minor scale: A scale of eight degrees consisting of whole steps except between the second and third scale degrees and between the fifth and sixth scale degrees — both of which are half steps. The tones A, B, C, D, E, F, G, and A form a minor scale.

Mixolydian mode: A scale pattern similar to major, but with a lowered seventh scale degree. The notes G, A, B, C, D, E, F, and G form a G mixolydian scale.

M.M.: An abbreviation for Maelzel's Metronome, sometimes used as a tempo indication (M.M. ♩ = 80).

Mode: (1) Any of the scale patterns that originated in the early centuries of Western civilization. The most commonly used modes are the Aeolian, Dorian, and Mixolydian. (2) A scale pattern made up of whole and half steps; major or minor.

Moderato: Moderate speed; faster than andante, but slower than allegro.

Modulation: Changing keys within a composition.

Molto: Much, very.

Monophonic texture: A style of music in which a single melody is presented without additional melodies or chordal accompaniments.

Mosso: Movement, motion; used with other words to suggest tempo changes.

Music: The intelligible combinations of vocal and/or instrumental tones into a composition having structure and continuity.

Natural: (1) The symbol (♮) that cancels the effect of a sharp or a flat. (2) A note that is neither sharped nor flatted.

Neck: The projection from the body of the guitar that has the fretted fingerboard on its upper side.

Neck strap: A strap attached to the guitar to enable the performer to stand while holding the instrument in playing position.

Non: Not.

Notation: A system of symbols that represent a "picture of the way the music goes." Notation of musical ideas gives the performer a visual representation of the duration, pitch, and loudness of a piece of music.

Note: The written designation of a tone consisting of a round head, possibly a stem, and possibly one or more flags or beams.

Note head: The round portion of all notes, which designates pitch by placement on a line or in a space of a staff.

Note value: The duration for which a tone is sustained.

Nut: The ridge over which the strings pass to suspend them above the fingerboard on a guitar.

Obbligato: An accompanying melody line added to enhance a song.

Octave: An interval that includes eight diatonic steps. C up to C, E down to E, and G up to G are examples of octaves.

Open D tuning: A special guitar tuning in which a D chord is produced by sounding the unfretted (open) strings.

Ostinato: A figure, usually melodic, that repeats throughout a piece.

Overtones: Subaudible tones that give pitches their characteristic tone color for each instrument. Overtones vibrate in exact multiples of the frequency of the fundamental. If the fundamental pitch vibrates at 55 cycles per second, then the first seven overtones vibrate at 110, 165, 220, 275, 330, 385, and 440 cycles per second, respectively.

p: Abbreviation for piano; soft.

Partner songs: Two different songs whose melodies and harmonies produce an agreeable sound when performed together. "Three Blind Mice"/"Are You Sleeping," "Rock-a My Soul"/"He's Got the Whole World," and "Skip to My Lou"/"Paw Paw Patch" are examples of partner songs.

Pedals: Foot levers on the piano. Depressing the right pedal (damper) releases all the dampers and allows the strings to ring freely and in sympathetic vibration. The left pedal (una corda) produces a softer volume.

Pentatonic scale: A five-tone scale that uses the first, second, third, fifth, and sixth degrees of the major scale.

Period: A musical structure containing two phrases, the first of which usually ends with a partial cadence, and the second of which usually ends with a complete cadence.

Phrase: A division of a melody comparable to a clause in a compound sentence. Depending on tempo and meter, phrases are usually two, four, or eight measures in length.

Phrasing: The clear rendition of the phrases of a song.

Piano: (1) Indication to play softly; p. (2) A keyboard instrument.

Pick: (1) A small, flat plastic or felt device used to pluck or strum the strings of a guitar or autoharp. (2) Finger picks and thumb picks are metal or plastic devices that fit on individual fingers or the thumb of the right hand and that are used to play on the strings of a guitar or autoharp.

Pickup note(s): See *Anacrusis*.

Pinch patterns: Guitar picking patterns that utilize the thumb and one other finger simultaneously plucking two strings.

Pitch: (1) The relative highness or lowness of tones, measured by frequency vibrations and having also the qualities of tone color and duration. (2) A note. (3) A tone. (4) An intonation reference; in-tuneness.

Poco, poco a poco: Little; little by little.

Polyphonic texture: A style of music in which the simultaneous occurrence of two or more melodies predominates.

Polyrhythmic: A piece in which two or more different rhythms are simultaneously performed.

pp: Abbreviation for pianissimo; as soft as possible.

Preparatory beats: Conductor's hand motions representative of beats given in anticipation of a group's performance.

Presto: Very fast.

Primary chords: The chords that are built on the first, fourth, and fifth scale degrees. In C major these would be the C, F, and G chords. They are named the tonic, subdominant, and dominant chords, respectively.

Progression: A succession of chords.

Pulse: The regular occurrence of accents in music that are analogous to the throbbing caused in the arteries by the contractions of the heart. See *Beat*.

Quarter note: A note (♩) equal to two eighth notes (♫) in duration.

Quarter rest: A symbol (𝄽) that indicates a duration of silence equal to the duration of a quarter note.

Quartet: A composition for four voices or instruments.

Rallentando: Gradually slower. Abbreviated "rall."

Range: The extent of pitch covered by a melody or lying within the capacity of a voice or instrument.

Refrain: See *Chorus*.

Relative keys: Major and minor keys that share the same key signature.

Repeat sign: A set of double bars and double dots (‖: :‖). A portion of music enclosed by double bars and double dots that is to be repeated. When the second sign (:‖) appears alone, repeat from the beginning. The double dots are always on the side of the double bar of the section that is to be performed again.

Resolution: Movement from an active, unstable, or dissonant sound to a more consonant or stable sound.

Resonance: The transmission of vibrations from one vibrating body to another, including the enhancement of tone by a soundboard or hollow box.

Rest: A symbol that indicates a duration of silence.

Rhythm: The temporal aspect of music. In this text, rhythm refers to the duration of notes and rests written on the staff.

Rhythmic motive: A short rhythmic idea that is repeated throughout a musical composition.

Ritardando: Abbreviated "rit." or "ritard." A gradual decrease in speed.

Root: The identifying tone of a chord, and the lowest sounding tone when all the tones are arranged in thirds.

Root position: A chord with the root sounding as the lowest tone.

Round: A melody that can be started by two or more performers at different times. Each performer can continuously repeat from the beginning, and the overlapping of the melody creates a chordal harmony. Every part imitates the melody presented by the first part to enter.

Scale: A succession of pitches built on an identifying tone to a particular pattern of whole and half steps. See *Major scale, Minor scale, Dorian mode, Mixolydian mode,* and *Pentatonic.*

Segno: Literally, "the sign." A symbol in the form of an "S" that indicates a point in the music from which the piece is to be repeated.

Semitone: See *Half step.*

Sequence: Repetition of a melodic idea at a different pitch level.

Seventh chord: A four-note chord containing a fundamental and three other tones a third, fifth, and seventh above the fundamental. The most important seventh chord is built on the fifth scale degree and is called the dominant seventh chord.

Sharp: (1) A symbol (♯) that raises the pitch of a note by one half step. (2) A tone that is higher in pitch than a comparison tone.

Sign: See *Segno.*

Signature: Symbols placed at the beginning of a song that indicate the key and the meter of the song. See *Key signature* and *Meter signature.*

Simile: Continue in the same manner.

Sixteenth note: A note (♬) equal to two thirty-second notes (♬) in duration.

Sixteenth Rest: A symbol (𝄿) that indicates a duration of silence equal to the duration of a sixteenth note.

Skip: A nondiatonic interval containing three or more letter names. C up to E and B down to F are skips.

Slide: See *Bottleneck.*

Slur: A curved line connecting two notes of different pitch that directs the performer to play in legato style.

Solo: A piece sung or played by one performer. Also, any piece in which a single voice or instrument predominates.

Song: A short musical composition for voice that is usually accompanied, has a poetic text, and is designed to portray the meaning and character of the text.

Soprano: The higher female voice.

Soundhole: An aperture in the form of a full circle in the top center of the body of the guitar, the purpose of which is to increase the sonority by opening up the interior of the body.

Staccato: Separated. Usually indicated by a dot placed over or under the note.

Staff: Five horizontal, parallel, and equidistant lines separated by four spaces, used for the notation of musical pitch and rhythm.

Stanza: A division of a poem consisting of more than two lines arranged together in a recurring pattern of meter and rhyme.

Stem: A vertical line attached to the head, or round portion, of all notes except whole notes.

Step: (1) A melodic interval of a second. (2) Also used synonymously with degree.

Strophic: A song in which all stanzas of text are sung to the same music.

Subdivision (rhythmic): The division of the duration of a longer note into two or more equal, shorter notes. The more common subdivisions are into two and into three.

Subdominant: (1) Fourth degree of a scale. (2) The chord built on the fourth scale degree.

Submediant: Sixth degree of a scale.

Supertonic: Second degree of a scale.

Suspension: A done held over from a preceding chord that is not one of the notes of the new chord. It is "suspended" until it resolves to a note of the new chord.

Syllables: Italian words used to represent scale degrees in teaching tonal memory. The first through eighth scale degrees are represented by do, re, mi, fa, sol, la, ti, and do. Numbers and syllables such as "and," "e," "na," and "ne" are used to represent rhythmic movement.

Symbols common in musical notation:

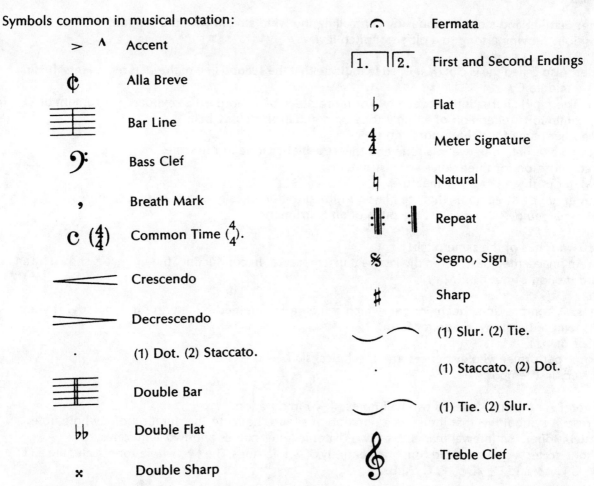

> ∧	Accent	
¢	Alla Breve	
(bar line symbol)	Bar Line	
𝄢	Bass Clef	
,	Breath Mark	
C (4/4)	Common Time (4/4).	
<	Crescendo	
>	Decrescendo	
.	(1) Dot. (2) Staccato.	
(double bar symbol)	Double Bar	
♭♭	Double Flat	
𝄪	Double Sharp	

⌢	Fermata
1. 2.	First and Second Endings
♭	Flat
4/4	Meter Signature
♮	Natural
(repeat symbols)	Repeat
𝄋	Segno, Sign
♯	Sharp
⌣	(1) Slur. (2) Tie.
.	(1) Staccato. (2) Dot.
⌣	(1) Tie. (2) Slur.
𝄞	Treble Clef

Syncopation: A rhythmic pattern in which the accent occurs on unexpected beats or parts of beats. Syncopation is created by (1) accenting a weak beat, (2) resting on a strong beat, and (3) sustaining from weak through strong beats.

System: A collection of two or more staves barred together for the notation of keyboard, choral, chamber, or orchestral music.

Tablature notation: A system of notation in which tones are represented by fingerings on an instrument rather than as notes on a staff.

Tempo: Rate of speed at which beats are performed. Usually indicated in number of beats per minute.

Tenor: The higher male voice.

Tessitura (of song): The general (most used) range of the greater proportion of a song's notes, not taking into account occasional high or low extremes.

Theme: A prominent melody in a composition.

Third: (1) An interval that contains three diatonic letter names. (2) The note in a chord that is three diatonic letters above the root.

Tie: A curved line that connects two notes of the same pitch, thereby making one tone of the combined durations.

Timbre: Tone quality of a sound as determined by its overtones.

Time signature: See *Meter signature*.

Tonality: The prominence of a single tone within a given song. Also, the chords grouped around and attracted by one central tonic chord.

Tone: A sound of definite pitch and duration.

Tone color or quality: See *Timbre*.

Tonic: (1) First degree of a major or minor scale. (2) A chord built on the first scale degree.

Tonguing: Starting and stopping tones by controlling the wind stream with the tongue.
Transposition: Moving a song to a different pitch level.

Treble clef: Also called the G clef (𝄞). Used to indicate that the second line of the staff represents the first G above middle C.
Tremolo: The rapid alternation between two or more notes of a chord on a keyboard instrument or the rapid, continuous reiteration of a single tone on a guitar or melody bell.
Triad: Another name for a three-note chord.
Trill: A rapid alternation between a tone and the next higher tone in the scale.
Trio: A composition for three voices or instruments.
Triple: Meter of three beats per measure.
Triplet: A group of three notes that are played in the duration usually occupied by two notes.
Tune: (1) See *Melody*. (2) To adjust the pitch of an instrument.

Unison: Two tones of the same pitch.
Upbeat: An unaccented beat; often the last beat in a measure. In conducting, the upbeat is shown by an upward motion of the hand.

Variations: A compositional technique in which a theme is modified by altering the melody, rhythm, meter, tempo, harmony, mode, or form.
Verse: See *Stanza*.
Virtuoso: A performer who evidences great technical skill.
Vivace: Very fast tempo.

Whole note: A note (○) equal to two half notes(♩ ♩) in duration.
Whole rest: A symbol (▬) that indicates a duration of silence equal to the duration of a whole note.
Whole step (tone): An interval made up of two diatonic letter names and two semitones.
Whole-tone scale: A six-note scale consisting entirely of whole steps. The two whole-tone scales are C, D, E, F♯, G♯, A♯ and C♯, D♯, F, G, A, B.

APPENDIX B
Song Analysis Test

Name_____ Song_____

Directions: Using the song supplied, answer the following questions.

1. Write the letter names of the note of the song. Write your answers below the staff.

2. Name the accidentals in the key signature in order.

3. In what key is this song written?

4. Is this key a major or a minor key?

5. Name the notes of the scale on which this song is based.

6. What is the pattern of whole and half steps in the scale of this song?

7. How many beats are there in one measure?

8. What kind of note receives one beat?

9. Draw the note which receives one beat.

10. Write the counting for the rhythm of the melody above the staff.

11. If a syncopated rhythm is used in this song, give the measure number of its first occurrence.

12. If a tie is used in this song, give the measure number of its first occurrence.

13. If a slur is used in this song, give the measure number of its first occurrence.

14. Name the root, third, fifth, and seventh (if applicable) of each chord in this song.

15.

16.

seventh	____	____	____
fifth	____	____	____
third	____	____	____
root	____	____	____
Chord Symbol	____	____	____

17. If you were conducting this song, what preparatory beat (or beats) would you give as a cue for the group to begin?

18. On the back of this page, draw the conducting pattern for this song, specifying the hand for which it is intended. Write in the beat numbers.

19. Transpose the first eight measures of this song into a key that can be played on guitar by a person
20. who knows only the D, A7, G, Em, and Am chords. Include the notes, key signature, and chords.

APPENDIX C
Playing Accompaniments on Baritone Ukulele

The ukulele, baritone ukulele, and tenor guitar — being less expensive and somewhat easier to play than the guitar — are used in music fundamentals classes at some institutions. In many situations, the lower cost and ease of playing are more compelling factors than the fuller sound and greater musical potential of the more widely used six-string guitar. This appendix explains the tuning and gives the left-hand fingerings of the chords that are used in Chapter 13, enabling ukuleles or baritone ukuleles to be substituted for, or used in conjunction with, regular guitars in that chapter. Except for cost, the baritone ukulele and the tenor guitar are similar instruments and are tuned exactly the same, like the four highest-pitched strings of the guitar. Both of these instruments are considered as baritone ukulele. The tuning of the baritone ukulele is given in the diagram. The subscript numbers indicate the particular pitch desired: Middle C is C_4, and the next C above middle C is C_5. All the tones from middle C ascending through B have the subscript 4.

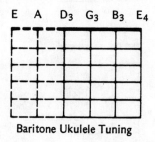

Baritone Ukulele Tuning

The ukulele is tuned in either of two ways: G_4, C_4, E_4, A_4, or A_4, D_4, $F\sharp_4$, B_4. The lower-pitched of these tunings is shown in the diagram and is used throughout this appendix.

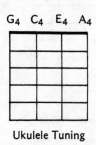

Ukulele Tuning

Open D tuning for these instruments would be accomplished as follows:

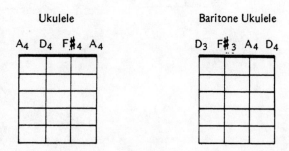

Ukulele   Baritone Ukulele

Strumming and finger picking techniques for the right hand are easily transferred from the guitar materials presented in Chapter 13.

Ukulele and Baritone Ukulele Fingerings for Guitar Chapter Chords

	Ukulele	Baritone Ukulele
D	1 2 3 0	0 1 3 2
A7	0 1 0 0	1 0 2 0
G	0 1 3 2	0 0 0 3
Em	0 3 2 1	2 0 0 0
Am	2 0 0 0	2 3 1 0

Classified Indexes

Index of Songs by Title

Index of Songs by Key

Index of Songs by Number of Chords Used

Index of Songs by Meter

Index of Songs by Instrument

SOPRANO RECORDER

Amazing Grace, 49
Ash Grove, The, 58
BAG, 43
Bile Them Cabbage Down, 55
Coventry Carol, 60
Dance, 45
Deaf Woman's Courtship, The, 157
ED, 44
GAB, 43
Go Tell Aunt Rhody, 48, 173, 179, 192
God Rest Ye Merry, Gentlemen, 62
Hey, Ho! Nobody Home, 52, 214
High E, 50
Hineh Ma Tov, 61
Hush Little Baby, 46
Indian Dance, 46
Jig, 54
Jingle Bells, 60, 132
Jolly Old Saint Nicholas, 44
Joy, 156
Kum Ba Ya, 59, 120
Largo, 48
Let Us Sing Together, 54
Little Bells of Westminster, The, 131
Long, Long Ago, 51
Lovely Evening, 219
Mary Had a Billy Goat, 83
Michael Row, 47
Minor Brother, A, 52
Ode to Joy, 50
Old Hundredth, 61
Pavane, 61
Polly Wolly Doodle, 180, 244
Psalm 23, 58
Riddle Song, 51
Round, 156
Se Vuol Ballare, 53
Shady Grove, 59
Skye Boat Song, 49
Song, 131
Sweet Betsy, 284
Tailor and the Mouse, The, 53
Theme from First Symphony, 47
Theme from Polovetsian Dances, 55
Worried Man Blues, 45, 248

GUITAR

Amazing Grace, 249
BAG, 43
Bear Song, The, 248
Bingo, 186
Dance, 45
Dona Nobis Pacem, 201
Down in the Valley, 242
Drill, Ye Tarriers, 99
ED, 44
GAB, 43
Go Tell Aunt Rhody, 48
He's Got the Whole World in His Hands, 117
Hey, Ho! Nobody Home, 52
Home on the Range, 224
Hush Little Baby, 46
I Remember, 250
Jig, 54
Largo, 48
Let Us Sing Together, 54
Little Bells of Westminster, The 131
Long, Long Ago, 51
Lovely Evening, 219
Mary Had a Billy Goat, 83
Miller of the Dee, The, 257
Miss Lucy Long, 254
Music Alone Shall Live, 103
Ode to Joy, 50
Old Rosin, the Beau, 256
On the Beautiful Blue Danube, 139
Once I Was a Poor Lost Soul, 255
Polly Wolly Doodle, 180, 244
Rock-a My Soul, 240
Roll On, Columbia, Roll On, 253
Scarborough Fair, 252
Since I Laid My Burden Down, 247
Six Little Ducks, 241
Song, 131
Stewball, 251
Sweet Betsy, 284
This Land Is Your Land, 246
Tom Dooley, 239
Was an Old Woman, 232
Worried Man Blues, 45, 248
Yellow Rose of Texas, The, 245

TWELVE-BAR AUTOHARP

(Note: All of the following songs can be played on the Fifteen-bar Autoharp.)

Acres of Clams, 110
Alouette, 89
America, 102
Battle Hymn of the Republic, The, 228
Bile Them Cabbage Down, 173, 183
Billy Boy, 109, 195
Chopsticks, 142
Clementine, 182
Cuckoo, The, 86
Drill, Ye Tarriers, 99
Drunken Sailor, 190
Every Time I Feel the Spirit, 115
Frère Jacques, 211
Go Tell Aunt Rhody, 173, 179, 192
Happy Birthday to You, 133, 134
Hey, Ho! Nobody Home, 214
Hineh Ma Tov, 61
Home, 104
Jingle Bells, 60
Kookaburra, 129, 130
Kum Ba Ya, 59
Little Bells of Westminster, The, 131
Make New Friends, 91
Minka, 223
My Bonnie Lies over the Ocean, 110
Oats, Peas, Beans, 217
Oh, Susanna, 185
On Top of Old Smoky, 32
Psalm 23, 58
Railroad Bill, 194
Rattler, 221
Reuben's Train, 178
Romance, 135
Sally Go 'Round the Sun, 127
Sandy McNab, 213
Shady Grove, 59
Skip to My Lou, 118
Theme from Symphony No. 94, 136
This Old Man, 101
When the Saints Go Marching In, 127
Wildwood Flower, 184, 193

FIFTEEN-BAR AUTOHARP

Amazing Grace, 249
America the Beautiful, 87
Ash Grove, The, 58
BAG, 43
Bear Song, The, 248
Bingo, 186
Blow, Ye Winds, 114
Coventry Carol, 60
Dance, 45
Dona Nobis Pacem, 201
Down in the Valley, 242
ED, 44
Ev'rything's Alright with Me, 188
GAB, 43
Go Tell Aunt Rhody, 48
Golden Slippers, 116
He's Got the Whole World in His Hands, 117
Home on the Range, 224
Hush Little Baby, 46
Jacob's Ladder, 98

General Index

NOTES

NOTES

NOTES

NOTES

NOTES

NOTES

NOTES

NOTES

NOTES

NOTES

NOTES

NOTES